SPIRIT OF THE

Royal Air Force

ONE HUNDRED YEARS OF EXCELLENCE

SPIRIT OF THE

Royal Air Force

ONE HUNDRED YEARS OF EXCELLENCE

An Anthology in Words & Works of Art

MICHAEL FOPP

BUCKINGHAM PALACE

I find it extraordinary to reflect that when I was born, in 1926, the Royal Air Force had existed for just eight years. Although the Service had been reduced in the aftermath of the Great War, it nevertheless played an important role in many theatres around the globe. In the 1930s, as war in Europe once again loomed, the Royal Air Force was much expanded and contributed greatly to the eventual victory of the Allied Nations in World War Two. The Cold War and Jet Age followed and then, in more recent times, the Service returned to the expeditionary operations that would have been familiar to the great-grandparents of today's men and women of the RAF.

Through this sweep of time, a great collection of aviation art has been amassed. In this, the centenary year of the RAF, I am interested to learn that the Royal Air Force Club is publishing a book entitled ''Spirit of the Royal Air Force – One Hundred Years of Excellence'', featuring works of art held by the Club and those of the many former British aircraft companies. I am sure that all who read the book will be reminded of the Royal Air Force's proud history over the last hundred years: a story of heroism, human endeavour and constant technical innovation, of indeed overcoming adversity to reach for the stars – *Per Ardua ad Astra.*

ELIZABETH R.
Patron, Royal Air Force Club

Portrait of HM Queen Elizabeth II
Denis Quentin Fildes
This artist's copy was commissioned for the Club in 1961 and presented by Hector Caird.

PREFACE

THE GENESIS OF this book came from initial discussions between Wg Cdr Michael Gilbert, the Chairman of the Royal Air Force Club's Art Committee and John Bulmer, in his BAE Systems company heritage role. Once the initial idea of an art book to celebrate the centenary of the RAF was identified a small working group was set up to examine the feasibility of using the Club's collections, other fine art collections, and a sponsor for the whole project. Very soon Howard Mason, BAE Systems Heritage Manager, brought BAE Systems on board and the project could start in earnest.

To tell the story it was imperative that we found pictures which not only illustrated the diversity of the equipment used by the Royal Air Force over its one hundred years, but also the lives of the people who served. We were determined that the book would not be a catalogue of aircraft, but would reflect the changing nature of the Service and its development. That development was so closely entwined with the growth and success of the British aircraft industry, and its people, that we soon realised that the Club's art collection would not suffice in isolation. As the inheritor of nearly all the famous British aircraft manufacturers, BAE Systems has recognised how important its antecedents are to its current operations. It has embraced the history and traditions of its predecessors and this is reflected in its own commissions of works of art over the years. A combination of the art collections of both the RAF Club and BAE Systems is therefore at the heart of this book. The text will give a concise canter through the one hundred years during which the RAF have played a major role on the world stage. The captions to the pictures add some additional information about their subjects, some detail about the specific image and, wherever possible, some facts which might not have otherwise occurred to the reader. Wherever possible the place of the RAF, its work and its people, has also been put in context with what was happening in the wider world – a necessary element in order to understand why, what or when.

The result is a book which all of us engaged in its production hope will bring enjoyment and pleasure to the reader whilst also demonstrating the fine achievements of the RAF over the past century.

Finally, I thank all the artists and/or their estates whose work we have used, for allowing us to reproduce their work in this book.

DR MICHAEL A. FOPP
Director General, RAF Museums, 1988–2010

INTRODUCTION

"Flying without feathers is not easy; my wings have no feathers."

PLAUTUS (C.254–184 BC)

THIS BOOK CELEBRATES the centenary of the Royal Air Force (RAF), and its Club, both founded only fourteen years after the first powered and controlled flight. Whilst balloons and gliders had preceded the Wright brothers' historic flight in North Carolina, this pioneering event relied heavily on the advice and research from colleagues around the world, particularly from the United Kingdom, Germany and France. Most new technologies are embraced by the military in a short time and such was the case with powered flight. However, no area of the world embraced it quite as quickly as those countries in northern Europe, facing, as they were, what would become known as 'The Great War'.

The British were the first to form an independent air force and therefore the RAF has a longer association with flight than any other air arm. Characteristically, the British way of doing things was to combine the regulation of both civil and military flying in a single government department. In so doing the development of aviation in the United Kingdom was greatly eased by an initial crossover of technology between the disciplines. Thus the RAF has pioneered almost every facet of flight and, at various points in its long and proud history, been the holder of world records for long-distance, high-altitude, and speed. It has been a beacon to other countries through its leadership and promotion of air power. In 1940 it was the first air force in the world to win a decisive battle fought solely in the air, the Battle of Britain, which stemmed the tide of the German advance across Europe and helped to win the peace and freedoms we all enjoy today. Later, innovative use of tactical support of troops on the ground in North Africa led the way to close air support operations which are still used today.

The RAF has developed from a policing force supporting the British Empire to become a major humanitarian and peacekeeping force around the world. Whilst not the largest air force, its skills and professionalism are widely acknowledged to be amongst the best. The RAF is much more than the sum of its aircraft; it is a highly trained force dedicated to national defence and international duty. The majority of its serving members are to be found on the ground in multiple roles supporting the aircraft.

This book is a celebration of that centenary; it not only marks an anniversary for the RAF, but also of the RAF Club. The Club was founded in October 1918 and the premises at 128 Piccadilly were extensively refurbished to provide facilities for dining, drinking and meeting. Accommodation was also created and the membership was open to all serving or retired officers. The building was formally opened, by the Duke of York, in 1922. In commemoration of the achievements of both, and with the co-operation and partnership of BAE Systems (the inheritor of the achievements of so many historic British aircraft companies), this history of the Service is illustrated using the art collections held by the Club and the BAE Systems plc.

The RAF Past and Present – Stained Glass Window

This window, installed in the RAF Club in 2008, is the generous gift of Sqn Ldr Ivan Heath, who served in the UK, Egypt and Italy during World War II. Created by artist Helen Whittaker and conservator Keith Barley of Barley Studios, it focuses on the wide range of activities in peace and war of RAF personnel, and their equipment throughout the history of the RAF and the RAF Club. Extending as it does over two floors, the window's narrative has been constructed so that the viewer's attention is taken from the lowermost register, rising up the window from right to left and right again, before coming to rest on the circular design in the upper arch. It also thereby caters for two distinct viewpoints: the ground floor and the first floor landing. In order to overcome problems of light variation, with good levels of natural light at the top diminishing to particularly dark conditions in the lower half, Barley Studios employed innovative techniques with gilded glass in the lower sections, which by reflecting internal light impart a vibrant and dramatic quality to the design. The Club is currently working with Helen on a project to commemorate the contribution of women in the service of the Royal Air Force. It will comprise two stained glass windows and will be installed in 2018.

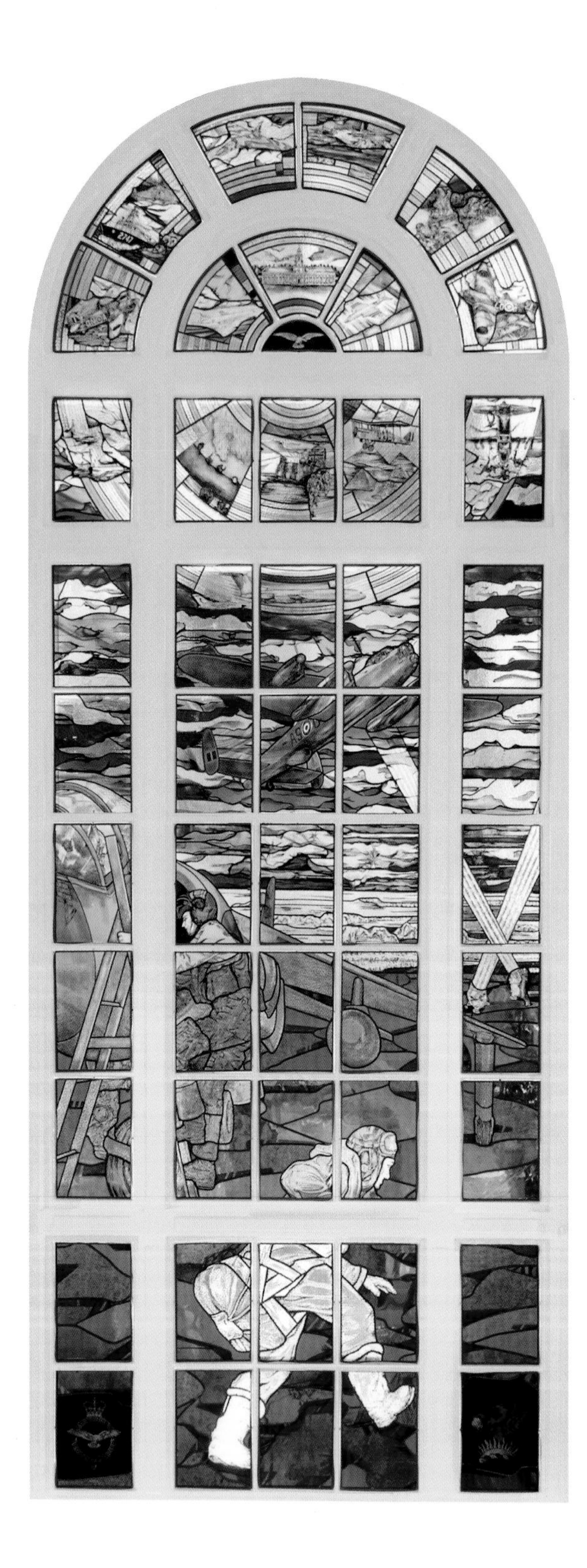

CONTENTS

CHAPTER I

THE FLEDGLING SERVICES ~ 1903 TO 1918

"If we all worked on the assumption that what is accepted as true is really true, there would be little hope of advance."

ORVILLE WRIGHT, 1903

THE 'father of aerial navigation' was an Englishman from Yorkshire, Sir George Cayley. At the age of 26, he suggested the wing of an aeroplane should be fixed and that, given an aerofoil shape, it could provide lift. Cayley had discovered the principles used in the modern aeroplane: a fixed wing, a man carrying fuselage, and movable tail surfaces. In 1804, at the age of 31, Cayley produced the world's first successful model glider incorporating these ideas. He followed it up with a full-scale aircraft five years later. During his life he developed the basic mathematical principles of heavier-than-air flight. He was the first to suggest the use of an internal combustion engine for aeroplanes, and the first to construct and fly a man-carrying glider. The first person to be carried aloft in a heavier-than-air craft in sustained, or gliding, flight was an unidentified young boy who became airborne in a glider constructed by Cayley in 1849.

The first Army balloon school was established at Woolwich in 1878, with the Balloon Factory and Training School established in 1882 at Chatham as a unit of the Royal Engineers. The factory was soon moved to Farnborough in Hampshire, thus beginning the town's long connection with aviation that continues to this day.

The first British Army Airship *Nulli Secundus* flew from Farnborough to London on 5 October 1907, but came back to Farnborough by road, deflated. More airships and balloons were built at Farnborough, but they were soon to be overshadowed by the aeroplane.

At the beginning of the 20th Century three principal pioneers were experimenting with powered aeroplane flight. These were the German Otto Lilienthal, the American Octave Chanute and the Englishman Percy Pilcher. But it was two unknown American brothers whose names have gone down in history as the inventors of the first aeroplane in the world to achieve man-carrying, powered and sustained flight. This was when *The 'Flyer*, designed and constructed by Wilbur and Orville Wright, flew on Thursday 17 December 1903, at Kill Devil Hill, Kittyhawk, North Carolina, USA. The flight lasted 12 seconds over a distance of 120ft. This short flight was the culmination of years of hard work by the Wright brothers. They, like their European colleagues, had been practising with gliders and models. The controllable, powered aeroplane had arrived and it was not long before military uses were discovered for this new form of transport.

On 16 October 1908 Samuel Franklin Cody, an American who was in England selling horses to the cavalry and experimenting with kites for army observation use, made the first officially recognised flight in Britain. Cody flew 1,390ft in British Army Aeroplane No1, built at Farnborough's Balloon Factory.

By this time governments on both sides of the Atlantic were looking more seriously at heavier-than-air machines. The Wright brothers separated, with Wilbur travelling to France to make public exhibition flights in Europe, and Orville remaining in the US and carrying out tests and demonstrations for the US Army.

Wilbur's demonstrations in France caused great excitement amongst aviators and the general public alike. Europe, rather than America, became the centre of the new sport of flight and in Britain, on 13 July 1909, A V Roe was the first man to fly an all-British machine. Just 12 days later the Frenchman Louis Blériot successfully completed the first cross-channel flight. This achievement showed that the English Channel might, in the not too distant future, no longer be an impregnable defence, policed for Britain solely by the Royal Navy.

The implications for the defence of the country did not go unnoticed by the military. On 1 April 1911 the Air Battalion of the Royal Engineers was forme; No 1 (Airship) Company was located at South Farnborough, and No 2 (Aeroplane) Company at Larkhill in Wiltshire. The Air Battalion's career was short lived, for a year later it became the Royal Flying Corps (RFC). Initially it was a joint-Service venture with separate Naval and Military Wings, a central flying school, a Reserve, and the Royal Aircraft Factory at Farnborough. The RFC was thus initially manned by men of both Services who were trained to fly and maintain aircraft at the world's first military flying training school at Upavon in Wiltshire. In 1914 the Royal Navy decided that the Naval Wing should become a separate air arm and formed the Royal Naval Air Service (RNAS).

The Army initially expected the new Flying Corps to provide only reconnaissance; other uses for military aircraft were not at that point being seriously considered. The aircraft were therefore designed primarily as machines to observe and co-operate with ground and sea forces. A range of aircraft types was in service in August 1914, when the RFC went to France at the start of World War I. This fledgling air force, with its motley collection of aircraft, consisted of just 63 aeroplanes, 105 officers and 95 motor vehicles. However, it very soon proved its worth, and provided valuable information more than once during the land battles in the early months of the war. Very quickly, with the development of aerial photography and wireless, aeroplanes became indispensable to both sides as the opposing armies waged their terrible industrialised trench warfare.

Aerial conflict began to develop at an ever-quickening pace, paving the way for a new type of aeroplane whose role was to seek out and destroy the reconnaissance aircraft. In 1915, the German Fokker monoplane fighter appeared. It was equipped with a synchronised machine-gun which fired forwards through the propeller, allowing the pilot to position his aeroplane and aim his gun with great accuracy. To counter this development Britain developed scout aeroplanes such as the Sopwith Pup. Designers produced stronger, faster aircraft with more powerful engines, notably the Sopwith Camel and the SE5a.

The primary function of the RNAS in Britain was to defend against attack by enemy airships and aircraft. The RNAS also went on the offensive by pioneering strategic bombing operations against German airship sheds and other targets. They also learnt to operate from warships, evolved the first true aircraft carriers, and attacked enemy shipping. Naval squadrons gave great aid to the hard-pressed Royal Flying Corps in France and shared the defence of the United Kingdom.

World War I showed the importance of this new technology. Not only could the aeroplane monitor the movement and disposition of the enemy, but it could also direct artillery fire, attack troops on the ground, bomb strategic and tactical targets, and provide rapid communication. The realisation of the importance of the aeroplane meant that it was developed at a prodigious rate during the four years of World War I. The aircraft that entered the war in 1914 were hard-pressed to achieve 75mph, yet by 1918 it was common for machines such as the Sopwith Snipe and Dolphin to achieve speeds in excess of 115mph, at much greater heights, and with increased manoeuvrability. These aircraft could carry automatic weapons and a bomb load, and were more mechanically reliable than their predecessors.

They not only operated over the Western Front, but also faced the rigours of the Middle East, providing air support for the land campaigns in Sinai, Palestine, Trans-Jordan, Mesopotamia (Iraq) and Syria. The RNAS also operated abroad with sea and land planes flying over the battlefields of the Dardanelles. Air campaigns were no longer the exception; they became the rule and aircraft flew from Macedonia, northern Italy, East Africa, Russia, India and many other parts of the world.

Managing this new war machine was not easy as there was long-standing rivalry between the Admiralty and the War Office. During 1916, the duplication and overlap between the roles of the RFC and RNAS, and competition between them for engines and aircraft, along with failures in the supply organisation, led to the suggestion that they might be amalgamated. Various attempts were made to solve this situation including creating the Air Board under Lord Cowdray, in January 1917, who centralised the supply within the Ministry of Munitions, rather than leaving it with the individual Services. Lord Cowdray had an excellent understanding of technical issues and was held in high regard by both Services. He also had a vision for the new Service which would soon be created and in October 1918 gave £100,000 "*... for the purpose of providing The Service Club for the Royal Air Force ...*". His generosity was followed by a further donation of £250,000 and, as a result the Royal Air Force Club was created.

Following an unopposed German daylight bombing raid on London's Docks on 13 June 1917, and another raid three weeks later, there was near-panic among members of the public. Prime Minister David Lloyd-George immediately appointed General Jan Christian Smuts, a South African Boer War veteran, to head an inquiry into London's aerial defences. Smuts' report recommended the re-organisation and amalgamation of the British air services and maintained that air power would one day cause the traditional concepts of Army and Navy power to be subordinated. He also recognised that the new Service should be directed by an Air Staff formed from a cadre of professionally qualified airmen.

Smuts detailed this vision for the independent use of air power as:

"*There is absolutely no limit to the scale of its future independent war use. And the day may not be far off when aerial operations with their devastation of enemy lands and destruction of industries and populous centres on a vast scale may become one of the principal operations of war, to which older forms of military and naval operations may become secondary and subordinate.*"

On 29 November 1917 the Air Force (Constitution) Act received Royal Assent and an Air Council was created. The first Chief of the Air Staff (CAS) was Sir Hugh Trenchard who had been in operational command of the Royal Flying Corps in France. His appointment did not last long since he found himself in almost constant conflict with the first Secretary of State for the Royal Air Force (the newspaper owner, Lord Rothermere), and in consequence he resigned after only two weeks. Nevertheless, on 1 April 1918 the Royal Flying Corps and the RNAS ceased to exist and were both absorbed into the new and separately administered RAF – the world's first independent air force had come into being.

Portrait of 2nd Lt Ronald Charles Wybrow Morgan

Solomon J Solomon

Ronald Morgan was an only child educated at Uppingham School. He was born in September 1897 and enlisted in 3rd Battalion, South Wales Borderers in July 1915. He was attached to the RFC a year later and gained his pilot's certificate in early 1917. In April 1917 he joined No 55 Squadron at Azelot, France flying DH4 aircraft. He died on 28 July 1917, from wounds he received during combat on the previous day. He is commemorated on a memorial at The Priory Church of St Mary and St Michael, Malvern, Worcs. A large stained glass window is also dedicated to his memory in St Saviour's Church, Westgate-on-Sea, Kent and he is buried in Hoogstade Belgium Military cemetery. The epitaph on his grave reads: "*His life on earth was short. He appears to fall, but is rising*". He was 19 years old at the time of his death.

The portrait is typical of the period, it is post-mortem and shows Ronald in a classic seated pose wearing his best uniform, the RFC 'Maternity Jacket', breeches and accoutrements, probably tailored at considerable expense and paid for by his proud parents. The chart spread across his knees points out that pilots are also navigators. His aircraft rests behind him.

Sopwith Triplanes On The Hunt
Mark Bromley

The Sopwith Aviation Company was one of the most important British aircraft companies during World War I. The aircraft was first flown on 28 May 1916 by Chief Test Pilot Harry Hawker who found it very agile, with effective and well-harmonised controls. In July the Triplane was sent to France for a successful evaluation by the Royal Naval Air Service (RNAS), which led to the Admiralty placing production contracts with Sopwith, Clayton & Shuttleworth Ltd and Oakley & Co Ltd who produced a total of 147 aircraft between them.

Acquiring the nickname 'Tripehound', or simply just 'Tripe', the Triplane was (contrary to the 'Red Baron' legend of the German Fokker version) the first triplane to see operational service. It had a successful introduction into combat as its high rate of climb and altitude gave it considerable advantage over contemporary German aircraft.

Despite its agility the Triplane had some weaknesses, for example it was armed with only a single synchronised Vickers machine gun, when its German contemporaries had two guns. Due to the rapid advances in technology, the Triplane's front-line career was fairly short, with its replacement in RNAS operational service by the Sopwith Camel completed by the end of 1917. However, it remained in use in a training role until the end of the war.

This painting depicts a flight of Triplanes, with the leading aircraft having the red painted fin and wheel covers sometimes associated with No 1 Naval Squadron.

BROMLEY

RNAS Sopwith Ships Camel Overflying a Dreadnought

Mark Bromley

The Sopwith Camel first flew in December 1916 and was developed as a faster and more heavily armed replacement for the earlier Pup, which, although only introduced into service that October, was already starting to be outclassed by the latest German aircraft. The humped fairing fitted over the twin Vickers machine guns to prevent them from freezing at altitude gave rise to the name Camel.

Designed by Herbert Smith and test flown by Harry Hawker, the Camel displayed exceptional manoeuvrability due to the close proximity of the engine, guns, fuel tank and pilot, which constituted most of the aircraft's weight. Unfortunately, this also resulted in the Camel gaining a reputation of being tricky to handle, especially for novice pilots.

The Camel saw operational service with numerous squadrons of both the RNAS and the RFC over the Western Front in France, and for Home Defence back in Britain. It was successfully used against Zeppelin airships and Gotha bombers, being adapted for night fighting when the German attacks became nocturnal. A specialised shipboard version was developed to operate from aircraft carriers, battleships fitted with platforms on their turrets and also aircraft lighters, which were modified barges towed behind warships. This painting shows Ships Camel 2F.1, serial No N8156, overflying a Dreadnought of the Grand Fleet, with the aircraft lighter visible in the distance.

The aircraft depicted was manufactured by Hooper and Company Ltd of London in late 1918. One of the last Camels to be produced, it was not completed in time to serve during World War I. It was, however, used by the RAF until 1925, when it was transferred to Canada along with six other Ships Camels.

This Camel was used by the RCAF for demonstration flights and as a training airframe. It was loaned to the Canadian War Museum in 1957, and was later stored and displayed at the National Research Council in Ottawa. Restored between 1958 and 1959, and made airworthy between 1966 and 1967, the aircraft was flown between May and June of that year before being transferred to the Canada Aviation & Space Museum, Rockcliffe Airport, Ottowa.

B
N8156
BROMLEY

Portrait of Viscount Cowdray
Sir William Orpen

The Peerage of Viscount Cowdray was created in 1917 for the industrialist Weetman Pearson, 1st Baron Cowdray, head of the Pearson conglomerate. Prime Minister David Lloyd George then asked him to become the President of the Air Board, which Cowdray agreed to, provided he received no salary.

During his time as President, he significantly increased the output of aircraft yet he was still criticised after a German raid in June 1917 which led to over 600 casualties. He resigned later in the year. He became active in both Liberal politics and philanthropy, making a significant financial contribution towards establishing the RAF Club initially with £100,000 to acquire the lease on 128 Piccadilly and subsequently with a further gift of £250,000 to carry out the necessary alterations to the building. Viscount Cowdray died aged 70 in his sleep at his house in Aberdeenshire on 1 May 1927.

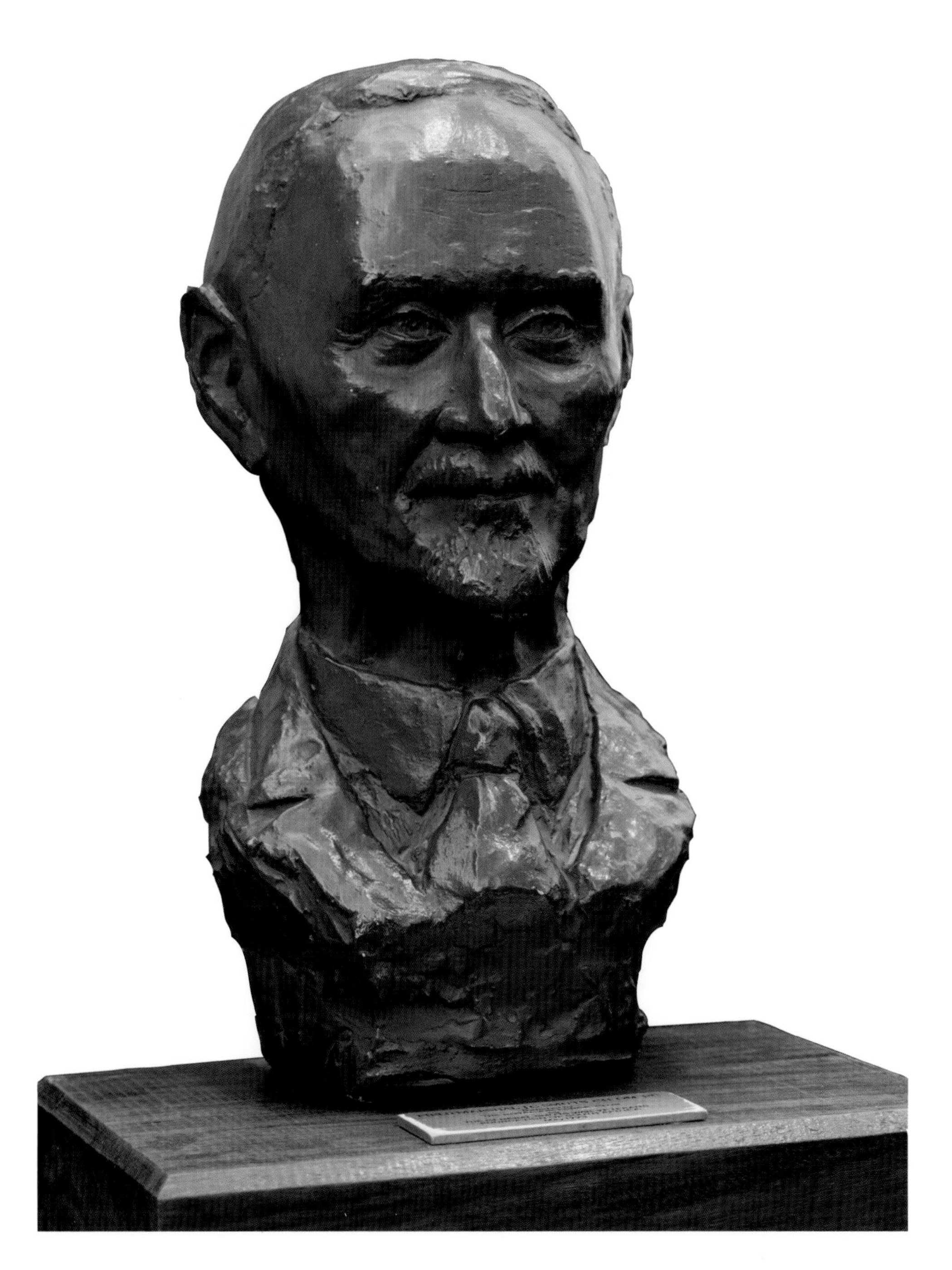

Bust of Field Marshal Jan Christian Smuts
The artist who created this sculpture is not known.

A painted plaster bust of Smuts who was born in 1870 in what is now South Africa. Smuts studied Law at Christ's College Cambridge, returning to South Africa in 1895, fighting against Britain in the Boer War. During World War I, he fought for Britain becoming a Lieutenant General and commanding the Allied forces in East Africa. He was appointed the South African representative at the Imperial War Conference and returned to Britain in January 1917.

With the German daylight bombing raids of London creating a public outcry against the inadequate state of Britain's air defences, Prime Minister Lloyd George turned to Smuts in July 1917, asking him to head a government committee to examine air defence arrangements and organisation. In this role he was supported by Sir David Henderson, the Director General of Military Aeronautics.

Smuts' committee issued two reports in July and August 1917, which recommended the formation of an Air Ministry, an Air Staff, and the amalgamation of the RFC and the RNAS into a new single Air Service that was independent of the Army and Navy. The Government accepted all these recommendations and the process of bringing the two services together began. This was achieved on 1 April 1918 with the creation of the Royal Air Force.

The reports are a milestone in aviation history, influencing the future direction of the development of air power in both Britain and many other countries. Smuts was a great personal friend of Churchill and a close advisor during World War II. At one point he was nominated as Churchill's successor should the Prime Minister die during the conflict. Smuts eventually reached the rank of Field Marshal and died in 1950 at the age of 80.

No 56 Squadron, Valheureux, France, 1 April 1918
Frank Wootton

This is one of a number of paintings which Frank Wootton made to commemorate 1 April 1918, the foundation day of the Royal Air Force. It illustrates his ability to include aircraft, vehicles, people and landscape in an informal and warm style. The painting depicts Royal Aircraft Factory Scout Experimental 5a aircraft (SE5a) of No 56 Squadron at their base in France. The SE5a, with its Wolseley Viper liquid cooled engine, was fast and manoeuvrable, and of comparatively strong construction, enabling it to dive at high speed.

The SE5a entered service with No 56 Squadron in March 1917, although the Squadron did not deploy to France until the following month. The scene in this painting shows the arrival of Trenchard and Smuts in their Crossley staff car. In the foreground is the aircraft flown by Major James McCudden, VC DSO* MC* and MM. McCudden was one of the most highly decorated British aces of World War I with 52 of his 57 victories achieved while flying the SE5a. Having previously been a mechanic, McCudden undertook considerable modifications to his aircraft, including increasing engine compression, shortening the exhaust pipe to reduce weight, fitting a spinner to the propeller and reducing the wing dihedral to increase agility. He was killed on 9 July 1918 when his SE5a crashed shortly after take-off and is buried in the Commonwealth War Graves Cemetery at Beauvoir-Wavans, France.

B4861
F
B4863
G

CHAPTER II

ESTABLISHING THE ROYAL AIR FORCE ~ 1918 TO 1921

"We want the man of initiative and the man of action, the methodical man and even the crank.
We open our ranks widely to all."

HUGH TRENCHARD

LITTLE changed on the Western Front following the formation of the Royal Air Force. Air power was still an essential component in defeating the German offensives and then in supporting the Allied armies in the counter-attacks that eventually resulted in The Armistice of 11 November 1918.

On 13 May 1918 the Independent Air Force (IAF) had already been created by bringing together RFC and RNAS units to undertake strategic bombing and operate independently of the land campaigns. With a force comprising De Havilland DH4s, DH9s, and Handley Page HP 0/400 (nicknamed 'Bloody Paralysers'), they had been conducting raids on Germany since the winter of 1917/18. Day and night raids were carried out and post-war analysis of this bombing suggested that the impact on the morale of the population, and the disruption to German production, was greater than the relatively minor damage caused. More significantly, perhaps, it was also found that, in addition, the raids ensured that large numbers of German forces were diverted into air defence units, which Germany could ill-afford when under such extreme pressures on the battlefield. These lessons would be carried forward to the next conflict.

Rather than being under the control of the Allied Supreme Commander, the IAF was commanded by Trenchard and its success confirmed his views, not only of the importance of employing airpower offensively, but also of the organisational issues that needed to be addressed to secure the long term future of the newly created RAF.

When the war was at last over, thousands of men were sent home, their aeroplanes were scrapped, and the new Service shrank almost overnight. The wartime strength of 188 operational squadrons, made up of nearly 300,000 men, 15,000 Women (of the, simultaneously formed, Women's Royal Air Force), together with over 22,000 aircraft, was reduced to a mere 33 squadrons in the first year following The Armistice. However, the end of the war did not mean the end of offensive operations for the RAF, which continued to support the White Russians against the Bolsheviks following the Russian Revolution.

A number of post war financial crises required the government to consider whether it could afford to maintain three independent services. Parliament, various committees and the press, publically debated the future of an independent air force and both the other services used the argument that savings could be made by axing the RAF and returning their flying services to them. However, a sound case in support of the RAF was made by Churchill and Trenchard; this led to the government accepting the case for the RAF's continued existence, albeit with a remit to define clearly its peacetime roles.

Valuable publicity for both the RAF and the British aircraft industry was achieved in June 1919, when the Daily Mail Prize of £10,000 for the first non-stop crossing of the Atlantic Ocean was won. The two successful RAF pilots, Capt John Alcock and Lt Arthur Whitten Brown, flying from Newfoundland in Canada to the west of Ireland using a modified Vickers Vimy bomber, were presented with the prize personally by Winston Churchill and received knighthoods from the King.

In March 1919 Trenchard had been re-appointed CAS and on 11 December 1919 the 'Trenchard Memorandum' outlined the principles for the permanent organisation of the RAF, and it was presented to Parliament by Churchill. Central to this was that:

"The principle to be kept in mind in forming the framework of the Air Services is that in future the main portion of it will consist of an independent force ... It may be that the Independent Air Force will grow larger and larger, and become more and more the predominating factor in all types of warfare."

Churchill explained that the first duty of the RAF was to garrison the British Empire, which led to the creation of 'Air Control' as a doctrine for undertaking the policing of large remote areas. The first campaign to test this came in 1920 in Somaliland against the insurgent forces of Mohammed Abdullah Hassan (derogatorily, often called 'The Mad Mullah'). Hassan was the Somali religious leader who had been operating in the hinterland for two decades and had built a number of fortresses to buttress his power and influence. The army had advised using a force comprising two or three divisions of troops, along the same lines as previous unsuccessful expeditions against Hassan by British, Italian and Ethiopian forces. This force would have cost several million pounds. Trenchard offered to undertake the operation using 12 De Havilland DH9s, in co-operation with local ground forces including the Somaliland Camel Corps, and in a matter of weeks drove the insurgents from their fortresses. Hassan, his power and influence fatally undermined, fled to the Ogaden where he died of influenza. The cost of Trenchard's successful expedition was around £77,000. This led to the campaign being described by Leo Amery, the Colonial Under-Secretary, as "*the cheapest war in history*". However, the strategic victory for the RAF lay in the proof it provided of the efficiency and affordability of Air Power whilst performing the key role of policing the Empire.

Thus, whilst Trenchard had very limited funds provided by Parliament to operate the fledgling Service, he constructed a permanent foundation for the RAF upon which future expansion could be accomplished, regardless of initial funding problems.

In placing the bulk of the operational squadrons overseas to 'police' the many Imperial and mandated territories then controlled by the British government following the Treaty of Versailles, the RAF continued fighting minor conflicts until the outbreak of World War II. This policing of Africa, the Middle East and India was part of Trenchard's great vision. He emphasised the need to create an 'Air Force Spirit' and to eliminate flying accidents by improving training. Thus he founded institutions to train technicians at Halton in Buckinghamshire, officers at Cranwell in Lincolnshire and senior officers at Andover in Wiltshire. Trenchard knew that high quality people were needed to provide the solid foundation for his new RAF. The engineering training of apprentices at Halton was a beacon of its day and Trenchard determined that the top three apprentices of each intake would be awarded scholarships to Cranwell. In an era when apprentices generally paid for their apprenticeships, RAF apprentice training was free and they were housed, fed, and paid good wages, whilst learning their trade. The training lasted three years, (longer than officer training) and apprentices were proud to be known as 'Halton Brats'. Many were subsequently commissioned, the most famous being Sir Frank Whittle, pilot and inventor of the jet engine.

Trenchard introduced three methods of entry as an officer into the new Service. There were permanent commissions via Cranwell from university or from the ranks. The Cranwell course lasted two years and was fee paying, intended for the future senior officers of the Service. The second entry method was for exchange officers from the other Services, with the intention of fostering close co-operation between the Army, Navy and Air Force. The final option was Short Service Commissions, which was a radical departure from what had been normal military practice up to that time. These officers did not go to Cranwell; they were taught to fly, served for four years, and were then held for a further six years in the Reserve. A permanent commission was open to them on examination and depending on the needs of the Service.

Trenchard's original plans were the cornerstones of the RAF and they enabled it to expand quickly and successfully in later years. The development of aviation and its commercial companies, and the links between the Service and that development, grew stronger still as the science and manufacture of aircraft became more sophisticated and the requirements of the RAF broadened. Simple things like creating a unified system of ranks, uniforms and an Ensign were every bit as important as the physical infrastructure, and perhaps more so in inculcating Trenchard's desired 'Air Force Spirit'. The designs for uniforms deserve particular mention. The initial officers' dress headgear was an allegorical ceremonial flying helmet complete with fur. The first officers' uniforms were made in a sky blue colour material sourced from cloth originally intended for the Russian Tsar's cavalry, but (like the original recipients) redundant to requirements and therefore affordable for the new Service. Closer scrutiny of the supplier's stock may have revealed how limited it was, for the supplies of material quickly ran out and were replaced by the present, more sober, shade of Air Force Blue in 1920.

Trenchard was conscious that he needed public support for his new Service and accordingly, on 3 July 1920, the first Royal Air Force Aerial Pageant was held at Hendon in north-west London. The pageants became an annual showpiece and by this means the RAF familiarised the public with its work and demonstrated the efficiency of its training whilst, at the same time, raising money for RAF charities.

Trenchard himself summed up his vision of airpower in the following words:

"The development of air power in its broadest sense, and including the development of all means of combating missiles that travel through the air, whether fired or dropped, is the first essential to our survival in war."

'Brisfit' Over the Western Front 1918

Mark Bromley

A 'Brisfit' (Bristol F.2B Fighter) circles above the Western Front in World War I, positioning itself to bring down a German reconnaissance machine below. Both the pilot and his gunner stare intently at their target. The German aircraft appears to be a Halberstadt CII which is identifiable by its single cockpit in which both pilot and gunner sit. The grouping of crew members together was common in German aircraft in both World Wars and was thought to improve cohesion and morale. Allied aircraft design separated the crews, positioning them where their duties required.

The first Bristol Fighters (F.2As) were delivered to No 48 Squadron of the RFC in December 1916, with the aircraft undertaking its first operation in March the following year. Unfortunately, the experience of operating previous two seat types led the RFC to continue to use the same tactics when flying the new aircraft and its early use suffered high casualties. However, once crews realised the F.2A was both structurally strong, with agile flying characteristics that gave it a performance more akin to a single seat fighter than a two seat observation or bomber machine, it proved to be a very effective aircraft. Fitted with a fixed forward machine gun for the pilot and one or two machine guns on a flexible mount for the observer, the Fighter had a good all round field of fire.

The F.2A variant was soon replaced by the definitive F.2B, with an uprated Rolls Royce Eagle engine that gave improved performance. By the end of World War I, and by then also known throughout the RAF as 'The Biff', the RAF had over 1,500 in squadron service. By the end of the war, Bristol Fighters of No 11 Squadron were fitted with radios, which allowed the flight commander to transmit Morse code messages to the other aircraft.

The F.2B was adopted by the RAF as its standard post-war aircraft for Army co-operation and continued in service for many years, with the final examples not being withdrawn from use with the RAF in India until 1932. Along with the De Havilland DH9A , the 'Brisfit' became well known for undertaking the aerial policing role across the British Empire. For this task it was modified to cope with the temperature extremes it encountered.

BROMLEY

Portrait of Sir Sefton Brancker

Sir John Lavery

Air Vice-Marshal Sir William Sefton Brancker KCB AFC, started his military career with the Royal Artillery in 1906 and served in both the Second Boer War and India. During his time in India he was responsible for the unloading of the Bristol Boxkites that arrived in 1911 for flying demonstrations. He subsequently flew as an observer, which enabled him to experience the benefits of aerial reconnaissance. While at the War Office under Sir David Henderson, he took up flying and was awarded his Aviators' Certificate by the Royal Aero Club (RAeC) in June 1913.

Apparently, whilst not a particularly good pilot, he was an excellent administrator and during World War I he held a number of important positions within the RFC. With the creation of the RAF and the Air Ministry, he was appointed a member of the Air Council as Controller-General of Equipment.

Retiring during the post-war run down of the RAF, he was appointed Controller of Civil Aviation in 1922 focusing on the development of air routes for airships and aircraft in Britain and across the Empire. In this he was a supporter of the pioneering long distance survey flights of Alan Cobham, served as Master of the Guild of Air Pilots (now The Honourable Company of Air Pilots), and also led to the RAeC forming the Light Aero Club scheme in 1925, which helped provide UK flying clubs with examples of new aircraft types such as the De Havilland DH60 Moth and the Avro Avian.

Sir Sefton Brancker was a passenger aboard the R101 for its inaugural flight to India in 1930. He died when the airship hit the ground in bad weather and burst into flames near Beauvais, France.

To GENERAL BRANCKER
FROM

No 221 Squadron, Russia, 1919

Anthony Cowland

For most pilots railway trains are an interesting subject, especially steam trains. Merely watching them from above, even in peacetime, is exhilarating. In war they are an enemy's means of logistical support and a prime target. However, attacking trains is exceptionally dangerous not only because of the low level which has to be flown to achieve success, but also because of the inevitable explosion from the locomotive's boiler if the attack is successful. Armoured trains, or those carrying military equipment, are even more dangerous because they return fire, as can be seen in this dramatic painting. This work shows a DH9 of No 221 Squadron attacking a Bolshevik train

Following the Bolshevik Revolution in Russia during November 1917, a civil war was fought until October 1922 between the 'Red Russians' led by Lenin and the 'White Russians' who were a loose coalition of forces, unified in their opposition to the Bolsheviks. Fearing that Russia's exit from World War I would allow Germany to redeploy significant forces to the Western Front and also access Russian bases, a number of nations, including Britain, provided forces to support the 'White Russians'. This support continued after the end of the War.

Amongst the RAF units involved, both Nos 47 and 221 Squadrons were sent to Russia in 1919 and undertook operations until being disbanded towards the end of the year. Both flew the De Havilland DH9 bomber, with No 47 Squadron flying a number of other types as well, including the Sopwith Camel, also visible in this painting.

The DH9 was designed by Geoffrey de Havilland and first flew in July 1917. It was a development of the earlier DH4, using the same wings and tail unit, but with a new fuselage that placed the pilot and gunner closer together, making communication between them easier. Unfortunately, the DH9 was plagued by engine problems and despite several different engine types being used, none was ever completely successful. Eventually, the American Liberty V-12 engine was fitted and the modified aircraft, known as the DH9A, became one of the most successful RAF aircraft of the interwar years, being used in many aerial policing operations.

Leaving the New World, 1919

Mark Bromley

As they climb slowly, overloaded with 865 gallons of fuel, John Alcock (1892–1919) and Arthur Whitten Brown (1886–1948) cross the Newfoundland coast bound for Europe. It is 14 June 1919 as they fly a modified World War I bomber, the Vickers Vimy. They face a 1,890 mile journey at an average speed of 115mph and flying in the most challenging of conditions. Their crossing was the first non-stop trans-Atlantic flight and ended less than 16 hours later, early the next day, in a bog in Clifden, County Galway Ireland – not far from their intended landing site. They won substantial cash prizes and were both knighted by HM King George V a few days after landing.

Only three Vickers Vimys had been delivered to the RAF by October 1918 and with The Armistice in November, the need for its strategic bombing role ceased. However, although its entry into service was slowed, it became the RAF's main bomber force throughout the 1920s, equipping squadrons both in Britain and overseas. Due to its long range and large payload it was also used for airmail services and to deliver newspapers during the 1926 General Strike. A commercial version was developed that entered RAF service as the first dedicated troop carrier. This version carried out the first strategic airlift of troops in February 1923, when they transported 500 troops into Kirkuk in Iraq after the town had been overrun by Kurdish forces. The final RAF Vimys were not retired until 1938.

The Vimy was used in a number of pioneering long range flights in the immediate post-war period. In December 1919 a Vimy was the first aircraft to fly from England to Australia, and in February 1920, from England to South Africa. Alcock and Brown's Vimy is displayed in the Science Museum, London.

Home Sweet Home

Mark Bromley

Coming into land across a peaceful and pastoral scene of summer harvesting. This image of a DH4 over the English countryside evokes an era of peace following the 'War to End All Wars'.

The Airco DH4 was designed by Geoffrey de Havilland as a two seat day bomber, which could carry a 460lb bomb load on external racks. Entering service with the RFC in January 1917, with No 55 Squadron, the DH4 soon established itself as a reliable aircraft with a very good performance, being able to achieve a speed and altitude that enabled many missions to be carried out without a fighter escort.

The DH4 was also used by the RNAS in France and overseas, being credited with shooting down a Zeppelin and sinking a U-boat. When America entered the War in 1917 it had no suitable indigenous combat aircraft and the DH4 was adopted by the United States Army Air Service. It continued in US military service until 1932. The DH4 was also manufactured in the USA and formed the backbone of the US Postal Service's early air mail service.

Following the Armistice, the RAF formed No 2 Communication Squadron, equipped with DH4s to take personnel between Britain and Paris for the Peace Conference. Several of these aircraft were modified with an enclosed cabin that could carry two passengers and were designated DH4As.

After the war, surplus DH4s were used extensively to establish passenger and air mail services across the world.

BROMLEY

Avro 504K In Flight
Mark Bromley

The first aircraft many early RAF pilots flew, the Avro 504K, has all the hallmarks of a machine built to withstand the trials and tribulations of student mishandling. Its distinctive ski-shaped skid, at the centre of its landing gear, stops the propeller hitting the ground and the hoops of bamboo under each lower wingtip avoid a similar fate should the aircraft topple on to a wing on the ground. It was a forgiving machine, much loved by those who flew it.

Having first flown in September 1913, the Avro 504 was already in service with the RFC and RNAS at the start of World War I. In August 1914, an RFC Avro 504 was the first to be shot down by the Germans. RNAS Avro 504s undertook a successful bombing raid on the Zeppelin works at Friedrichshafen in November 1914.

The rapid technological advances during the war soon made the Avro 504 obsolete for combat roles over the Western Front and a new role was found for it in pilot training. It was discovered to be ideal for this purpose and continued in production for many years, serving with the RAF until 1933.

Many surplus aircraft went onto the civil register in Britain and overseas and were used for a number of roles, including pleasure flights and banner towing. A small number of civilian examples were even brought back into RAF service during the early part of World War II.

The aircraft depicted here, H5199, was built in 1918 as a K version and was converted to an N, being sold to Air Publicity, at Heston Aerodrome in August 1935. It was taken back onto RAF charge in 1939 and used in conjunction with glider towing experiments, before being finally struck off charge in June 1942. In July 1955, it was converted back to K standard by Avro apprentices for use in the film *Reach for the Sky* about the life of Gp Capt Sir Douglas Bader. Although now carrying different markings, this aircraft is owned by the Shuttleworth Collection and regularly flies from their airfield in Bedfordshire.

H
5199
H5199
BROMLEY

Sopwith Snipe Over Kingston Bridge

Mark Bromley

The Sopwith Snipe started to equip the RAF in France from August 1918 when it replaced the Sopwith Camels of No 43 Squadron. The Squadron flew its first operational missions with the Snipe in September, but saw relatively little combat prior to the end of the War.

In October 1918, Canadian Major William George 'Billy' Barker, who was attached to No 201 Squadron, was flying a Snipe over the Western Front. This Snipe, E8102, had been brought with him to France for a 10 day evaluation of the latest combat techniques in use, to assist him in his role at the OC Fighter Training School at Hounslow Heath. On his last flight before returning to England he shot down a German Rumpler two seat aircraft and was then attacked by at least 15 Fokker D.VIIs, one of the finest fighter aircraft of the war. In the ensuing dogfight, Barker managed to shoot down three of the Fokkers despite being wounded three times and losing consciousness twice. He made a forced landing on the Allied front lines and was awarded the Victoria Cross for his actions.

This painting shows a Snipe, in the markings of Barker's machine, flying over Kingston Bridge with Sopwith's Ham, Surrey, factory in the distance. Built by the Ministry of Munitions as the National Aircraft Factory No 2 through the winter of 1917, Ham was then leased by Sopwith to more than double their manufacturing capacity. From April 1918, Sopwith was producing aircraft, including Snipes, Dolphins and Salamanders at the factory. The factory became part of Hawker Aircraft Ltd in 1948 and continued in use by Hawker and its successor companies until it closed in 1992.

Following The Armistice, Snipes were used as part of the British Army of Occupation in Germany, eventually returning to the UK during 1919. Although Snipes continued to replace Camels, the rapid post-war rundown of the RAF meant that, by the end of 1919, only No 80 Squadron was still equipped with the Snipe. As part of the British intervention in the Russian Civil War to support the 'White Russians', Snipes were deployed as part of the RAF's mission in northern Russia. The Snipe served with the RAF until 1926.

BROMLEY

Portrait of Lord Trenchard

Sir Oswald Birley

Marshal of the Royal Air Force Hugh Montague Trenchard, 1st Viscount Trenchard, GCB OM GCVO DSO (3 February 1873 to 10 February 1956). Trenchard is widely regarded as the 'Father of the Royal Air Force', although he was known to dislike the reference, believing that Lieutenant General Sir David Henderson, KCB KCVO DSO (11 August 1862 – 17 August 1921) better deserved the accolade.

After a difficult academic career, Trenchard was commissioned into the Army and served in both India and the Boer War, where he was badly injured. Following recuperation, he re-joined the Service and also learned to fly in 1912 with the Sopwith School of Flying at Brooklands, becoming second in command of the Central Flying School.

He was the first Chief of the Air Staff (CAS), before taking over command of the Independent Air Force in France, where he developed links with the American Air Service, advising them on advanced bombing techniques and providing support to them on operations.

In 1927, he became the first Marshal of the Royal Air Force, a rank that only a further 26 men have held, 22 of whom have been RAF Officers and five, members of the Royal Family. Retiring as CAS for the second time in 1930, he was made a Baron and entered the House of Lords, took up a directorship and became the Metropolitan Police Commissioner. As Commissioner he was keen to modernise police training and, mirroring his achievements at Cranwell, Andover and Halton, he determined to build a Police College. In deciding a location, he knew of an ideal site in North London next to RAF Hendon. The Metropolitan Police College was built using the redundant Grahame-White Country Club and ancillary buildings of the aerodrome which were no longer needed by the RAF.

During the 1930s, his Baron status was upgraded to Viscount and in 1937, one of his overseas visits led to him being hosted by the Chief of the recently created German Luftwaffe, Herman Göring. Always a supporter of the offensive use of air power through bombing, Trenchard had reservations about the expansion era focus on defensive fighter aircraft at the expense of bombers.

He did not return to command during World War II. However, as a peer, a friend of Churchill, and with close connections to the Air Staff, Trenchard made many morale boosting visits to RAF stations and squadrons, championing the cause of air power and the RAF. The war brought the loss of two stepsons and his own eldest son, although his younger son, Thomas, survived.

Post war, he was asked by several American generals to brief them in support of the debate about establishing the United States Air Force, which was created in 1947.

Trenchard died in February 1956 and, following his funeral in Westminster Abbey, his ashes were buried there, in the Battle of Britain Chapel. His legacy lives on in the RAF today, through Trenchard Hall at RAF Cranwell, Trenchard House at Farnborough, home of the Farnborough Air Science Trust museum and Trenchard Lines, part of the Army's HQ Land Forces, at the famous former RAF Upavon, Wilts.

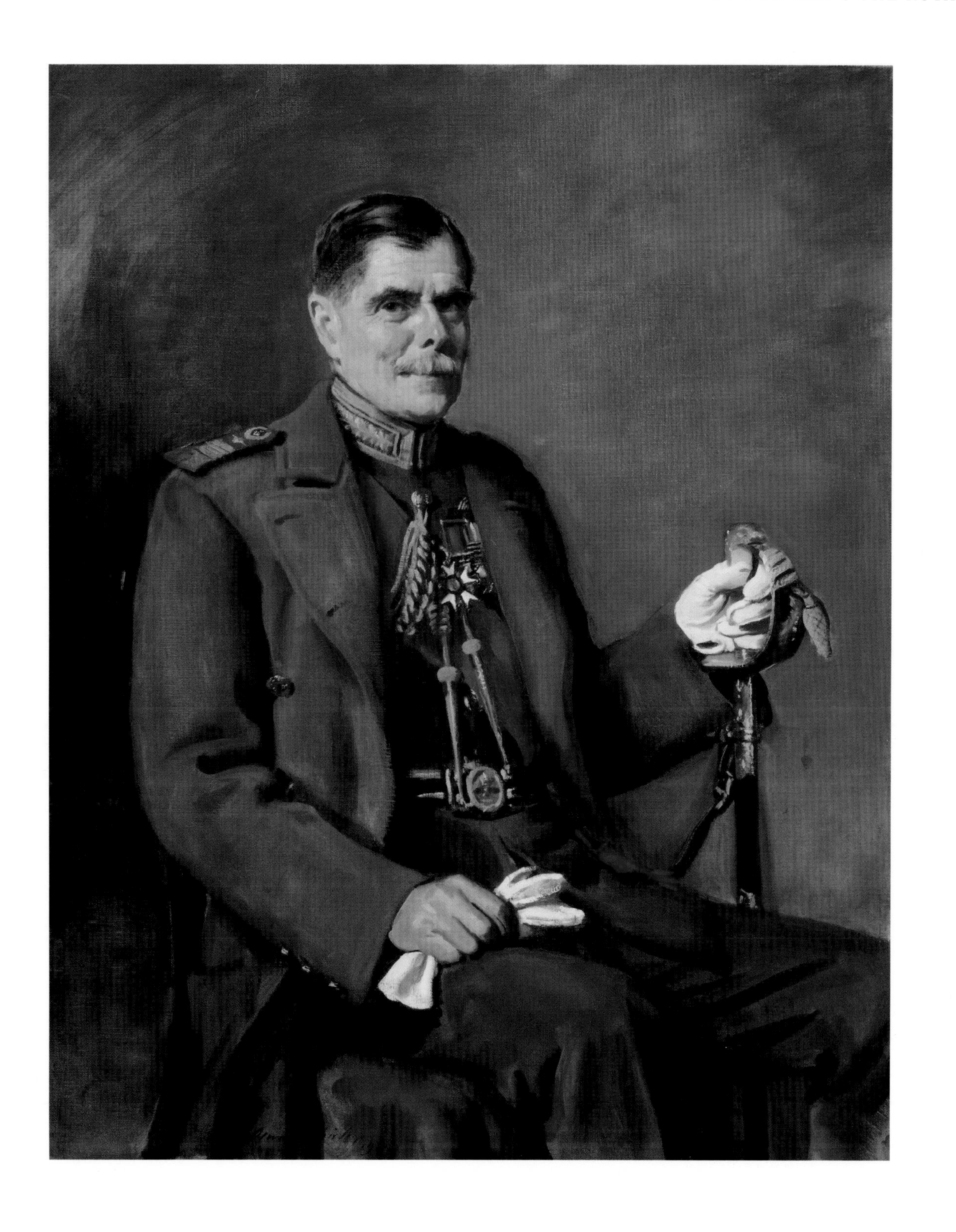

CHAPTER III

HOSTILE ENVIRONMENTS ~ 1922 TO 1932

"The word Trenchard spells out confidence in the RAF. We think of him as immense not by what he says ... and not by what he writes ... but just by what he is. He knows."

AIRCRAFTSMAN SHAW (T E LAWRENCE)

THE struggles with the other Services continued throughout the early 1920s. However, the RAF was starting to prove to the Government the continued value of its new independence.

Following the operation in Somaliland and with Winston Churchill now the Colonial Secretary, the RAF was used on a much larger scale in Iraq, where there was considerable unrest and instability. Under the command of AVM Sir John Salmond, the RAF deployed eight squadrons of aircraft, comprising DH9 bombers, Bristol Fighters and Vickers Vernon transports. The only ground forces to remain in Iraq were a single brigade of British and Indian troops, along with four companies of RAF armoured cars, which formed the origins of today's Royal Air Force Regiment. Prior to this, the Army had deployed 33 infantry battalions and six cavalry regiments, so Trenchard's value-for-money philosophy was, once again, evident to the Treasury.

In September 1922, a revolt in the northern province of Iraq led Salmond to authorise the world's first air evacuation. Vernons and DH9s were used and, in a five hour period, some 70 people and a dog were moved from Sulamaniya to Kirkuk. Ever more active Turkish and local support to oppose British rule threatened the small garrison at Kirkuk, leading Salmond to undertake the first troop airlift when the Vernons moved around 480 troops in to reinforce the garrison. As the rebels had not believed it would be possible for the British to send additional troops, their forces drifted away into the mountains and while they remained an irritant for many years, with Turkey's backing fading, they became much less of a threat. Sir John Salmond would later be promoted to Air Marshal and succeed Trenchard as CAS. Another notable officer involved in this campaign was Sqn Ldr Arthur Harris, who commanded the Vernons of No 45 Squadron and went on to lead Bomber Command during World War II. An early example of Harris' character can be seen from his modification of his Vernon transport aircraft to provide an offensive capability, by ordering his engineers to cut bomb aiming windows in the aircraft and arrange for weapons to be carried.

In 1923 a committee was appointed to examine the relationship between the RAF and the Royal Navy. Following its report, on 1 April 1924, the Fleet Air Arm of the Royal Air Force was formed from units normally embarked on aircraft carriers and other ships. However, the separation of the aviation aspects of operations from the Royal Navy delayed the speedy development and potential of naval aviation. This was done in a number of ways, but principally by both Trenchard (CAS) and Churchill (who had until recently been Secretary of State for Air), claiming that many of the responsibilities assigned to the Navy could be carried out more cheaply by the RAF and, more importantly, that neither the battleship nor the aircraft carrier had much of a future stating: *"Carrier ships are expensive and vulnerable, and with suitable aerodromes the main routes of the Empire can be largely covered"*. However, the arguments were also quite trivial at times with Lord Londonderry, the Under-Secretary of State for Air, telling Trenchard there was nothing personal in the Navy's attacks on him; their actions were *"... the dread that an air officer might one day be Commander-in-Chief."*

Whilst this was going on, in addition to the Middle East situation, the Government was also becoming concerned with the possibility of air attack, or simply the threat of such an attack during diplomatic crises, from Europe and in particular from France. This led, in June 1923, to the decision, by Prime Minister Stanley Baldwin, that a Home Defence Air Force to protect the United Kingdom from attack was required. The plan to bring the RAF up to the strength to undertake this required the Service to expand to 52 squadrons.

Unfortunately, the continued pressure on defence spending and a Government policy still based on the 'Ten Year Rule', adopted in August 1919, trusting that *"... the British Empire would not be engaged in any great war during the next 10 years"*, meant that the completion of the 52 squadrons was delayed until 1935–36. However, the aim further strengthened the case for independence and gave Trenchard the opportunity to start to put into practice his ideas on the development of bomber squadrons for offensive operations. Therefore, the strength was divided between 17 air defence squadrons, equipped with fighters, and 35 bomber squadrons.

Meanwhile, the short service commission scheme was proving effective in providing both the manning for these squadrons and an instantly available trained reserve. The first Auxiliary Air Force Squadrons were formed in 1925, with the initial University Air Squadrons (UAS) at Cambridge, London and Oxford following shortly afterwards. In a speech at Cambridge in 1925, Trenchard explained the aim behind the UAS stating that *"It will give the brains of the country a chance of being used for aeronautical purposes which will be an important factor in home defence"* – a prophesy which would soon become self evident.

1925 also saw the creation of the unified Air Defence of Great Britain, which brought together the RAF's Metropolitan Air Force, the Army's heavy anti-aircraft guns and searchlights, and the newly formed Observer Corps.

The Middle East continued to provide a source of trouble for the British Empire and a large scale rebellion in 1928 cut off Kabul in Afghanistan and threatened foreign nationals in the city. The effectiveness of the RAF in humanitarian operations was demonstrated when 586 people, of many nationalities, were evacuated from the city over a two month winter period, with the loss of one Vickers Victoria transport aircraft in a forced landing, but with no casualties.

With the Directorate of Civil Aviation being part of the Air Ministry, the RAF was very influential in the development of British civil aviation and in particular the creation of the air routes to the Middle East, Africa, India, Hong Kong, Singapore and Australia. The first major route between Cairo and Baghdad commenced in 1921, when a convoy of cars from Amman met roughly halfway another convoy that had set off from Baghdad; both were accompanied by aircraft. The convoys' physical wheel tracks provided a navigation aid until a more permanent path could be marked ploughed. Subsequently, landing grounds were created along the route and underground fuel tanks provided. Africa was being opened up in a similar way, with flights made through Sudan, Kenya and down to South Africa. These became established civil air routes, when, in 1924, the Government established Imperial Airways to develop economic commercial air transport. The first route launched in 1927 being that between Cairo and Baghdad.

Owing to the vast distances that would be flown over oceans, the opening of the routes to the Far East was carried out by flying boats, such as the Supermarine Southampton and the Blackburn Iris.

Probably one of the most notable of these flights was that undertaken by four Southamptons of the Far East Flight. The Flight had been specially formed to undertake a journey to Australia and the Far East. Previous long range 'cruises' had established the durability of the flying boat and, between 17 October 1927 and 18 September 1928, the Flight covered approximately 23,000 miles from Felixstowe to Singapore, around Australia and back to Singapore.

The RAF undertook a further succession of pioneering flights and record-breaking adventures. In April 1929 Sqn Ldr A D Jones Williams and Flt Lt N H Jenkins set off in a specially designed Fairey Monoplane of the Long-Range Development Unit (LRDU). They flew non-stop from Cranwell to Karachi, then in India, a journey of 4,030 miles. They had hoped to fly even further, but headwinds hampered their progress. A second attempt was made later in the year, flying from England to South Africa, but the aircraft crashed en-route killing both these two officers. The LRDU persisted and set a new World record between Cranwell and Walvis Bay (South Africa), a distance of 5,430 miles; this record stood until 1938. Thus routes now taken for granted were proved possible at this time by the Royal Air Force and Imperial Airways, the national airline.

Not only long range flying but high altitudes and greater speeds were achieved. In 1927 the RAF competed for the first time in the Schneider Trophy, sponsored by the French industrialist, financier, balloonist and aircraft enthusiast, Jacques Schneider. First held in 1913, it was intended to encourage the development of sea planes and flying boats. The Air Ministry recognised the research potential offered by the race and in 1927 formed the RAF High Speed Flight (HSF). The British aircraft industry also recognised the opportunity that the races provided, with Gloster and Shorts both developing aircraft. However, the Supermarine company and its Chief Designer, Reginald J Mitchell, became the most successful and are forever associated with the Schneider Trophy.

The 1927 race was held in Venice and was won by Flt Lt S N Webster AFC, flying a Supermarine S.5 at an average speed of 281.66mph, with another S.5 taking second place. Also flying was Flt Lt S Kinkead DSO DSC* DFC*, whose Gloster IV retired after five laps.

In March 1928, Kinkaid was in command of the HSF and flew an S.5 to make an attempt on the world air speed record. Unfortunately, this ended in tragedy when, on the approach to the start line for his record attempt, the aircraft crashed into the Solent killing him instantly.

For the 1929 race, held at Cowes, two new all-metal Supermarine S.6s, fitted with the new Rolls Royce R engine, were in direct competition with the Italian Air Force who were under orders from their Fascist Dictator, Benito Mussolini, to win. However, Fg Off H R D Waghorn, flying S.6 N247, won at a speed of 328.63mph.

With these two consecutive wins, Britain only needed to win a third time, in 1931, to retain the trophy permanently. Yet, with the country suffering another financial crisis, the Government withdrew financial support. However, public outcry and donations, led by Lady Houston's £100,000, financed the entry and the Government changed its position, reforming the High Speed Flight.

With only seven months until the race in September, Supermarine and Rolls Royce could only update the S.6 by strengthening the airframe, lengthening the floats and increasing the engine power. Two new S.6Bs were built and the S.6s modified to S.6A standard.

All the other nations had dropped out leaving the HSF unchallenged and Flt Lt J N Boothman, flying S.6B S1595, won at a speed of 340.08mph. With this victory work then began on a further attempt at the world speed record which was flown by Flt Lt G Stainforth on 29 September 1931 in a specially prepared S.6B fitted with a 'sprint' version of the R engine and using a specially prepared fuel mixture. He achieved a new record of 407.5mph, being the first man to travel faster than 400mph.

The great technological progress achieved through the Schneider Trophy races was to provide Supermarine and Rolls Royce with the experience to develop the Spitfire fighter and Merlin engine, which would become such a formidable combination during World War II.

Ensuring a spirit of 'air mindedness' was maintained in members of the public the Hendon Pageants continued. As the decade advanced this included the addition of a New Types Park which showcased the aircraft manufacturers and their latest products. Each year the very latest machines would be displayed and the public informed of the advances that had been made. As the years unfolded this annual event became ever more popular and important, not only for the public, but also for the RAF and its industry partners. This practice has continued to this day with the major shows around the world, including Farnborough and Paris. Industry and the RAF continue their long tradition of encouraging young people to consider careers in science and engineering through the modern science, technology, engineering, and mathematics (STEM) initiatives

Despite this 'golden era' of aviation, the failure of the Geneva Disarmament Conference and the rise of fascist and militaristic powers in both Europe and the Far East foretold the need to expand the RAF to prepare it to fight yet another war. In the early years of the 1930s a further expansion and re-equipping was therefore both necessary and urgent.

Portrait of Sir John Salmond
Cuthbert Orde

Marshal of the Royal Air Force Sir John Maitland Salmond, GCB CMG CVO DSO* (17 July 1881–16 April 1968) graduated from Sandhurst in 1901 as a Second Lieutenant and took part in the Boer War. He learned to fly with the Central Flying School (CFS) in August 1912 and was then seconded to the RFC, becoming a flight and then squadron commander. He also set the solo British altitude record of 13,140ft, in December 1913.

During the early stages of World War I he served as a squadron commander and became Commander of the Training Brigade in July 1916, and then General Officer Commanding Training Division from August 1917. During his tenure he opened many flying schools, determined minimum training standards and introduced modern teaching methods. In January 1918, Salmond became General Officer Commanding the RFC in the Field.

After the war he was promoted to Air Chief Marshal and appointed Air Member for Personnel in January 1929. He succeeded Trenchard as CAS in January 1930 and, with a further promotion to Marshal of the Royal Air Force in January 1933, served as CAS until April 1933 when he handed over to his brother Sir Geoffrey Salmond. However, Sir Geoffrey was suffering from incurable cancer and died less than a month later, so that Sir John returned as CAS for a further month until a new CAS was appointed.

During World War II, he was Director of Armament Production at the Ministry of Aircraft Production (MAP) and also chaired the committee of enquiry into Britain's night air defences and was appointed Director-General of Flying Control and Air Sea Rescue. He retired as a result of ill health in 1943. He was President of the RAF Club for 23 Years and Honorary Air Commodore of No 3618 (County of Sussex) Fighter Control Unit of the RAuxAF.

Air Control of Mesopotamia

Alan Fearnley

A painting which depicts 'Aerial Policing' in the mandated territories during the inter-war period evoking the role which secured the independence of the Royal Air Force when it was at its most vulnerable. The 'affordable' nature of air control, as opposed to large numbers of troops on the ground, gave Trenchard the advantage whenever the Army or Navy sought to return the air services to their command.

The DH9A, known as the 'Ninak', was the RAF's standard post-war light bomber, continuing in service until 1931. Aircraft used overseas were frequently modified to cope with the extreme conditions, for example with an additional radiator fitted under the fuselage to cope with the high temperatures. Before the widespread use of wireless some machines were equipped with a long bamboo pole with a hook at the end. This was suspended under the fuselage and could be lowered by a crew member in order to pick up written messages hung on a line between two poles a few feet above the ground. Additional water containers and spares (including spare wheels lashed to the fuselage) were carried in case the aircraft were forced down in the desert.

Singapore Via Southamptons
Alan Fearnley

The RAF Far East Flight, led by Gp Capt Henry Cave-Browne-Cave, flew four Supermarine Southampton flying boats from England to Australia. It is a notable example of the pioneering work undertaken by the RAF between the World Wars to open up the air routes across the British Empire.

The Flight left Britain in October 1927 and via numerous staging points including Iraq, India and Singapore, arrived in Australia in June 1928, reaching Darwin in August. With long range flying in its infancy, an RAF base party of officers and men travelled ahead with fuel and spares, and a spare Southampton was shipped to Singapore.

Following their time in Australia, the Flight returned to Singapore, via a number of countries including Thailand and Vietnam, reaching RAF Seletar again in September 1928. A Further 4,500 miles were flown on a final leg, a return trip from Singapore to Hong Kong, in November and December of 1928.During the 14 month period since leaving Britain, the Flight had covered some 27,000 miles at an average speed of 80mph. The Flight was disbanded in January 1929, becoming No 205 Squadron, which was the first squadron to be based in the Far East and remained at Seletar.

The Supermarine Southampton was designed by R J Mitchell who would go on to design the Schneider Trophy seaplanes and the Spitfire. The wooden hulled Mk I version first flew in 1925, but the Far East Flight used the later metal hulled Mk IIs which were modified for their journey. This included having the capacity of the engine cooling and oil systems increased and the hulls painted white inside and out. In addition, all armament, fittings and bomb racks were removed to save weight. The success of the flight provided much valuable publicity for both Supermarine and Napier, the engine manufacturer.

Allan Fearnley 79

Long Distance Heroes
Cuthbert Orde

These two portraits honour men who, as the crew of an experimental aircraft, were part of the pioneering work undertaken by the RAF during the inter-war period. Both died in their quest to set a world distance record.

Sqn Ldr Arthur Gordon Jones-Williams OBE MC* (1898 – 17 December 1929) was born in Wales, and following service as a 2nd Lieutenant in the Welsh Regiment, was seconded to the RFC during early 1917. He achieved his first eight victories while flying Nieuports with No 29 Squadron during 1917, before being transferred to No 65 Squadron and the Sopwith Camel, with which he achieved a further three victories during 1918.

In April 1929, along with Flt Lt Norman H Jenkins, OBE DFC DSM, he made the first non-stop flight from England to India in the Fairey Long-range Monoplane. The aim was to reach Bangalore, but strong headwinds meant that they landed at Karachi after nearly 51 hours in the air. Although the flight was successful, the great circle distance of 4,130 miles was short of the world record that had been set by Italy the previous year. It was decided to make another record attempt later that year, even though the record for flying from England to South Africa had subsequently been raised to 4,912 miles by the French.

This flight took off from RAF Cranwell in December 1929, but crashed near Tunis. Both these men were killed and the aircraft completely destroyed.

Despite this setback, a second Fairey Long-range Monoplane was produced for another attempt on the record. On 27–28 October 1931, Sqn Ldr O R Gayford (officer in charge of the RAF Long Range Development Unit), with Flt Lt D Betts as Navigator, flew from RAF Cranwell to Abu Seir in Egypt. The 2,557 miles (4,115km) was completed in 31½ hours. From 6–8 February 1933, Gayford and his navigator Flt Lt G E Nicholetts flew non-stop from Cranwell to Walvis Bay, South West Africa. This was a world long-distance record of 5,410 miles. The record stood until August 1933.

Flt Lt Norman H Jenkins OBE DFC DSM

Sqn Ldr Arthur Gordon Jones-Williams OBE MC*

Portrait of Samuel Kinkead
George Harcourt

Flt Lt Samuel Marcus Kinkead DSO DSC* DFC* (1897 – 12 March 1928) was born in South Africa and joined the RNAS in September 1915. He was posted to the Dardanelles in 1916 and, flying with No 3 Naval Wing, scored his first three victories flying aircraft including the Bristol Scout. In 1917, after recovering from malaria, he was posted to France and saw action on the Somme and at Ypres while serving with No 1 Naval Squadron, which became No 201 Squadron of the RAF. Flying the Sopwith Camel, Kinkead ended the War as No 201's highest scoring ace.

After the war he continued to fly the Camel with No 47 Squadron and scored several more victories during the Russian Civil War, for which he was awarded the DSO. He was a member of the RAF High Speed Flight in 1927 when it competed for the Schneider Trophy, but after five laps in the Gloster IVB had to retire with engine problems. However, his third lap speed of 277.18mph was the fastest biplane seaplane flight ever recorded.

The following year, he commanded the High Speed Flight but was killed when attempting to break the world speed record in his Supermarine S.5 at Calshot.

The Schneider Trophy Winning Team of 1929

Fred May

A caricature is a rendered image showing the features of its subject in a simplified or exaggerated way through sketching, pencil strokes, or through other artistic drawings. Caricatures can be insulting or complimentary, satirical or humorous and can serve a political purpose or be drawn solely for entertainment. Military caricatures were extremely popular in the RAF until fairly recently. They allowed an element of irreverence in an otherwise disciplined environment and provided amusing decoration in crew rooms and messes.

This caricature of the RAF High Speed Flight team which won the Schneider Trophy race in 1929 was sketched by Fred May and signed in September 1981 by D'Arcy Greig. The following members of the team are identified, going from left to right and top to bottom, with details where available:

Flt Lt E F Turner

Gp Capt E R C Nansen CBE DSC AFC

Flt Lt J C May (Adjutant)

Lt Cdr Harold Ernest Perrin CBE (1878–1948) was the Secretary of the Royal Aero Club from 1903 to 1945 and in this capacity signed more than 20,000 private pilots licenses.

Flg Off H R D Waghorn (1904–1931) entered RAF Cranwell in 1924 and was the winner of the Sword of Honour. Waghorn was exceptionally conscientious, but reserved. He won the 1929 race in a Supermarine S.6B at an average speed of 328.63mph, for which he was awarded the Air Force Cross (AFC) in September of the same year. Waghorn was killed in May 1931 while flying a Hawker Horsley biplane with an experimental engine that encountered very high winds.

Flg Off R L R 'Batchy' Atcherley (1904–1970) entered RAF Cranwell in 1922 and was judged to be the best pilot in his year. It would seem that he and D'Arcy Greig were the practical jokers of the team. He went on to have a notable career in the RAF throughout World War II, taking part in operations in Europe, the Western Desert and eventually the Commandant of the Central Fighter Establishment. Post War, he became the Commandant of RAF Cranwell and then CAS for the Royal Pakistani Air Force in 1949, eventually retiring after being the Air Officer Commanding-in-Chief at Flying Training Command. In retirement, he was Sales Director at Folland Aircraft Limited. Air Mshl Sir Richard Llewellyn Roger Atcherley, KBE CB AFC* died in April 1970.

Flt Lt D'Arcy Greig DFC AFC (1900–1986) served with the RFC and RAF during 1918. He was shot down behind enemy lines in September 1918 but evaded capture and walked home through the lines. He was granted a permanent commission in September 1919 and by June 1924 he was a QFI at the CFS. When asked for his opinion on pilots for the High Speed Flight, he named three of the pilots from his Hendon Display Flight of the previous year, which accounted for Stainforth, Waghorn and Atcherley being on the team. He published his autobiography under the title *My Golden Flying Years* and died in 1986.

Sqn Ldr Augustus Harry 'Orly' Orlebar AFC (1897–1943) joined the RFC in 1916 after service with the Army at Gallipoli, where he was wounded. In March 1918, he shot down and severely wounded Ltn Lothar von Richthoften, brother of Manfred, *The Red Baron*, and ended the war with seven victories to his name. He served as a test pilot at the Aeroplane and Armament Experimental Establishment at RAF Martlesham Heath. He took command of the High Speed Flight and, in 1929, set an air speed record of 357.7mph in a Supermarine S.6. During World War II, he was the Director of Flying Training before joining the Air Staff at HQ Fighter Command in October 1940, becoming AOC 10 Group in July 1941, and finally Deputy Chief of Combined Operations from March 1943.

Flg Off T H Moon – Technical Officer

Flt Lt George H Stainforth (1899–1942) was a former Sandhurst cadet and a crack shot who joined the RAF in 1923. In 1928, he was promoted to Flt Lt and posted for duties with the High Speed Flight. Stainforth was to fly the Gloster VI during the 1929 race but it was withdrawn for technical reasons shortly before the competition, which was won by Waghorn in the Supermarine S.6B. The following day, Stainforth flew the Gloster VI to a top speed of 351.3mph and achieved a world speed record of 336.3mph. The record was only held briefly as it was raised to over 350mph by the Supermarine. He flew the Supermarine S.6B in the 1931 race, which won the Schneider Trophy outright for Britain and in September 1931 became the first man to travel at over 400mph when he achieved a top speed of 407.5mph in the Supermarine. During World War II, he flew a captured Messerschmitt Bf109 against Spitfires for comparison trials. Posted to the Middle East at the end of 1941, Wg Cdr George Hedley Stainforth AFC was killed in action in Egypt in September 1942 while flying a Bristol Beaufighter.

THE SCHNEIDER TROPHY WINNING BRITISH TEAM 1929

OUR AERIAL TRIPLETS, THE O.C. AND OTHERS—BY FRED MAY

Empire Air Day, Hendon 1937
Mark Bromley

This pilot and his crewman are about to perform at the Empire Air Day of 1937 when No 600 (City of London) Squadron RAuxAF gave its first display with their new Hawker Demons at its home base of Hendon. No 600 also took part in the 'set piece' (a major feature of each day of the show) when, as *Flight* magazine's correspondent put it at the time:

"*The erection represented Port Hendon, complete with lighthouse and a ship in dock. The broadcast came from the control room of the Fighter Command, and one heard the reports coming in of a Blueland raid flying inland very fast and evidently making for Port Hendon. The A.O.C. ordered up No 3 (Fighter) Squadron to meet it, and we saw the Gladiators leap into the sky and make off for their patrol line. Then came in reports of a second raid, and yet a third. After waiting a moment to make sure of its direction, the A.O.C. sent up No 600 (City of London) Squadron to deal with it, and off went the Auxiliaries in their Demons.*"

No 600 Squadron had only just replaced their Hawker Hart bombers and become a fighter squadron with the Demons. They were very keen to show their proficiency with the new aircraft at the 1937 Empire Air Day.

The first flight from Hendon was made in a balloon in 1862, with other balloon ascents taking place regularly in and around the area until April 1910 when the first powered flight was made by Frenchman, Louis Paulhan, using the open field as his departure point for his successful attempt on the *Daily Mail's* competition to fly between London and Manchester for a prize of £10,000. His co-competitor in that race was the British aviator Claude Grahame-White who established his Aviation Company on the Hendon site shortly after these flights. In September 1911, the first official airmail was flown between Hendon and Windsor as part of the celebrations of the coronation of King George V. The two most famous pilots of the early years, apart from Grahame-White himself, were Bentfield Hucks and Gustav Hamel. Hucks was the first British pilot to loop-the-loop and Hamel was said to have swooped so low that the tail of his "... *plane knocked a policeman's helmet off!*". Because of their notoriety a dinner was held in their honour at the Royal Automobile Club. The 'Upside Down Dinner' consisted of ten courses working backwards from cigars and coffee. The menus were printed in reverse and placed upside down on the tables. Upon arrival the guests observed that their chairs were neatly placed upside down upon the tables

In 1912 the first Aerial Derby started and ended at Hendon, with an estimated three million people watching across London, with 45,000 of them having paid for admission to the enclosures. During World War I Hendon was used for pilot training and also, from 1915, for the aerial defence of London.

Following the War, the first 'RAF Pageant' was held in 1922 and these annual events became increasingly popular. By 1924 an estimated 100,000 people were coming to watch the displays and aerobatics of the latest RAF aircraft. From 1925, the event was known as the 'Royal Air Force Display' and from 1937 'The Empire Air Day', until World War II brought the shows to an end. Post-war, with the increasing proximity of housing and the short runways, the use of Hendon declined. The Avro Ansons of the last flying unit, the Metropolitan Communications Squadron, left for RAF Northolt in November 1957. RAF Hendon closed in 1987 although the RAF presence remains through the RAF Museum.

BROMLEY

CHAPTER IV

EXPANSION AND RE-ARMAMENT ~ 1933 TO 1939

"I think it is well for the man in the street to realise ... whatever people may tell him ... the bomber will always get through. The only defence is in offence."

STANLEY BALDWIN

THROUGHOUT the 1930s the RAF continued its investigations into both high altitude and long range flying. At Farnborough in September 1936 Sqn Ldr F R D 'Ferdy' Swain, flying a specially constructed and unique Bristol 138 wooden monoplane, reached a new world record height of 49,967ft. This record was pushed even further in June 1937 when Flt Lt M J Adam, flying the same aircraft, climbed to 53,937ft. The pressure suits worn by these men were 24 years in advance of those worn by astronauts in the conquest of space and recognised, subsequently, by NASA, as the first of their type. In November 1938 the LRDU once again set a new world record with a non-stop flight from Britain to Australia. Two out of the three Vickers Wellesley single engined bombers managed to complete the journey of 7,162 miles in 48 hours. The Wellesley was designed by Barnes Wallis and pioneered the geodesic structure subsequently used for the Vickers Wellington bomber, which was a mainstay of the RAF's bomber force during the early years of World War II.

During the middle 1930s the threat of aggression from Germany became apparent and in 1935 the British government published proposals for greatly expanding the RAF. It was intended to treble the RAF's strength of 580 aircraft within two years, thereby achieving theoretical parity with France and the recently announced German air force. 71 new squadrons were needed for the defence of Britain, which required 2,500 pilots and 20,000 other additional personnel. The RAF in Great Britain was reorganised in July 1936 into four new Commands: Bomber, Fighter, Coastal and Training. The development of equipment was poor by comparison with those of our near European neighbours. Aircraft flown by the RAF were little different from those they had inherited at the end of World War I and the operational tactics relied much upon the experience gained from air-to-ground attacks in colonial policing.

The RAF had become rather set in its ways. However, between 1934 and 1939, the Government embarked on a series of expansion programmes to address the upgrading and building of airfields, development and acquisition of new equipment and increases in manpower. Despite a slow start, by mid-1939 the cost of the building programme alone was more than treble the entire cost of the RAF in 1934.

New designs of modern monoplane fighters and bombers were being developed. The most significant of these were the Hawker Hurricane and the Supermarine Spitfire, soon to prove themselves in the Battle of Britain. At the same time scientists were working on new technologies which were to have a huge impact on the course of history. Radio Direction Finding (RDF), later known as radar, was developed in secret. The Observer Corps, formed in 1925, also used a network of observation posts located throughout the countryside and urban areas to report on enemy aircraft which passed behind the new radar system. A method of reporting on incoming raids was set up under the direction of Sir Hugh Dowding and Sir Keith Park whilst they both had responsibility for RAF Research & Development. They would soon direct the defence of the country in the Battle of Britain. The 'Dowding System', as it became known, enabled commanders to pin-point the positions of intruders in real time and direct the defending squadrons effectively and precisely. It was, unlike RDF, a total mystery to the Germans throughout the crucial months of 1940.

Navigation aids were also being developed to allow bomber crews to find targets in the dark and through cloud. The rise of Adolf Hitler and his Nazi party, coupled with the unveiling of the secret German air force, the Luftwaffe, prodded the decision-makers in Britain to increase spending on the RAF, as it was clearly seen to be the 'thin blue line' between freedom and defeat. A widespread belief that the "... *bomber will always get through...* " (said by Prime Minister Stanley Baldwin in Parliament in 1932), led not only to improvements in Britain's defences, but also to specifications for offensive aircraft which would, in a few short years, devastate huge areas of occupied Europe and Germany. The big four-engined bombers designed specifically for strategic bombing, such as the Short Stirling and Handley Page Halifax, were on the drawing board just before war broke out.

To support this massive increase in aircraft manufacturing requirements, the Government set up the 'Shadow Factory' scheme. This involved the building, often by leading motor companies such as Austin, Humber and Morris, of huge factories for the mass production of aircraft and engines. Some shadow factories are still in use. Supermarine built Castle Bromwich near Birmingham to build the Spitfire and it is currently a main manufacturing plant for Jaguar Land Rover cars. The English Electric Company built one at Samlesbury in Lancashire, which was first used to manufacture the Handley Page Hampden. This site remains in use today by BAE Systems, manufacturing sub-assemblies for the Eurofighter Typhoon and a proportion of the Lockheed Martin F-35 Lightning II.

In 1938 agreement was given for the RAF to buy aircraft from the USA and in June it was announced that 400 aeroplanes (half of these were Lockheed Hudsons) had already been purchased. It was the start of an increasing use of American-built aircraft during the next few years. This provided an opportunity for the American aircraft industry to be revitalised following years of depression. Further impetus to the hasty re-arming of the RAF came with the Munich crisis in September 1938, when Britain came to the very brink of war with Hitler's Germany. PM Neville Chamberlain has been derided for his appeasement of Hitler and the so-called 'sacrifice of Czechoslovakia', but at the time of his meeting with Hitler the RAF was totally unprepared for war. Chamberlain's "... *peace in our time...* ", gave at least a year of grace in which the RAF could continue to expand for the war which was now inevitable.

In 1939 new flying training schools were opened and three further Commands were added: Balloon, Maintenance and Reserve Commands. A Women's Royal Air Force that had been formed with the RAF in 1918 was disbanded at the end of World War I. However, women were brought back in on 28 June 1939 when King George VI gave Royal Assent to the formation of the Women's Auxiliary Air Force (WAAF). By September the first trained WAAFs were being posted to RAF stations. As in World War I there were distinct reservations about women in uniform in these pre-war months but, within a year, these doubts were dispelled by the calm courage displayed by the young women during the bombing of Fighter Command bases in the Battle of Britain.

With continued Admiralty frustration over control of naval aviation, responsibility for Fleet Air administration was returned to full Admiralty control, with the Fleet Air Arm (FAA) being a wholly naval entity from 1939.

On 24 August 1939, a general mobilisation of the RAF was called, placing the Service on a war footing. On that date the RAF could claim a total of 157 squadrons – nearly 2,000 first-line aircraft and of these, 34 squadrons were at bases scattered throughout the Empire while only 40 squadrons were equipped with fighters. For Home Defence, there were 270 Hurricanes and 240 Spitfires. The remaining fighters were either out-moded biplanes or converted twin-engined bombers, such as the 120 Gloster Gladiators and the 111 Bristol Blenheims shown on official records. For offensive operations Bomber Command possessed nearly 500 Hampdens, Whitleys and Wellingtons, but it had many more of the inferior Blenheims and Fairy Battles. On 1 September 1939 Hitler's armies invaded Poland and two days later Britain was again at war with Germany.

Bulldog Taxis Out
Mark Bromley

Aircraft like this Bulldog operated from grass airfields, taking off and landing in whatever direction was directly into the wind. Early versions of the Bulldog had no brakes and relied on their tailskid to arrest their progress, and on airmen on the ground to assist by holding their wingtips. Even when brakes were fitted ground crew were needed. This Bulldog has just completed its power checks before take-off, the pilot has signalled that he is ready to go and one airman is holding the wing whilst the other pulls the chocks from beneath the wheels.

The Bristol Bulldog was one of the RAF's front-line fighters for nine years, entering service in 1929. It was famous for its performances during the annual RAF Air Displays held at Hendon. This Bristol Bulldog IIA was operated by No 41 Squadron from October 1931 through to August 1934.

During the period it operated the Bulldog, No 41 Squadron was based at RAF Northolt, which would later become an important station for RAF Fighter Command during the Battle of Britain.

The Bulldog was operated by a number of other Squadrons, including No 23 Squadron and it was in an aircraft of this Squadron that Douglas Bader crashed in December 1931 while undertaking unauthorised aerobatics. As a result of this crash, he lost both his legs but, after a long recovery and much lobbying, he returned to flying with the RAF in 1939.

K
2209
BROMLEY

Hawker Biplanes Fly Together

Roy Cross

Designed by Sydney Camm, the Hawker Hart was a very successful two-seat biplane light bomber of the inter-war period. The versatility of the Hart's design led to a wide range of variants being produced, including the two shown in this painting.

In the foreground is the fighter version of the Hart, the Demon. The aircraft shown, K3976, is in the markings of No 29 Squadron, which nearly twenty years after it was first raised, received its Demons in March 1935 while based at RAF North Weald. During the Abyssinian Crisis the Squadron was detached to Egypt from October 1935 to September 1936, finally retiring its Demons in 1938.

The aircraft shown in the background is a Hawker Osprey S1699 which was the naval version operated by the Fleet Air Arm (FAA) in the fighter and reconnaissance roles. The Osprey joined the FAA in 1932 and was operated with a wheeled undercarriage from aircraft carriers and floats from catapult equipped warships. The Ospreys' final use with the FAA was as a trainer and the last examples were withdrawn in 1944.

K
3976
ROY CROSS

Faithful Annie

Anthony Cowland

These Avro Ansons are part of Coastal Command's No 217 Squadron and are shown flying over an estuary performing General Reconnaissance duties. The aircraft in the front carries tail number K8785, which served with No 217 Squadron, 3 Air Observers School, 3 Observers Advanced Flying Unit before being struck off charge in August 1944. The all-over silver scheme and No 217 markings date the scene as being prior to April 1939, when the squadron codes 'YQ' were introduced.

Having flown De Havilland DH4 bombers during World War I, No 217 Squadron was disbanded at the end of the war, being reformed in March 1937 at RAF Boscombe Down. Moving to the newly built airfield at RAF St Eval at the start of World War II in order to conduct coastal and anti-submarine patrols over the Western Approaches. From May 1940 the Ansons started to be replaced by the Bristol Beaufort torpedo bomber, but the final Anson did not leave the squadron until the end of the year.

Avro developed the Anson from their earlier 652 airliner to meet a 1933 Air Ministry requirement for a relatively cheap aircraft to carry out coastal duties, supplementing the more capable, but expensive, flying boats that undertook maritime reconnaissance. The prototype carried out its maiden flight in March 1935 from Avro's Woodford Aerodrome and was selected for production in May 1935, with the first aircraft flying in December.

The Anson was notable for being the RAF's first aircraft fitted with a retractable undercarriage although, as this was originally hand driven, crews often left it down. When retracted the wheels still protruded sufficiently to avoid major damage if a crew were forced to land wheels-up. The aircraft was much-loved by its crews and earned the name 'Faithful Annie' as it brought so many home under difficult circumstances. Rapidly becoming obsolete for front-line duties during the early years of the war, the Anson found a new role as a training aircraft and continued to serve throughout the war as part of the Commonwealth Air Training Plan. After the war the Anson was developed and became a well-used small commercial transport. The RAF used it as a VIP and communications aircraft and civilian operators carried passengers and freight. The RAF's final Ansons were not retired until June 1968.

217
O
217
K8785
K
8785

The First of the Few
Frank Wootton

This image is a classic Wootton masterpiece, illustrating, as only he could, an aircraft in all its simplicity against a perfect cloudscape. A pre-war MkI is seen in its early dark green/earth camouflage of 1939. It is the first production Spitfire (K9787) with test pilot Jeffery Quill at the controls. It is extremely unlikely that Wootton was able to view this scene in order to paint this early image of the aircraft as he did not join the RAF until after the event took place. However, publicity photographs were taken for Supermarine by Charles E Brown, one of the greatest air-to-air photographers, shortly after the first flight, and this painting was possibly referenced by the artist from that series of shots.

Probably the most iconic fighter aircraft ever built, the Supermarine Spitfire was designed by R J Mitchell, drawing on the experience he had gained with aerodynamics and stressed metal construction with the S.5 and S.6 seaplane racing aircraft built for the Schneider Trophy competition. It was the only Allied fighter to remain in continuous production throughout World War II (1939/45).

The first Spitfire Mk Is entered service with No 19 Squadron at RAF Duxford in August 1938 and the aircraft became famous during the Battle of Britain in 1940. Its reputation was further enhanced by the numerous 'Spitfire Funds' established across the world during the War, in which countries, companies, communities and individuals bought presentation aircraft for the RAF.

Spitfire production was dispersed across Britain, which was fortunate as Supermarine's works in Southampton were early targets during the Blitz and had been destroyed by September 1940. The most well-known of these 'Shadow Factories' was that at Castle Bromwich in the West Midlands, which is still in use for car production.

WOOTTON

CHAPTER V

THE FEW ~ 1939 TO 1941

"May it not be that the cause of civilisation itself will be defended by the skill and devotion of a few thousand airmen? There never has been, I suppose, in all the world, in all the history of war, such an opportunity for youth."

WINSTON CHURCHILL, 4 JUNE 1940

ON 2 September 1939, 10 Fairey Battle squadrons were sent to France. All 10 units (160 aircraft) immediately prepared for their war role. This was far from clear cut. Formally, they comprised the Advanced Air Striking Force and were part of Bomber Command, and the positioning of their bases in the Champagne area reflected the Air Staff view that they were likely to be used for direct attacks into Germany, which they could only reach from eastern France. Practically, there were likely to be only limited results from such attacks and they were more likely to be involved in direct or indirect tactical support of the British Expeditionary Force (BEF) which was due to follow shortly and which would deploy along the Belgium border with accompanying RAF units of its Air Component. Whilst these aircraft were flying to France, the RAF dispersed its other aircraft throughout Great Britain and crews stood by in 'readiness' awaiting their operational orders. In fact, the war in the west got off to a very slow start. Missions were flown by both sides, mostly rather desultory reconnaissance, but the expected assault by Germany on its western neighbours did not take place. However, the Allies had seen how quickly Hitler's armies, supported by the Luftwaffe, had defeated Poland. This was a blitzkrieg or 'lightning war', where fast-moving mechanised armies were supported by aerial artillery, in the form of Ju87 Stuka dive-bombers, attacking just in front of the advancing troops, and medium bombers attacking airfields and communications. The British and French armies waited for the attack, but nothing happened until Hitler invaded Denmark and Norway on 9 April 1940.

The RAF attempted to support operations in Norway but eventually withdrew, leaving behind the burnt-out wrecks of unserviceable Gloster Gladiators on frozen fields and lakes. Knowing how valuable their flyable aircraft were, the squadron commanders of the two fighter squadrons elected to fly their aircraft out of Norway and on to *HMS Glorious* to keep them from being destroyed in the evacuation, in spite of the fact that none of the pilots had landed on an aircraft carrier before. Ten Gladiators of No 263 Squadron were flown aboard during the afternoon of 7 June and the 10 Hurricanes of No 46 Squadron were flown aboard in the early evening. This was the first time that high-performance monoplanes without tail hooks had been landed on an aircraft carrier. This courageous and skilful effort was all in vain, since *HMS Glorious* was sunk a few hours later, by the German battleships *Scharnhorst* and *Gneisenau*, with the loss of 1,207 men; all but two of the RAF pilots, perished.

The 'phoney war', as it was known, abruptly came to an end at dawn on 10 May 1940 when German troops and their Luftwaffe 'umbrella' began a devastating blitzkrieg against the Low Countries. The RAF immediately launched itself into the attack but was out-gunned and out-numbered by an enemy with superior equipment. The Air Component and the Advanced Air Striking Force (AASF) displayed extraordinary courage and bravery in the face of overwhelming odds, by attempting to delay the advance with attacks on enemy communications, road and rail junctions and other key locations such as the vital bridges over the River Meuse and the Albert Canal. The attack on the latter resulted in the posthumous award of Victoria Crosses to Fg Off Patrick Garland and Sgt Thomas Grey. Garland was one of four brothers, all were killed or died in service with the RAF during the War; Grey was an ex-Halton apprentice.

The RAF suffered substantial casualties in the Battle of France; between mid-May to early June 1940 they lost nearly 1,000 aircraft destroyed, 320 pilots killed or missing and 115 pilots who were made prisoners of war. During the evacuation of the British Expeditionary Force (BEF) from Dunkirk between 26 May and 4 June, Fighter Command alone lost 106 aircraft and between 75 and 80 pilots.

The Commander-in-Chief of Fighter Command, Sir Hugh Dowding, knew that sending more fighters to France would further deplete his own reserves and therefore his ability to defend Britain when France, as he foresaw, inevitably fell. Nevertheless, he continued to receive orders, insisting he despatch more fighters to France. During the evacuation of the BEF from Dunkirk, aircraft from bases in Britain had flown across the channel to provide air protection. This was because 10 days before, on 16 May, Dowding had written to the Under Secretary of State for Air (Sir Archibald Sinclair), knowing that the message would go to Churchill and the Cabinet, advising that he believed no further aircraft should be sent to France, for he considered the war there was lost and that every RAF aircraft would be needed at home. He was supported in this view by Sir Cyril Newall, the CAS. Only Hurricanes had served in France as the Spitfire had always been considered too valuable. By the end of the Battle of France the RAF had lost 959 aircraft of which 477 were fighters.

By 18 June 1940, the RAF and its aircraft had been evacuated from France to England in order to re-group, re-equip and have their losses replaced. Everyone believed it could only be a matter of time before the real battle for Britain's survival, the Battle of Britain, would begin. The summer of 1940 became Great Britain's, and the RAF's, *"finest hour"*. Britain stood alone against Germany, with Luftwaffe bases in Norway, the Low Countries and France – a mere 23 miles across the Channel. Luftwaffe strength was approximately 3,500 aircraft, including bombers, dive bombers, single and twin engined fighters as well as reconnaissance aircraft. It was estimated that about two-thirds would be available for operations each day.

Facing them, Fighter Command had 60 squadrons with 700 operational aircraft, of which just 400 were Hurricanes and 200 Spitfires, with the balance being types such as the Gloster Gladiator bi-plane, twin-engined Bristol Blenheim or the vulnerable Boulton Paul Defiant with its rear gun turret. Only the Hurricane and Spitfire could hold their own against the German Messerschmitt Bf109s and Bf110s.

Luftwaffe operations against England started with a night raid on the 4/5 June 1940 and continued throughout the summer.

The opening phase was used by the Luftwaffe to test Britain's defences, her radar and, unbeknown to the Germans, the fighter control network perfected by Dowding and his team just before the war began. In July the Luftwaffe made attacks on convoys passing through the Straits of Dover and launched tentative raids to assess anti-aircraft guns, searchlights, balloons and the Hurricanes and Spitfires of Fighter Command.

The first major assault on the RAF was set for 13 August and known by the Germans as Adlertag or 'Eagle Day'. 749 British fighters faced a Luftwaffe force of 2,550, of which 1,029 were fighters. The Battle of Britain began in earnest. It was during this phase that the Luftwaffe made determined attacks on airfields in their attempt to bring Fighter Command to battle, destroy it in the air and on the ground just as they had the Polish Air Force, and leave Britain defenceless from the air.

The attrition rate was high. In only 14 days, from 24 August to 6 September, the main period of assault against Fighter Command airfields, the RAF lost 103 pilots killed and 128 seriously injured, with an overall loss of 466 Spitfires and Hurricanes either destroyed or in need of major repairs.

The most intense day of the entire battle was 15 August when the Luftwaffe flew 1,786 sorties against Britain, which were opposed by 974 flown by Fighter Command, in a series of battles running from the north-east down to the south coast, over both land and sea. In the last week of August and the first week of September, the Luftwaffe concentrated its main effort on the south-eastern stations of Sir Keith Park's No 11 Group, including such famous airfields as Biggin Hill, Debden, Hornchurch, Manston, North Weald and Tangmere. These were the two most critical weeks throughout the Battle but, with Fighter Command at its lowest ebb, just as things seem to be going extremely badly for Britain, Hitler ordered a complete change in strategy.

In response to the accidental bombing of London by the Luftwaffe on 24/25 August, Churchill ordered the RAF to bomb Berlin with a mixed force of Hampdens, Wellingtons and Whitleys. The reaction of the Nazi leadership, some of whom believed the RAF to be on the verge of collapse, was out of proportion to the slight damage caused. Hitler revoked his previous prohibition on the bombing of London, and Herman Göring, the Chief of the Luftwaffe, after consulting his senior commanders, elected to undertake a full scale assault on the capital. The first raid took place on 7 September when over 300 bombers, escorted by 600 fighters, attacked the city. What became known as 'The Blitz' had started.

Meanwhile, the invasion barges continued to build up on the enemy-occupied coast and the date of the invasion was set for late September. Bomber Command carried out nightly raids on these preparations, sinking some ten percent of the assembled barges at their moorings, but Herman Göring, continued to boast that he would crush the RAF.

In the first week of September, Fighter Command's control systems quickly adapted to the daylight attacks on London. The bombing caused considerable damage, but the Luftwaffe was being harried by RAF squadrons on its way to the targets, and all the way back to the Channel, and part of the way across. The Battle reached its climax on 15 September, when Göring launched the raids he claimed would finally destroy the RAF. However, Fighter Command had recovered, revised its tactics and was more flexible in its formation attacks and the distribution of its forces. Wherever possible the Hurricanes were now directed to attack the bombers, and the Spitfires the escorting fighters. On this day, which has since been commemorated annually as 'Battle of Britain Day', the Luftwaffe provided five escorting fighters for every bomber sent over. In spite of this the RAF destroyed a quarter of the Luftwaffe bomber force sent against England. Such losses were unsustainable for the Germans.

It was becoming increasingly obvious to the Luftwaffe that it could not survive daylight raids over London since its main defensive fighter, the Messerschmitt Bf109, had sufficient fuel to operate for no more than 10 minutes in combat over the capital. Göring had further hampered their effectiveness against the RAF fighters by ordering them to stay close to the bombers. The RAF was retaining control of the air over Britain and two days later Hitler postponed his invasion plans.

The German switch to round-the-clock bombing of London, and the night bombing of other important industrial towns, gave the RAF the breathing space it needed. After months of terrible casualties, the skies, during the day, became relatively quiet. As German losses rose and the weather deteriorated, the Battle of Britain petered out at the end of October 1940, leaving only the night bombers still at work. During the Battle of Britain, between 10 July and 31 October 1940, the RAF lost 1,023 machines against 1,887 of all types lost by the Luftwaffe. Fighter Command aircrew casualties were 544 killed and roughly the same number wounded whilst the Luftwaffe suffered 2,662 airmen killed as well as large numbers of prisoners and wounded.

The Battle of Britain was one of the most significant campaigns of the war; if the RAF had been defeated by the Luftwaffe, Britain could have been occupied, meaning it would not have been the eventual Allied base for the liberation of Europe. It was also the first battle to have been decided by air power alone and was won by the efficiency of Dowding's integrated air defence system, as well as the skill and courage of the fighter pilots. They are forever remembered through the words of Churchill's speech *"... never in the field of human conflict was so much owed by so many to so few"*.

There were nearly 3,000 aircrew with almost 600 from abroad. They came from the Commonwealth, the Dominions and from among those who had escaped from the occupied countries of Europe, such as Belgium, Czechoslovakia, France and Poland; pilots also came from the neutral countries of Ireland and the United States. They were not all RAF as over 20 pilots were seconded from the FAA to RAF Squadrons, and Nos 804 and 808 Squadrons served under Fighter Command during the Battle. Whilst 544 were killed in the Battle itself it must also be remembered that another 790 did not live to see the end of the war in 1945. Their average age was 21 years.

It should also be remembered that there were many men and women, service and civilian, in support roles, including ground crew, those in the operations rooms, and workers repairing infrastructure including vital telephone lines. Civilian aircraft manufacturing also outstripped German capacity fourfold as a result of huge increases in production and the utilisation of Shadow Factories and the services of non-RAF aircrew from the Air Transport Auxiliary. The losses from within Bomber and Coastal Command during the period of the Battle of Britain exceeded those of Fighter Command – a testament to the bravery and hard work being done in attacking German invasion preparations and keeping the sea lanes clear.

The Battle of Britain may have been won, but the battle for the night sky over England was about to start. The Blitz on London and other cities continued until May 1941. It was at this time that the RAF perfected its night fighter tactics, with new aircraft such as the Bristol Beaufighter being introduced.

Both sides devoted considerable resources to the electronic and scientific war. A radar set small enough to be carried in an aircraft was developed almost simultaneously by Britain and Germany. During the early period of the Blitz of 1940/41, most interceptions made by RAF aircrews at night were visual, but soon Airborne Interception Radar enabled night fighter pilots to 'see in the dark', and interceptions began to increase.

The Battle of the Atlantic had been the very first theatre of World War II and in the first month German U-boats had sunk 41 ships. Coastal Command's original role was primarily reconnaissance over the North Sea, but with only 230 aircraft, primarily Avro Ansons and Bristol Blenheims, they lacked the range and bomb load to have any noticeable impact on enemy shipping or the U-boats. The only long range aircraft were the small number of Short Sunderlands, one of which participated in the first U-boat sinking in January 1940.

Coastal Command would grow as the war progressed, and in these first months the major achievement was the increasing willingness to combine RAF and Royal Navy assets. This would result in mutual co-operation between the two Services, which would go on to flourish in a battle over the oceans and seas of the world until the end of the war.

During the Battle of Britain it had been found that, even with the help of the Royal Navy and civilian vessels, aircrew who came down in the North Sea or English Channel had only a twenty percent chance of survival. With the increase in Bomber Command operations, it was clear that something needed to be done. In early 1941 the RAF created the Directorate of Air Sea Rescue to improve the chances of locating and recovering downed airmen. Using a mixed collection of aircraft that had been withdrawn from front-line use as obsolete or 'war weary' they patrolled in search of aircrew, dropped supplies and dinghies and, using amphibious aircraft such as the Supermarine Walrus, could land on the sea to carry out rescues. The development of High Speed Rescue Launches, used by the RAF Marinecraft Section also ensured that the recovery of aircrew could be carried out when amphibians were either not available, or the sea state made it impossible for them to land. The Air Sea Rescue Service plucked 5,721 airmen from home waters by the end of the War as well as 4,665 others, mostly sailors, and 277 German and Italian airmen.

In spite of all this, the end of the Battle of Britain was the beginning of a massive effort to take the fight back to Germany. The only way this could be done was through the strategic bombing of Germany and occupied Europe by Bomber Command. The Handley Page Halifax demonstrated fully the farsightedness of the pre-war decision to order heavy bombers. It began operations with No 35 Squadron on 11/12 March 1941 and went on eventually to share, with the Stirling and Lancaster, the task of maintaining the RAF's great night bomber offensive.

Italy's entry into the War in June 1940 threatened Britain's empire and friendly nations in the Mediterranean, North Africa and Middle East. The small, strategically vital, but valiant island of Malta was besieged from June 1940 until November 1942, following an Axis decision to starve it into submission. Churchill called it *"... an unsinkable aircraft carrier"* and German General Erwin Rommel (Commander of the Afrika Korps), declared that *"Without Malta the Axis will end by losing control of North Africa"*. He was completely correct as the island withstood the siege and went on to play a major role in the eventual Allied success in North Africa. In April 1942 the George Cross was awarded collectively to Malta and it still features in that island's flag.

However, while Italian invasions of Greece were defeated, once German forces came to their assistance, both Greece and Crete were occupied by mid-1941. While the RAF had fought valiantly, it was significantly out-numbered and had been mainly equipped with obsolescent aircraft types that were no match for those of the Axis powers. Similar events unfolded in North Africa, when early Allied success against Italian forces equipped with much the same vintage equipment as the RAF, would be swiftly reversed once German forces, including the Luftwaffe, came to their aid.

The war also affected the Middle East and in particular Iraq, which had been a focus of so much RAF effort during the years between the wars. While Iraq had broken off diplomatic relations with Germany, it did not do the same with Italy, which then used its continued presence to create anti-British feelings amongst the Iraqi people. Following a coup in early 1941, the new Iraqi regime asked Germany for assistance in the event of war with Britain. Following the failure of diplomatic efforts to secure a peaceful solution, Iraqi forces surrounded the major RAF base at Habbaniyah and laid siege. This led to a series of land and air battles throughout May, initially fought by the RAF largely using training aircraft, until Allied forces defeated the Iraqis and secured an armistice that returned a pro-British leader to power.

During the Battle of France the Germans had unleashed an extremely effective new weapon which took the defending French completely by surprise. Dropping parachute troops and gliders directly on top of the Maginot Line fortresses, and behind the French lines, accelerated the advance significantly. Churchill seized on this new form of attack, saw in it a huge potential for the future and ordered the formation of a force of at least 5,000 paratroopers immediately. The result was that, while the Germans were amassing invasion barges on the coast of France in June 1940, Squadron Leader Louis Strange was appointed commanding officer of the newly created Central Landing School (CLS) at RAF Ringway near Manchester. This unit was charged with the initiation, development and organisation of the UK's sole parachute training facility, which later pioneered the parachute training curriculum of all Allied airborne forces. The unit was later redesignated No.1 Parachute Training School RAF (PTS). Using the techniques developed under Strange, the PTS trained over 60,000 Allied personnel and paratroopers at Ringway, between 1940 and 1946. Strange managed this incredible feat because of his compete disregard of official channels. His vision to make parachute training a wholly RAF function, and to insert it within the Physical Training Branch, was inspired. To this day all airborne troops from the three services are trained at No 1 PTS Brize Norton and the skills of the instructors form the nucleus of today's RAF Falcons Parachute Display Team.

The final descent into global conflict came in December 1941 when Japan made near-simultaneous attacks on the US Navy at Pearl Harbor, and on British territories such as Hong Kong in the Far East. Already struggling to meet the requirements for modern aircraft types for European and North African conflicts, the RAF strength in the Far East was pitifully small; only 181 serviceable aircraft of all types were available. This force included a number of obsolete types such as the American Brewster Buffalo fighter and the Vickers Vildebeest biplane torpedo bomber, with the most modern fighter in the RAF's inventory being the Hawker Hurricane, which was still out-performed by Japanese aircraft such as the Mitsubishi Zero.

Incredibly, Hitler immediately declared war on the United States, so by Christmas 1941, war had struck the far reaches of the globe and, though there were still dark days ahead, Britain and her Dominions were no longer fighting alone.

Fairey Battles at the Albert Canal, 1940

Geoffrey Crompton

When the Battle of France began in May 1940, Fairey Battles were called upon to perform unescorted, low-level tactical attacks against the advancing German army. This type of mission placed the aircraft at risk of attack from Luftwaffe fighters and within easy range of light anti-aircraft guns. In the first of two sorties carried out by Battles on 10 May 1940, three out of eight aircraft were lost, while a further 10 out of 24 were shot down in the second sortie. All the surviving aircraft suffered varying degrees of damage. However, despite bombing from as low as 250ft, their attacks were recorded as having had little impact on the German advance.

Crompton's painting features 12 May 1940 when, in spite of the losses of the previous days, five Battles from No 12 Squadron attacked two vital bridge crossings across the Albert Canal. Facing very heavy enemy ground fire, the crews pressed home their attacks with extraordinary valour and managed to damage one of the bridges. Yet the action resulted in the loss of all five aircraft involved and the first RAF Victoria Crosses of World War II were awarded posthumously to Fg Off D E Garland and his Observer, Sgt T Gray, for their respective parts in that action.

Designed by Marcel Lobelle and first flown in March 1936, the Fairey Battle was originally designed to replace the Hawker Hart as a daytime light bomber. The Battle was the first aircraft powered by the legendary Rolls Royce Merlin engine.

By the outbreak of war in 1939, over 1,000 Battles were in RAF service and No 226 Squadron's Battles were the first RAF aircraft to be committed to the defence of France as part of the RAF's Advanced Air Striking Force. Despite being only four years since its first flight, the operational performance of the Battle was deemed disappointing. Following the losses in France the Battle was withdrawn from front-line duties. Yet, with over 2,000 built for home and export customers, the Battle would go on to serve the RAF until 1949 in a range of other secondary roles such as training and target towing. Many were also passed to the Soviet Union following the German invasion of June 1941. This painting was presented to the RAF Club by Fg Off Garland's niece, Caroline Crompton.

PH K
PH J
PH N
Geoffrey Crompton 1992

Britain First, The Blenheim IV 1940

Mark Bromley

The crew of a Bristol Blenheim Mk IV discuss their luck having survived a particularly arduous mission. The pilot points out a tear in his flying jacket to his crew and the aircraft still smokes from the damage to its left engine. Bullet holes to the nose and flak damage to the left wing show how determinedly they carried out their task. The pilot has quickly removed his parachute to check on his physical condition and they enjoy a welcome cigarette before they move away for an intelligence de-brief. Under normal circumstances parachutes were rarely placed on the ground, but stored and carefully kept out of reach of any small animal, especially rodents, for obvious reasons. On smaller aircraft they are usually placed on the tailplane and larger ones thrown inside the aircraft. In this case, the arrival of the fire section and its crew serve to illustrate how serious their situation had been mere minutes before.

The Blenheim was spawned from a challenge, championed by Lord Rothermere, to British industry to develop the fastest commercial airliner in Europe. The civilian Bristol Type 142, christened 'Britain First', had its maiden flight in April 1935 and turned out to be faster than the front-line RAF fighters of the period. Impressed by this performance, the Air Ministry ordered a development which would enter service with the RAF as the Bristol Blenheim in 1937.

Designed by Frank Barnwell, the Blenheim was one of the first RAF aircraft to utilise an all-metal, stressed-skin construction, retractable landing gear, powered turret and variable-pitch propellers. No 114 Squadron at RAF Wyton received the RAF's first Blenheim in the summer of 1937; its revolutionary design made it one of the world's most advanced bombers at that time.

The Blenheim IV performed a number of important missions for the RAF in the early years of the war, but it also incurred heavy losses. The Blenheim in all its versions performed key roles during its wartime service being used not only as a light tactical bomber but also as a heavy night fighter, reconnaissance and training aircraft. Serving in all the major theatres of war some 4,422 Blenheim had been produced by 1942, with the final RAF Blenheim retiring in 1944.

BROMLEY

Spitfire Scramble 1940
Frank Wootton

This painting is part of Wootton's World War II triptych commissioned by the RAF Club. It illustrates a Fighter Command airfield under direct attack as a squadron scrambles to intercept. In such situations the objective was to get every aircraft into the air as soon as possible – pilots felt safer in the air than on the ground and their aircraft were less vulnerable. This resulted in squadrons dispersed around an airfield, often taking off in opposing directions. This situation was dangerous for those on the ground too, as the field ambulance crew attend to the damaged Spitfire's pilot whilst bullets and bombs encircle them.

Key to the Spitfire's success was its advanced design built around a stressed all-metal airframe that was both lightweight and strong. The Spitfire was blessed with superb handling qualities and excellent power generated originally by a Rolls Royce Merlin engine. Upon the outbreak of war in Europe in September 1939, 306 Spitfires were operational with the RAF with around another 2,000 on order. Soon enough, RAF Spitfires were engaged in action in the defence of Britain's airspace. In October 1939, Spitfires from Nos 602 and 603 Squadrons intercepted nine Junkers Ju 88 bombers over Rosyth, Scotland. During the subsequent action, two Ju 88s were destroyed and another heavily damaged. This was the first combat action for the Spitfire.

The Spitfire has become synonymous with the Battle of Britain in 1940 and an RAF icon in its own right.

Aircrew On Standby 1940
Mark Bromley

'The Few' epitomised in Bromley's painting of RAF fighter crews standing at readiness, a common scene on RAF Fighter Command bases during the Battle of Britain. Exhausted crews wait, ready to respond to the scramble call that would be received via telephone, followed by the constant ringing of the bell as the crews raced to their aircraft. Many recalled that, even in later life, they still jumped at the sound of a telephone.

Whilst well equipped with the Hurricanes and Spitfires they flew, their personal kit was out of date and replaced as soon as the battle was over. They were expected to fly in their everyday uniforms. Their life preservers (named 'Mae Wests', after a voluptuous actress of the day) could only be inflated by blowing into a rubber tube and were a dull grey/green colour; many of the men painted them yellow in order that they might be seen if floating in the sea. Their standard issue goggles were often made of flammable material (they would buy their own motorcycle versions) and they were often expected to wear their starched, stiff, uniform studded collar and tie whilst flying. Their oxygen masks were made of canvas and leaked, and they had neither a rubber dinghy nor a first aid kit in their aircraft. If they came down in the sea they had little chance of rescue and the majority were saved either by the RNLI or the Germans.

In this picture they are fortunate not to have to comply with some squadron commanders' strict uniform requirements and are wearing comfortable clothing, more suitable to the action they are expecting any minute. They are also fortunate to be occupying semi-permanent accommodation; many would detach to an empty farmer's field at first light each day to wait for a call on a field telephone whilst sheltering in a bell tent. Dispersal of RAF squadrons was a lesson learned earlier in the year by the squadrons in France.

Their day, at the height of the Battle, began at 0400 when they were woken and went to dispersal, often still wearing their pyjamas under their uniforms. Their readiness increased as soon as first light appeared and they did not rest until the sun had set. It was not unknown for the busiest squadrons to take to the skies four or five times a day. Whilst they flew the general population went about their daily lives below them, including going on holiday and even an occasional industrial dispute leading to a short strike over pay.

Although they were hard pressed the commanders knew that days off were important and, even at the height of the Battle, pilots were still granted passes. Most went to London and enjoyed the theatre, cinema and the bars of London's hotels. If they were shot down, unlike their enemy, they would land on friendly

soil, but because of the many nationalities amongst their number, they would often have to convince the local people that they were not German. If uninjured they would be issued with a travel warrant and make their way back to their squadron by public transport, a journey which, in most cases, could be hundreds of miles. They would be expected to keep all their kit, especially their parachute, with them and upon their return to their unit they might well be flying again the next day. Their average age was about 21 years and they were considered very experienced if they had more than 50 hours flying time on their operational aircraft.

TUESDAY
READINESS
BROMLEY

Bombing Up

Mark Bromley

One of the very few Allied aircraft to see operational service throughout World War II, the Vickers Wellington started life as a long-range medium bomber, entering service in 1938. Yet, like the ground crew depicted in Bromley's art, the Wellington was exceptionally versatile and ended the war having performed a myriad of roles and, excelling in particular, in the night bombing offensive and over the sea against the U-boat threat.

The Wellington's strength was literally built within, the airframe design utilising the geodesic structural concept that Barnes Wallis had experimented with before the war. On 24 September 1939, 24 hours after the outbreak of war, Wellingtons from Nos 9 and 149 Squadrons performed the first RAF bombing mission of the war alongside Bristol Blenheims, with 14 aircraft attacking German shipping off Wilhelmshaven. Unfortunately during that raid, two Wellingtons also became the first RAF losses of the war.

Wellingtons continued to take the war to the Reich and occupied Europe throughout 1940, performing both low level daylight strikes and high altitude night raids. Poor defensive armament became an issue, as Wellington losses mounted, yet the bombers continued to reach their targets, especially at night. On 25 August 1940, Wellingtons performed the first raid on Berlin. In May 1942, Wellingtons joined the first 1,000 bomber raid on Cologne. They performed 47,409 missions delivering 41,823 tons of munitions on operations with Bomber Command.

By 1942, with heavier more modern bombers coming into service, the ample Wellington force shifted focus to anti-submarine warfare and became an integral part of Coastal Command's efforts during the Battle of the Atlantic. With over 11,000 built between 1936 and 1945, the final Wellington ended RAF service as a training aircraft in 1953 and is now in the RAF Museum collection.

BROMLEY

"*Tally Ho!*" September 1940
Frank Wootton

Another of Wootton's triptych paintings illustrates Hawker Hurricanes of B Flight of No 17 Squadron descending to intercept a raid over London in September 1940. No 17 Squadron was based at Debden in Essex at this time and the aircraft in the foreground, with the code letters YB-W, was the personal mount of Plt Off H A C 'Birdy' Bird-Wilson.

Entering RAF service in December 1937 with No 111 Squadron at RAF Northolt, the Hawker Hurricane represented the vanguard of RAF Fighter Command at the outbreak of war in 1939. Sydney Camm's design proved exceptionally stable and rugged, qualities that would define it during the early months of the war.

As RAF squadrons were committed to the defence of continental Europe, four squadrons of Hurricanes were deployed to France, starting in September 1939. Increasing numbers of Hurricanes would operate from there right up until the evacuation from Dunkirk in June 1940.

Yet it was in the role of defending Britain's air space that the Hurricane earned its hard fought reputation. The Hurricane's first combat action came on 21 October 1939, but its performance in the Battle of Britain (when it represented 60 percent of RAF Fighter Command's strength) was demonstrated by the fact that three out of five enemy aircraft brought down by all forms of defence were victims of this superb machine. Whilst the Spitfire was expected to take on the escorting German fighters, the Hurricane attacked the massed bombing formations, often, as in this image, whilst being hugely outnumbered. By the end of the Battle, Hurricanes had accounted for 656 enemy aircraft.

Development and production of the Hurricane continued until 1944, by which time over 14,500 Hurricanes had been built in the UK and Canada, with further licensed production undertaken in Belgium and Yugoslavia. The Hurricane operated in every major theatre of World War II.

YB L
YB W
YB A

Hurricanes In Winter, 1940/41

Frank Wootton

The winter of 1940–1941 was the one of the most severe on record, with temperatures reaching their coldest in over 45 years. The RAF had to contend with this extreme weather whilst also maintaining air defence coverage of the British Isles.

A testament to the ground crews who kept the squadrons active during this challenging time is that the RAF managed to maintain its capability throughout the period. This was achieved even when a spate of major snowstorms struck in November 1940.

Wootton's painting depicts this effort, with crews performing their duties in the severest conditions, ensuring that Britain, even when faced by natural challenges as well as those of the enemy, was still able to defend itself effectively. The aircraft in the foreground is the personal Hurricane of the Squadron Commander of No 257 (Burma) Squadron, based at North Weald in Essex. Sqn Ldr R R 'Bob' Stanford-Tuck joined this squadron on 11 September after achieving combat successes flying Spitfires with No 92 Squadron. By mid-November 1940, Tuck had scored a total of 25 confirmed and probable victories and this was recorded by a row of white swastikas under the left side of the cockpit. In order for his squadron to recognise him instantly in the air he had the front portion of his propeller spinner painted red.

DT

The 'Flying Porcupine', Sunderland On Convoy Patrol

Ron Lackenby

The Battle of the Atlantic was the longest running single battle of World War II, starting on the first day and only finishing after the German surrender in May 1945. This painting shows a patrolling Sunderland flying boat with the distinctive smoke of the convoy it is protecting behind it. The smoke of the ships, and the fact that Germany could read the Royal Naval ciphers until well in to the fourth year of the war, helped the U-boat packs to find the convoys. However, the radar and vigilance of the Sunderland crews helped them to engage the U-boats. The cost was huge with 32,000 merchant seamen and 30,000 U-boat crews losing their lives and over 3,000 airmen failing to return from their lonely patrols.

Developed by Short Brothers (and also produced by Blackburn Aircraft Ltd) as a long-range maritime patrol aircraft, the Sunderland first flew in October 1937. Powered by four Bristol Pegasus XVIII engines, the Sunderland represented one of the most powerful and purposeful aircraft of its class and quickly became the backbone of RAF Coastal Command. Although designed to hunt and destroy enemy submarines, the Sunderland's initial entry into service underlined its utility as a rescue aircraft for ships attacked by the growing U-boat threat. In September 1939, two Sunderland aircraft rescued the crew of the torpedo stricken merchantman, the *Kensington Court*.

Blessed with long range and excellent patrol qualities, the Sunderland soon began inflicting casualties on the enemy's U-boat fleet. Key to this was the installation of Air to Surface Vessel (ASV) Radar that allowed the Sunderland to hunt U-boats on the surface from a distance and then rapidly transit to the target at low level. Taking the U-boat by surprise, the Sunderland would then use its comprehensive gun and depth charge armament to engage the vessel. Uniquely for such a large aircraft the Sunderland had not only turret guns, but also four fixed forward firing machine guns aimed with a ring and bead sight by the pilot. Because of its formidable armament the Germans gave it the nickname 'Flying Porcupine'.

The first unassisted U-boat sinking by a Sunderland occurred on 17 July 1940 by an aircraft of No 10 Squadron Royal Australian Air Force. Sunderlands operated with distinction in all theatres and continued to serve the RAF up to the 1950s.

'Whaleback' & 'Shagbat' to the Rescue

Patrick Donovan

Depicted in Donovan's painting is a 'Whaleback' Type Two High Speed Launch (HSL), built by British Power Boat Company. It is seen co-ordinating with a Supermarine Walrus to recover a downed pilot. Over 300 HSLs would be operated by the RAF during World War II, the largest such fleet in operation anywhere in the world.

Aircrew were a scarce and vital commodity and every effort was mobilised to recover downed crews by the RAF, using both its air and marine assets. The positive effect of knowing an extraordinary effort would be made to recover downed aircrew naturally improved morale.

However, Britain started the war with no co-ordinated effort in terms of air sea rescue capability. The problem was highlighted to stark effect during the Battle of Britain, with aircrew having only a 20 percent chance of surviving if they baled out into the North Sea or English Channel. 200 aircrew were lost at sea during the Battle of Britain.

The RAF responded and on 14 January 1941 the Directorate of Air Sea Rescue Services was established to co-ordinate downed aircrew recovery efforts. Later that year the first specialist Search and Rescue Squadrons were established and the Supermarine Walrus, designed by R J Mitchell and nicknamed 'The Shagbat' by its crews, became a mainstay of RAF search and rescue operations and critical to its vital life-saving role.

By the end of World War II, 8,000 aircrew and some 5,000 civilians had been rescued by RAF aircraft and Marinecraft Section High Speed Launches, throughout the world.

127

The Sea Shall Not Have Them

Anthony Cowland

This is a panel from Anthony Cowland's triptych, commissioned by the Royal Air Force Club to commemorate the cessation of Royal Air Force Air Sea Rescue Services in 2016. The image illustrates the situation when a pilot came down in the English Channel during the first years of World War II. One of the downed pilot's squadron chums has remained circling over him whilst a Lysander equipped with dinghy packs attached to its wheel spats stands guard. A Marine Craft Section high speed launch has arrived at the scene and is manoeuvring next to the red and yellow Air Sea Rescue Float.

These Floats were not manned or armed, but were designed to hold up to six men, and equipped with signal apparatus, bunks, cooking stove, clothing and food. The stern of the Float was sloped down from the hatch to the water to enable a man to climb aboard with the least difficulty. In addition, ladders, extending below the water line were fitted either side of the bow and strong hand-rails led to the cabin hatch. Inside the Float were full instructions for the crews to follow to ensure a speedy rescue. A radio was fitted, there were distress signals, flags, a lamp and whistle. In addition complete changes of dry clothing, food, drink, books and games, also cutlery, plates and drinking mugs were installed. These Floats were moored in the English Channel and parts of the North Sea, but very few were ever used. They were called 'Cuckoos' by those who serviced and maintained them.

The Westland Lysander entered service with No 16 Squadron at Old Sarum in June 1938. Designed specifically as a purpose-built army co-operation aircraft, the Lysander quickly gained a reputation for outstanding reliability and versatility.

The Lysander provided a vital reconnaissance, co-ordination and support asset during the battles in France in 1940, but its slow speed made it vulnerable.

New roles included target tug, training and highly secret covert flights in support of the Special Operations Executive (SOE) and supplying Allied Resistance forces during their struggle in occupied Europe. The Lysander's handling and short landing performance proved invaluable for such missions.

BA
127

The Battle of Habbaniyah, 1941

Stuart Brown

Force protection has always been a key role for the RAF. Brown's painting emphasises this and the role of RAF ground forces in protecting Air Force assets, especially on expeditionary operations.

With its origins dating back to the early 1920s, No 1 Armoured Car Company RAF, was equipped with some 18 Rolls Royce Armoured Cars and deployed to Iraq to protect RAF bases there. In 1936, the Company arrived at its new base of RAF Habbaniyah after transferring from RAF Hinaidi. Their role would prove vital during the Anglo-Iraqi War of 1941.

Early in May Iraqi rebel government forces, seeking to take advantage of the UK's difficulties in Europe, surrounded and lay siege to RAF Habbaniyah, demanding its surrender. Despite being significantly outnumbered, RAF base commander AVM H G Smart refused to give up the base and instead opted to use his aircraft in a surprise attack against the massing rebel forces. For four days Habbaniyah and No 1 Armoured Car Company held off rebel attacks and artillery, whilst a motley collection of aircraft mounted bombing operations both around Habbaniyah's proximity and against rebel outposts across the country. After suffering significant casualties and being taken completely by surprise, the rebel forces evacuated and withdrew. By the end of May 1941, the Iraqi rebel threat had been removed completely.

The spirit, traditions and concepts of force protection that No 1 Armoured Car Company portrayed so vividly at Habbaniyah continue today with the RAF Regiment. Indeed, that unit became No 1 Squadron, RAF Regiment in 1947.

CHAPTER VI

THE MANY ~ 1942 TO 1945

"The Nazis entered this war under the rather childish delusion that they were going to bomb everyone else, and nobody was going to bomb them.... They sowed the wind, and now they are going to reap the whirlwind."

ARTHUR HARRIS, 1942

WHILE Bomber Command was gearing itself towards a massive offensive over occupied Europe, the RAF was also actively engaged in Africa, the Middle East and the Mediterranean. Even before the Battle of Britain, Italy's Benito Mussolini, taking advantage of the fatal blows inflicted on France by the German invasion, entered the War on Germany's side on 10 June 1940. The RAF in the Middle East immediately commenced battle with the Italian forces in North and East Africa, and the campaign for the strategic island of Malta began in earnest. In 1941, following the attack on the American fleet at Pearl Harbor, the Japanese swept down through south-east Asia, capturing airfields occupied by obsolete RAF aircraft. Hurried reinforcements, including 51 Hurricanes, arrived too late to alter the course of events. Hong Kong surrendered on Christmas Day. By 9 February 1942, only eight Hurricanes remained in Singapore to engage the Japanese raiders, but these were withdrawn to join other surviving aircraft in the Netherlands East Indies, and Singapore surrendered on the 15 February .

The first units of the American Eighth Army Air Force arrived in Great Britain in the spring of 1942. Not only did Britain now have access to American equipment, which had been agreed through the Lend-Lease Bill on 11 March 1941, but also their fighting forces were now on British soil. The Allies could now progressively mount offensive operations with ever increasing resources.

Establishing the necessary training schools to cope with the vast expansion required, whilst attempting to maintain the highest technical and professional standards, was a significant challenge. A notable success was the British Commonwealth Air Training Plan (BCATP), the single largest aviation training programme in history. Known simply as 'The Plan', nearly 300,000 pilots and other aircrew were trained between May 1940 and March 1945. The BCATP was primarily operated in Canada, which had over 300 schools and trained nearly 138,000 aircrew, but training was also delivered in Australia, Bermuda, New Zealand, South Africa, Rhodesia and Britain. Other training schemes like 'The Arnold Scheme' also took advantage of the climate and size of the USA and many aircrew were trained in the peaceful, and comparatively luxurious, American bases in the southern US States of Florida, Georgia and Alabama.

Clearly, schemes of this magnitude required large quantities of basic training machines such as the De Havilland Tiger Moth, and multi-engined types like the Avro Anson and Airspeed Oxford. While many aircraft were delivered from Britain, significant manufacturing operations were established in Canada to build these aircraft locally, including carrying out modifications to use more readily available US engines and other equipment. Some pilots learned on robust US manufactured aircraft such as the Boeing Stearman, the North American AT6 (known as the 'Harvard' in RAF service), and Cessna Crane. The scale of training was huge and the efforts to ensure high standards were complex using formal instructional documents, visual aids and humour.

The regular distribution of the light hearted *Training Memorandum* promoting good airmanship and known as *Tee Emm* had, as its central character, the hapless 'Plt Off Percy Prune', created by cartoonist Bill Hooper. Prune was totally accident prone, ignoring standing orders, never bothering to read flight manuals, always making mistakes and damaging or crashing aircraft. Needless to say, the RAF loved him and his antics; Prune became a major part of improving flight safety awareness. His legacy lives on in the modern world with his name being an intentional acronym for the Professional Pilots Rumour Network website forums (PPRuNE).

In early 1942 Air Mshl Sir Arthur 'Bomber' Harris was appointed as Commander-in-Chief Bomber Command and the Avro Lancaster, designed by Roy Chadwick, entered operational service. Bomber Command now had the leader who would develop its strategic air offensive and the most capable of its four-engined bomber aircraft.

Whilst both the Short Stirling and Handley Page Halifax were highly regarded by their crews, the Lancaster, with its large bomb bay and higher service ceiling, proved the most adaptable of the three types. It was modified to carry the RAF's largest bomb, the 22,000lb 'Grand Slam' and, most famously of all, the 'Bouncing Bomb' (code named *Upkeep*), both designed by Barnes Wallis.

The use of *Upkeep* in the Dams Raid of 15/16 May 1943 by No 617 Squadron, under Wg Cdr Guy Gibson, has become one of the most famous raids of World War II. This was one of the first examples of a low-level precision attack undertaken by the RAF, breaching 2 of the 3 dams bombed. However, the cost in crews and aircraft was very high, with 8 of the 19 aircraft failing to return. However, the enormous morale boost for both the RAF and British public ensured that the raid passed into popular legend, giving the squadron the name 'The Dambusters', and creating an enduring reputation.

The introduction of the De Havilland Mosquito into service provided the RAF, and the USAAF with one of the most versatile Allied aircraft of the whole war. Its low level attacks on key targets throughout Europe, its incredible photo-reconnaissance ability and shipbusting capability, coupled with its use as both a fighter and a bomber, made it both popular with its crews and in high demand by operational planners. As a high flying, fast, unarmed transport it was also used by the British Overseas Airways Corporation (BOAC) to carry vitally important people and cargo back and forth to Sweden.

In August 1943, a mixed Bomber Command force comprising all three heavy bombers undertook the first attack on the German research centre, on the Baltic coast at Peenemunde, to disrupt German secret weapon development. RAF photo reconnaissance and intelligence had identified the Peenemunde site as the centre of the research and development programme of the world's first cruise missile, the V-1, and long range guided ballistic missile, the V-2 rocket.

Harris' appointment coincided with the decision to implement a policy of all-out attack on German cities, and in mid-1942, the Path Finder Force (PFF) was established to mark targets with flares for the main bombing force. Additionally, rapid technological developments led to continuous upgrades to improve the effectiveness of attacks. These included improvements in navigational aids, blind bombing devices, airborne radar and radar jamming.

Despite these efforts, and the use of the 'bomber stream' in an attempt to overwhelm German defences, the scale of Bomber Command's operations came at an enormous cost in terms of both aircrew and aircraft brought down by night-fighters, flak guns and weather. By the end of the war more than 57,000 airmen of Bomber Command were lost, either on operations or in training, whilst nearly 10,000 became POWs in the Third Reich's notably bleak prison camps.

For the aircrew who managed to bale out of their aircraft, or who survived a crash landing, there was the perilous attempt at escape and evasion to avoid being captured. With the valiant support of civilians and resistance fighters in occupied countries some aircrew did manage to escape back to Britain, but most spent the rest of the war in the POW camps.

The Special Operations Executive (SOE), also known as 'Churchill's Secret Army' or the 'Ministry of Ungentlemanly Warfare', supplied and supported the Resistance in occupied countries. In carrying out these tasks, it was sustained by RAF aircrew operating clandestine missions, using Westland Lysanders, Lockheed Hudsons and Handley Page Halifax's. The Lysanders, often landing and taking off from unprepared fields in the heart of enemy occupied territory on moonlit nights, were flown by dead reckoning, by single pilots. There can be few other missions as dangerous and as lonely than these.

Since the beginning of the war Britain's supply lines had been under attack by German surface ships and submarines. However, Coastal Command with its Short Sunderland and Consolidated Catalina flying boats, coupled with land-based aeroplanes such as the Lockheed Hudson and the Consolidated B-24 Liberator, ranged far and wide for up to 13 hours across the grey waters to protect convoys from attack. The Battle of the Atlantic reached its peak in March 1943 and eventually the very long range types were finally able to cover what had previously been called the mid-Atlantic gap, the U-boats' favourite hunting ground. Along with the Vickers Warwick and Short Sunderlands already in service, the Catalina also provided the long range search and rescue capability to pick up survivors far out to sea.

Coastal Command also undertook perilous low level attacks on Axis shipping, originally with Blenheims, Beauforts and Handley-Page Hampdens, which suffered heavy casualties. Later anti-shipping squadrons were re-equipped with the Bristol Beaufighter and De Havilland Mosquito. During the second half of the war, these aircraft were formed into Strike Wings, armed with torpedoes, rockets and bombs. They undertook devastating attacks on German shipping from Norway to the Bay of Biscay. With multinational crews they flew daily low-level sorties across the formidable North Sea to attack ships sheltering in inlets and fjords. Their pro rata losses were even greater than those of Bomber Command.

Reflecting the rapid development of technology during all aspects of war, many Coastal Command aircraft were fitted with Air to Surface Vessel (ASV) radar to improve the chances of finding U-boats in the vast expanses of sea in the Atlantic and Bay of Biscay. The introduction of the aerial depth-charge and low-level bombsight gave the accuracy and firepower necessary to destroy the U-boat whether on the surface or submerged. The war in the Atlantic fluctuated as the Germans, in turn, equipped their U-boats with radar detection devices, more anti-aircraft guns and a device enabling the U-boat to remain under the surface for longer periods of time. Greater and more effective armament, with large calibre cannon, rockets and sophisticated depth charges, enabled Coastal Command to turn the tide by attacking U-boats more effectively. Bomber Command further reduced the submarine menace by bombing maintenance pens and construction yards. Although never completely eliminated, by mid-1943 the tide had turned in the Allies' favour and the U-boat menace never again seriously threatened an Allied victory.

Whilst armadas of British heavy bombers were relentlessly attacking Germany by night, USAAF B-17 Flying Fortresses and B-24 Liberators continued the fight by day. This Combined Bomber Offensive had a devastating effect on German industry, communications and morale. The concerted and devastating attacks on Germany's oil refineries from mid-1944 onwards meant that by 1945 total oil production was reduced by some ninety per cent, rendering the Wehrmacht's famed panzers nearly immobile and grounding large parts of the Luftwaffe.

In other theatres of war the tide was also turning, particularly following El Alamein and Operation Torch, which led to the final defeat of the German and Italian forces in North Africa and, eventually, the landings in southern Italy and the slow progress towards Rome. In all these campaigns the RAF flew with courage and determination to carry out strategic bombing and tactical support of ground troops. In North Africa, after some initial teething problems, the RAF developed new techniques for supporting the ground forces and it was here that Rommel first learned to be fearful of the significant impact the RAF could have on his army, a lesson he was to re-learn in Normandy. At El Alamein not only did the RAF successfully offer significant direct support to the Army, but aircraft from Malta crippled Rommel's supply lines across the Mediterranean, sinking a high proportion of the Axis oil tankers and supply ships.

In the Far East, the Japanese had rapidly advanced through most of the countries of the European empires during 1942, with British and Allied forces fighting a retreat to India. The rebuilding of RAF strength in India for the 3rd Tactical Air Force (3TAF), established in December 1943, was a slow and difficult process. Initially, the 3TAF relied heavily on US aircraft supplied under the 'Lend Lease' programme. These included the Curtiss Mohawk, Consolidated B-24 Liberator and the Republic P-47 Thunderbolt. Manufacturing capabilities were also established in Australia, where versions of the Bristol Beaufort, Beaufighter and De Havilland Mosquito were built.

Due to the often inhospitable nature of the terrain, with few roads, many mountains and the frequent monsoon weather systems, aerial re-supply became a major aspect of the war in the Far East. The Commander of the British 14th Army, General 'Bill' Slim, imaginatively used it to both stabilise his front line and to launch the counter attacks that would liberate Burma. This included delivering supplies to the 'Chindit' operations of General Orde Wingate, which carried out guerrilla warfare against Japanese forces deep inside occupied territory.

During 1944 the Allied air forces progressively established air supremacy over the Japanese and, as in other theatres of the war, the increased co-operation between air and ground forces began to turn the conflict in the Allies' favour. In March 1944 the 155,000 men at Kohima and Imphal were surrounded, being resupplied solely by air. Over a two month period, approximately 250 tons of supplies a day were delivered with the loss of only two Dakotas and one Wellington.

The training, camaraderie and esprit de corps of Trenchard's pre-war RAF was now paying dividends. In the deserts of North Africa, the jungles of the Far East and over the waters of the Atlantic and the Mediterranean, the RAF was playing a decisive role in the overall Allied victory.

The US Army Air Forces also played a vital part, with Republic P-47 Thunderbolt and the North American P-51 Mustang fighters ranging far and wide over occupied Europe and deep into Germany seeking out targets of opportunity. By the summer of 1944 the Allies had achieved total aerial superiority in western Europe. The Luftwaffe was forced to devote most of its efforts to the defence against the continued, combined bombing raids against its homeland. In advance of the invasion of Europe in 1944, the RAF established the 2nd Tactical Air Force (2TAF) to provide direct support to the Allied invasion forces. Air Mshl Sir Arthur Coningham, who had led the RAF Desert Air Force in North Africa was appointed to command 2TAF: it comprised four Groups flying a mix of Hawker Typhoon, North American Mustang and Supermarine Spitfire fighters, along with De Havilland Mosquito, Douglas Boston and North American Mitchell bombers. Prior to the invasion, the Allied heavy bomber and tactical air forces devastated the railway system in western Europe, crucially disrupting the Germans' ability to move reinforcements and supplies quickly to Normandy from other fronts. German units were forced to unload from trains, as far back as the borders of Germany and central France, and to proceed to the battle by road, consuming precious time and fuel in so doing.

On 6 June 1944 Operation *Overlord* was launched against Hitler's Fortress Europe. On 'D-Day', over the invasion beaches, the Allied air forces achieved complete air superiority. There were no less than 14,674 sorties flown, 5,656 by the RAF, for the loss of just 113 aircraft. The Luftwaffe had completely failed to defeat the Allied air forces.

While the Germans had pioneered the use of airborne assault using parachute troops and gliders, Britain had quickly developed its own capabilities and undertook operations in North Africa, Italy and the Normandy invasion, with increasing effectiveness each time. On the night before D-Day five out of six Airspeed Horsa gliders came within yards of their intended target, the moveable bridge at Bénouville over the Caen Canal (subsequently re-named 'Pegasus Bridge' in honour of the airborne troops who captured it).

The lessons of supporting the Army from the campaigns in Africa, Sicily and Italy had been well learned. With air superiority, and an effective system for controlling and directing fighter-bombers against ground targets, the Allies dominated the skies over Normandy to such an extent that the German armies were increasingly unable to manoeuvre in daylight. When the Allied breakout came the German troops trapped in the Falaise 'pocket' were subjected to relentless and unceasing strafing attacks from Allied aircraft and suffered heavily, especially from the rockets and cannon of the formidable RAF Typhoons.

It was to be nearly a year before Germany finally capitulated, but first it had other surprises for the British people.

On 13 June 1944, at 4.00am, the first of 7,547 V-1 flying bombs fired landed on British soil. Fighter Command quickly developed tactics to counter the V-1 menace, with the new Hawker Tempest fighters achieving particular success due to their high combat speed. The Gloster Meteor, the only Allied jet to see service in the war, also came into its own in dealing with these fearful weapons. The pioneering work in developing the jet engine for this aircraft had been undertaken by former RAF Cranwell apprentice and cadet, Air Cdre Sir Frank Whittle. Whittle had first suggested, in 1928, that a new type of engine would be necessary to achieve the higher speeds, altitudes and ranges required as aircraft designs continued to advance. Following successful trials of the engine, the Meteor evolved, powered by two of Whittle's Rolls Royce Welland engines. The Meteor entered service in mid-1944, just in time to deal with the arrival of the V-1. A total of 1,847 V-1s were destroyed by fighters.

Hitler's second 'Vengeance Weapon', the V-2 rocket, first fell on London in September. These weapons could only be destroyed by attacking their places of manufacture or actual launch sites. Fighters and bombers played their part in mounting massive attacks on both types of site. These disrupted both the V-1 and V-2 offensives, but it took a combination of air and ground attacks to, eventually, remove the threat of these weapons entirely.

In an attempt to speed up the advance north from Normandy to Germany Allied airborne operations were mounted at Arnhem in 1944, which aimed to seize the bridges over Dutch rivers and, crucially, the Rhine to open a route into Germany. Operation *Market Garden* was unsuccessful despite the gallantry of the troops on the ground and the continued aerial re-supply by Transport Command's Dakotas.

On New Year's Day 1945, a last ditch attempt to delay the Allied advance was made by Germany when Operation *Bodenplatte* (Baseplate) was launched. About 800 Luftwaffe aircraft attacked airfields on the Continent and destroyed many Allied aircraft on the ground. However, whilst a shock, it was a minor setback for the Allies who were able to replace their losses quickly; but it proved the death knell for the Luftwaffe which could not so easily replace their own heavy casualties, particularly their pilots. Although the War dragged on for another four months nothing further could be done to alter the inevitable defeat of Nazi Germany.

As the war in Europe drew to a close, Bomber Command found itself involved in humanitarian missions to deliver food to Dutch civilians facing starvation in occupied Holland. Known as Operation *Manna* by the British and *Chowhound* by the Americans, it began on 29 April 1945. In just over a week the Allies dropped over 11,000 tons of food to the Dutch people still living under German occupation.

The European war ended on 8 May 1945, with that in the Far East following on 15 August, by which time the RAF had grown out of all recognition, both in terms of its size and capabilities. At the start of World War II, the RAF had 2,600 aircraft, 173,958 officers and men, and 1,734 women. By the end of the war in Europe, its numbers had grown to 9,200 aircraft, 1,079,835 officers and men, and 158,771 women. They came from Britain and around the globe and 193,313 were aircrew. Of these 102,000 RAF men and women were killed during the war.

The RAF had formed a strong alliance with the US Army Air Forces and those of the many nations who had fought with it during World War II. However, one of the wartime Allies, The Soviet Union, was increasingly to take the form of a future enemy and an exhausted, victorious, but virtually bankrupt Britain faced an uncertain post war era. An era which saw not only a continuation of the privations of war carried into peace, by way of rationing and austerity, but also a change in government as the 1945 election saw a radical transformation in the political landscape of Britain.

The Many of Bomber Command
Mark Bromley

Bromley's painting of a Lancaster crew underlines so many aspects of Bomber Command's aircrew experience during World War II. Cramped working conditions and extreme environmental hazards made missions intense challenges for aircrew whose average age was 20 years old. The emphasis here is men and machine working in cohesion and that most vital element – teamwork. In the foreground is the Wireless Operator sitting at his R1155 Receiver and T1154 Transmitter sets. The crew have not yet reached their operating altitude as they have yet to put their oxygen masks on fully, and are not yet wearing their thickest gauntlets. The large control knobs on the wireless sets were designed so that the operator could adjust them with thick gloves. The Operator's role was to receive Morse coded messages throughout the flight and update the pilot with the information received. He would very rarely transmit anything, except emergency messages if the aircraft was in trouble. In front of the Wireless Operator is the Navigator, working with electronic aids and dead reckoning (compass, watch and chart), sitting at his table and communicating with the pilot, visible at the front of the cockpit on the left side. Behind the pilot's head is a 1/4 inch thick steel armour plate upon which can be seen a yellow circle. The yellow circle was a gas indicator patch which would change colour if the aircraft flew through poisoned gas.

Under the stewardship of leaders like Air Mshl Charles Portal and Air Chf Mshl Sir Arthur 'Bomber' Harris, a total of 126 squadrons served in Bomber Command during the course of World War II. Amongst these were 32 squadrons which were officially non-British units; there were 15 Canadian, 8 Australian, 4 Polish, 2 French, 2 New Zealand squadrons and 1 Czechoslovak squadron. Hundreds of foreign aircrew also served in other Bomber Command squadrons. These mixed crews gave an esprit de corps out of all proportion to the public relations benefit some may have thought they commanded. Crews enjoyed each other's company and bonds forged in war have been sustained for years in peace.

Over 364,500 sorties were flown by Bomber Command crews during the entire war, and 8,325 aircraft were shot down. Bomber Command suffered a very high casualty rate with some 57,205 men lost in action, and a further 8,403 wounded – accounting for some 60 percent of Bomber Command's total crew strength. Another 9,838 aircrew would become prisoners of war after being brought down and captured. Yet, these volunteers – a requirement for all Bomber Command crews – consistently took the war to the enemy and did so even when few other options were available for a beleaguered Allied cause. Indeed if occupying a civilian, important, 'reserved occupation' the only option open to a man insisting on serving in the armed forces, was in Bomber Command. Thus a sizeable number of Police Officers served in bombers and those who survived returned to life on the beat after the war with significant bravery awards visible on their chests. The courageousness, commitment and sacrifice of Harris' 'Bomber Boys' is remembered today at the Bomber Command memorial, opposite the RAF Club, in Green Park, London.

First of the Heavies, Short Stirling
Alex Hamilton

Representing a significant leap in RAF heavy bomber capability upon its introduction in 1940, the Short Stirling was the first four-engine heavy bomber to enter RAF service.

The Air Ministry's Specification B.12/36 called for a high-speed, long-range bomber that could be rapidly designed and introduced into service. Specifications stipulated a bombload of 14,000lb, carried to a range of 2,000 miles with a cruising speed of 230mph. Also, the requirement demanded a capability of carrying 24 soldiers in a secondary troop transport role.

On 14 May 1939 the first Stirling took to the air. No 7 Squadron at RAF Leeming became the first operational squadron with the aircraft in January 1941 and was committed to the RAF bombing effort the following month. By the end of 1941, 150 Stirlings were in RAF service, with three squadrons operating the type in both daytime and night operations. By 1941, Stirling bombers were being used to formulate the Pathfinder tactics that would help to define the RAF's bombing doctrine for the rest of the war.

The Stirling gained a reputation as a robust performer and its thick wing also blessed it with exceptional turning capability for an aircraft of its size, often outmanoeuvring smaller enemy heavy fighters. It was a 'first generation' heavy bomber and was not as economical to build as its successors, neither did it have the advantage of an uncluttered bomb bay which meant it could not to carry the new 4,000lb bombs when they came into service. Its lacklustre performance at high altitude also ensured it would be relegated to other, equally important, duties. However, between 1940 and 1943 the Stirling, along with the Halifax and Wellington, represented the vanguard of RAF Bomber Command.

After its withdrawal as a heavy bomber, the Stirling continued to give an excellent account of itself as a glider tug. In addition, from late 1944, 160 Stirling Mk V transports were put into service, dropping paratroopers and their fuel/equipment. Special duties versions also dropped agents and supplies into occupied Europe. The Stirling was retired from RAF service in 1946.

Operation *Jericho* and All That, Mosquito Low Level Raids

Mark Bromley

A typical low level precision attack is seen in this painting. Mosquito fighter bombers are flying towards a specific target such as the Amiens Prison (named Operation *Jericho* as the mission required the accurate breaching of the prison walls), or the Philips Electronics Factory, to cause maximum damage as part of the war effort and minimal damage to the local population and infrastructure.

Conceived as a fast un-armed bomber De Havilland's Mosquito represented, upon its introduction in 1941, an end to the RAF's reliance on older, increasingly obsolete heavy fighters and medium bombers. Known as the 'wooden wonder' due to its predominantly wooden construction, the Mosquito was a robust, hard-hitting and exceptionally versatile machine that could outperform even some lighter single-engine enemy aircraft, as a fighter, and heavier bombers, as a strike platform. Overshadowed by aircraft such as the Spitfire, Hurricane and Lancaster the Mosquito can rightly take its place as the most versatile and effective British aircraft of World War II.

However, the original design of the Mosquito was proposed before the outbreak of war, in 1936, yet was largely ignored in preference to other designs like the Blenheim, an aircraft the Mosquito would go on to replace in front-line squadrons. It would take the Air Ministry until 1940 before they re-prioritised the De Havilland design. The first Mosquito took to the air in November 1940. In July 1941, the first production Mosquito entered service with No 1 Photographic Reconnaissance Unit (PRU), followed by the first bomber versions with No 105 Squadron in November 1941.

Mosquitos immediately started long-range raids against enemy targets across Europe, its two Rolls Royce Merlin engines affording it astonishing speed, range, survivability and low-level performance.

BROMLEY

Peenemunde, 1943
Frank Wootton

Arguably one of the most significant bombing campaigns of the entire Second World War, Operation *Hydra* – part of the RAF's *Crossbow* Campaign targeting German V-Weapon facilities – commenced with a major wave of strikes on the Peenemunde Army Research Centre during the night of 17/18 August 1943. Peenemunde was situated on the German Baltic coast at the very limit of Allied bombing range from Britain. There were several novel features about this first attack on the site. This was the first occasion that Bomber Command's Pathfinder Force used the 'Master Bomber' technique where one aircraft controlled the progress of the entire raid while orbiting above the target area. It was the only occasion in the second half of the war when virtually the whole of Bomber Command attempted a precision raid by night on such a small target.

The strikes included 324 Lancasters, 218 Halifaxes, 54 Stirlings and were obscured by a number of disrupting missions including Operation *Whitebait*, a group of Mosquitos that launched a diversionary raid on Berlin to distract Luftwaffe night fighter defences. Long range intruder missions by Beaufighters against Luftwaffe airfields caused further confusion and Halifaxes added to the German workload by carrying out a number of supply drops to resistance groups in Denmark. Over Peenemunde, and flying lower than normal to ensure bombing accuracy, the bombers were also relying on moonlight for waypoint accuracy as the target was out of range of the RAF's GEE beam navigation equipment.

The strike that night severely damaged the German V-Weapons programme, both in terms of the loss of key scientific personnel and of facilities. The V-Weapons programme, that at one point threatened to turn the tide of the war, was delayed by at least two months. 40 RAF bombers were lost during the raid, of which 23 were Lancasters. 215 RAF aircrew paid the ultimate price and were killed during the operation.

Contemporary claims that key facilities escaped damage during Operation *Hydra* may be true and V-Weapon testing did indeed restart quickly after the raid. However there is no doubt that Peenemunde never managed to develop any further V-Weapon systems following the attack.

Those Who Helped Us In Our Hour of Need

Elizabeth Harrison

Elizabeth Harrison was the former secretary of the RAF Escaping Society (RAFES) and her sculpture lies within the crypt of the RAF Church of St Clement Danes on The Strand, London. The sculpture depicts a downed airman being assisted by two helpers (an elderly man and a very young woman), with a second airman parachuting down close by. The plaque pays tribute to all those who helped Allied airmen to evade and escape capture.

Additional plaques are in place at the RAF Museum, Hendon, the War Museums in Ottawa and Canberra, the Musée de L'Armée in Paris, the National Resistance Museum at Overloon, the Netherlands, and the Basilica in Brussels, Belgium. This final plaque resides in the RAF Club in London and was presented by Andy Sowerby, grandson of Fg Off 'Al' Day RCAF. As Sergeant A D Day RCAF, on the night of 5 August 1941, 'Al' was serving on No 77 Squadron flying in an Armstrong Whitworth Whitley when he was shot down over Belgium and became the 10th (of 288) evader to be taken over the Pyrenees by the 'Comet' escape line. After being looked after through a serious bout of pneumonia, he was sheltered by the people in 'Comet' for over four months before reaching neutral Spain. The 'Comet' line inspired the 1970s TV series *Secret Army* and its most famous member was the 24 year old Andrée de Jongh (codename 'Dédée'), who survived two concentration camps to receive the George Medal in 1946.

ON THE 21ST JUNE
WORLD WAR II
WITHOUT THOUGHT OF DANGER TO
COMMONWEALTH
AIR FORCES TO ESCAPE AND RETURN TO THIS COUNTRY AND SO
PAID WITH THEIR LIVES. MANY MORE
ENDURED THE DEGRADATION OF CONCENTRATION CAMPS. THEIR NAMES ARE REMEMBERED
TO FIGHT A LONGER BATTLE. TO MARK ITS DEBT OF GRATITUDE THE ROYAL AIR FORCES ESCAPING SOCIETY ERECTED THIS MEMORIAL AS A
LASTING TRIBUTE AND ALSO TO SERVE AS AN INSPIRATION TO FUTURE GENERATIONS.

Clandestine Motive

Michael Turner

The moon shines through a cloudy sky above a field, somewhere in occupied Western Europe. Delivering agents or supplies demanded basic map reading and dead reckoning navigation by the pilot of this Lysander, he also needed moonlight to achieve an accurate position and arrive at the spot dimly illuminated by partisans on the ground. A stop watch, compass, chart, and very accurate flying, made this highly dangerous job a very specialised business. The rugged and reliable Lysander made it possible. It was part of Britain's role in sustaining the resistance on occupied mainland Europe, using members of the Special Operations Executive (SOE), 'The Baker Street Irregulars', to infiltrate the enemy heartland.

No 138 (Special Duty) Squadron was formed in August 1941. Among its fleet, the Lysander Mk III (known as the 'Lizzie') was one of the few aircraft types in the squadron that had the short, rough field qualities to land on occupied soil. The Mk III was specially equipped with a ladder to allow for quick access to the rear cockpit and a 150 gallon fixed cylindrical fuel tank under the belly to extend the Lysander's range. No 138 Squadron Lysanders were also painted matte black as most missions took place at night.

The RAF built secret airfields for their Lysanders at Newmarket and Tempsford, although fuelling for missions usually took place at regular RAF airfields. In early 1942, a second unit, No 161 Squadron, was raised to facilitate more special duties operations.

Lysander special duties operations continued until the liberation of France in 1944. By this time, 101 agents had been inserted into occupied Europe by Lysander and a further 128 agents and downed aircrew were recovered.

'The Flying Suitcase', Hampdens Attack a Convoy 1942

Anthony Cowland

Employing a distinctive slim pod and boom design, the Handley Page Hampden first flew on 21 June 1936. Designed to satisfy the Air Ministry's Specification B.9/36, the Hampden, at 254mph, was one of the fastest medium bombers in service with the RAF during World War II and, despite being smaller than the heavier bombers, could carry a bombload almost equal to the Wellington. This ability gave it the nickname 'The Flying Suitcase' by its crews.

Entering service with No 49 Squadron at RAF Scampton in September 1938, initial wartime operations in the daylight reconnaissance and strike role proved disappointing and several Hampdens were lost as tactical and operational shortcomings became apparent. However, in early 1940, Hampdens began to be employed in coastal patrol role and as minelayers. Within a year, Hampdens from No 5 Group had performed 1,209 minelaying sorties and delivered over 700 mines. That role was especially important during the Norwegian Campaign of April 1940.

Hampden pilot Flt Lt R A B Learoyd from No 49 Squadron (known as 'Babe' by his chums because of his youthful looks) became Bomber Command's first Victoria Cross recipient after his efforts on, 12 August 1940 to destroy an aqueduct of the Dortmund-Ems Canal. Interviewed by the author in 1980, Learoyd revealed that, at the exact moment he attacked his target, his Navigator reported on the intercom that their carrier pigeon had laid an egg. He thought that, as he was trying to do exactly that with his bombs, it was perfect timing by the pigeon. Nearly a month after Learoyd's mission, on the night of 15 September, No 83 Squadron's Hampden gunner Sgt John Hannah also won the Victoria Cross. Hannah was aged 18 and remains the RAF's youngest recipient of the award.

By 1942, and as depicted in Cowland's painting, Hampdens were transferred permanently to Coastal Command and employed on convoy operations, in particular protecting the critical Northern Russia-bound merchantman carrying supplies to a beleaguered Soviet Union. The Hampden was also converted to carry torpedoes and a number were ferried to Russia for use by the Soviet Air Forces. By the close of 1943, Hampden squadrons began to re-equip with more modern types such as the Bristol Beaufighter, and by 1944 Hampdens had been retired from operational roles.

L KM

Air Sea Rescue and All That

Anthony Cowland

The development of Coastal Command's Air Sea Rescue role, as depicted in another panel from Cowland's triptych, is illustrated by the increasing importance of heavy aircraft types, as part of the efforts to maintain an effective rescue capability for both downed aircraft and lost ships alike.

Increasingly obsolete as bomber types, aircraft like the Lockheed Hudson, the Wellington and its larger sibling the Warwick, which had the range that allowed them to patrol far out over the ocean, were pressed into service as air sea rescue types.

The painting also shows the developments that had been made in rescue equipment towards the end of the war: inflatable rafts, droppable airborne lifeboats and other survival equipment, items developed after the hard-learnt lessons of the Battle of Britain and the Battle of the Atlantic. Visible in this scene are a number of small orange containers. These are carrier pigeon cages with their round apertures and carrying handles. Many multi-crewed RAF aircraft carried pigeons to be released with a message should the aircraft come down in the sea or a remote area. The pigeon cages were identical to the containers used prior to the war for dispensing potato crisps in Public Houses. When it was realised that these containers would be ideal for pigeon carrying in aircraft the manufacture was 're-purposed' for the duration of the war. The animal equivalent of the Victoria Cross is the Dickin Medal; since it was instituted in 1943, 67 Dickin medals have been awarded with the majority (32) going to pigeons.

Shipping Strike
Frank Wootton

Frank Wootton captioned this painting in his book *The Aviation Art of Frank Wootton* as follows:

"Led by Wing Commander Neil Wheeler, 27 Beaufighters of the North Coates Wing attacked a heavily escorted convoy off the Dutch coast on June 22, 1943. High level protection for the Beaufighters was provided by Spitfires and Typhoons of Fighter Command. The role of 143 and 236 Beaufighter Squadrons was to attack the escort vessels of the convoy with rockets, cannon and machine gun fire in order to enable 254 Squadron, which carried torpedoes, to attack the larger merchant vessels."

The Coastal Command 'Strike Wings', as they became known, operated against shipping from Cornwall, Lincolnshire and Scotland, attacking ships as far afield as the Bay of Biscay and Norway. They were highly successful, sinking over 300,000 tons of shipping. Their own loss rate was the highest, pro rata, of any branch of the RAF, with 450 airmen (out of 700) and 250 aircraft lost. The North Coates Wing also supplied the means to carry out one of the most audacious missions of the War. On 14 June 1944, in a bid to upset the Germans and invigorate the public in Paris, a single Beaufighter flew a few feet above the Avenue des Champs-Élysées, dropped a tricolour flag on the Arc de Triomphe de l'Étoile and machine gunned the Kriegsmarine's Paris HQ. Operation *Squabble* was flown by Flt Lt Ken Gatwood and Sgt George Fern of No 236 Squadron; they were awarded the DFC and DFM respectively for their achievement.

The Bristol Beaufighter was a product of improvisation designed by Roy Fedden and Leslie Frise to meet an urgent pre-war requirement for a heavy fighter. To rapidly meet the demand, Bristol took the Beaufort torpedo-bomber – itself a development of the Blenheim – and within days drafted what would become the Beaufighter. Within eight months of this draft, the first Beaufighter took to the air in July 1939.

Built around an all-metal airframe and cantilever mid-wing, the Beaufighter was initially powered by Bristol's own Hercules radial piston engine. The real strength of the Beaufighter however lay in its versatility and ability to mount various weapons to suit different roles, from heavy long range interceptor to night fighter and anti-shipping strike aircraft, as depicted here.

By 1940 three production lines were mass producing the Beaufighter – Bristol's plants at Filton and Weston-Super-Mare along with Fairey's plant at Stockport. The first Beaufighter entered RAF service in July 1940. Nos 25 and 29 Squadrons received their first examples of the aircraft in September that year. They would both be operational and engaged at night against the enemy within four weeks; the Beaufighter scored its first aerial victory against a Junkers Ju 88 on 19 November 1940.

Exceptionally flexible and very robust, whilst also blessed with excellent handling and performance, the Beaufighter served with 59 RAF squadrons and over 5,900 were produced before production ceased in 1946. The versatile Beaufighter would serve on as a target tug until 1960.

Hot, Humid, Deadly and Dangerous, The Far East 1945

Trevor Lay

Lay's painting depicts a tropicalised Spitfire Mk VIII wearing the distinctive markings of the RAF's Far East Air Force, interdicting enemy railway lines in the Chittagong Region, a setting that exemplifies the South East Asian theatre of World War II. The railways were the artery for enemy communications, logistics and especially its vital oil supplies. The scene is of a No 273 Squadron aircraft, based at Mingaladon, Burma (now Yangon International Airport, Myanmar) during the summer of 1945, just after its aircraft were equipped with wing mounted bombs. It is flying at very low height over difficult and challenging terrain which is typical of the areas of operation found in wartime Burma and Malaya. Disrupting communications was a vital element of the war and a key objective of the RAF in the Far East. So successful were the RAF's attacks on Japanese railway traffic, that by late 1943, the enemy was forced to operate its trains by night and hide their rolling stock by day. The disruption effectively reduced the enemy's supply capability.

Formed as Air Command, South East Asia in 1943, the Far East Air Force, as it was more commonly known, came under the command of Lord Louis Mountbatten, as Supreme Allied Commander South East Asia and part of Allied Forces South East Asia. Success in 1943 would lead to the Command, by late 1944, being at the forefront of the Burma Campaign and to the eviction of Japanese forces from that absolutely vital theatre.

MS C
MT730

Strike Hard, Strike Sure
Mark Bromley

Underlining the Mosquito's versatility, the aircraft eventually went on to serve not only as a tactical bomber but also in the coastal strike role, as a heavy fighter, photo reconnaissance and night fighter. It has since been recognised as the aircraft with the fewest casualties, pro rata, than any other Allied aircraft.

Bromley's illustration shows a sight that was common for the Mosquito in the mid to late years of World War II: a single aircraft and crew operating at range over enemy territory. Whether the mission was reconnaissance, raiding, or as a pathfinder guiding heavy bomber groups, the Mosquito's qualities of speed, robust strength, hard hitting defences, and the élan of its crews, meant that the chances of achieving a successful mission outcome were always high.

Such qualities made the Mosquito popular with its crews. The effect on the enemy was the total opposite, with the Mosquito identified early in its service career as a key threat by the Luftwaffe. Mosquitos accounted for some 487 enemy aircraft, with the vast majority scored by night fighter variants. It was also particularly effective, again at long range, against convoys hiding in Norwegian fjords with the reconnaissance and reporting for these dangerous missions being carried out by Norwegian crews. In the Light Night Striking Force, Bomber Command used the aircraft as an intruder, stalking enemy airfields and strategic sites on free-ranging interdiction. These missions diverted defences away from the Main Force and, importantly, undermined the morale of the enemy who never knew when and where a Mosquito might appear.

Production of the Mosquito ran until 1950, by which point some 7,781 Mosquitos had been built. The last Mosquito left RAF service in 1961.

BROMLEY

The Falaise Gap Closed, a Typhoon 'Cab Rank'
Frank Wootton

Close Air Support – the importance of which is underlined in Wootton's rendition of Falaise in August 1944. Following the D-Day landings and the establishment of a beachhead, the Allied ground forces around the Falaise pocket had become bogged down as the Germans rallied after the initial surprise. Six weeks after the initial landing, the British forces, under the command of General Bernard Montgomery, began a major offensive in an attempt to envelop the Wehrmacht's Army Group B. Close to two weeks of fighting followed, with the 50,000 German troops being almost surrounded before forced into a major retreat. By 21 August German losses, especially in terms of armoured vehicles, were huge, primarily as a result of the efforts of rocket-armed Typhoons. This was a result of the RAF's development of the 'Cab Rank' system of air support, whereby a squadron of Typhoons was, like taxis awaiting a customer, constantly available to be called upon for ground support. This method of air support is still an operational choice for commanders today.

Designed originally as an interceptor, and taking to the air for the first time in February 1940, the Typhoon originally failed to deliver the performance Hawker promised for the interception role. However, due to the arrival of the Focke-Wulf Fw190, and the Typhoon being the only RAF aircraft capable of catching it at low-level, there was a reprieve for the Hawker aircraft. In time, the Typhoon would gain its fearsome reputation as a ground attack aircraft, where its low-level performance would come into its own. Armed with 20mm cannon and RP-3 rockets, some 26 squadrons of Typhoons were serving the 2nd Allied Tactical Air Force by D-Day.

The Meteor's First Blow, 4 August 1944
Frank Wootton

Within days of the D-Day landings in Normandy the first vengeance weapons started to arrive in and around London. This new weapon necessitated fresh tactics and very soon it was discovered that the standard form of attack (firing guns from directly behind the target) was extremely dangerous for the attacking aircraft. A successful shot would blow the V-1 into thousands of exploding pieces which would then envelope the attacker. A solution was soon found. A fast diving Spitfire or Tempest would catch up with the weapon, fly alongside for a few seconds and, at the right moment when the wing tips of each aircraft were aligned, a swift upward movement of the attacker's wing would produce enough air pressure to lift the wing of the missile and topple its levelling gyroscope.

Wootton's illustration shows this novel tactic being employed on 4 August 1944 by a Meteor F1 of No 616 (South Yorkshire) Squadron AuxAF over an un-populated area. In this particular case the pilot, Flg Off 'Dixie' Dean, had little choice as his guns jammed as he was diving towards the V-1 near Tonbridge in Kent. He employed the alternative manoeuvre and, in so doing, was the first jet pilot in the world to score an aerial victory over a missile. A few minutes later Dean's colleague Fg Off J K Roger, whose guns had functioned properly, became the first Allied airman to shoot down an enemy aircraft in a jet fighter. By the close of the war, and with the V-1 threat diminished, the Meteor had managed to destroy 14 flying bombs.

The only Allied jet fighter to see combat service during World War II, the Meteor first took to the air in March 1943 and was introduced into No 616 Squadron at Culmhead in July 1944. The aircraft's ground-breaking Rolls Royce turbojet engines blessed the Meteor with superior speed and performance compared to the piston engine fighters of the time.

Meteors would go on to prove a major success in RAF service, with over 3,900 built for UK and export markets. Used in a myriad of roles, particularly as a test bed for a large number of post-war innovations in engine and ejection seat development, the last RAF Meteor (a shepherd aircraft for Jindivik target drones) was retired in the 1980s. The Meteor is still used for ejector seat testing by the Martin Baker Company.

YQ E
WOOTTON

"*Thank you for coming boys.*" Operation Manna, Holland, 1945
Alan Fearnley

The starving people of the Netherlands wave, cheer and hold flags to thank the Allied crews dropping supplies of basic foodstuffs to them in the Spring of 1945. With the war not yet over, but with the northern Netherlands bypassed by the advancing allies and still occupied by the Germans, the population was starving to death. Operation *Manna* was undertaken by the RAF (the same missions were flown by the USAAF under the name *Chowhound*) and took place between April and May 1945 They were organised to relieve the three million Dutch nationals facing starvation as a result of food shortages caused by the Germans flooding their agricultural land and supplies being cut off by the isolation of the area.

The operation was sanctioned by PM Winston Churchill and Supreme Allied Commander Dwight D Eisenhower. Prince Bernard of the Netherlands negotiated a truce with the remaining German occupying forces who agreed not to fire on aircraft dropping aid in certain designated air corridors.

On the morning of 29 April 1945, a sole Avro Lancaster launched Operation *Manna*, despite the German ceasefire agreement not yet being in place. Flying at an extremely low level to avoid enemy anti-aircraft ordnance, the 'Bad Penny' succeeded in dropping its cargo of food aid and returned safely home. The crew reported that the German anti-aircraft guns followed their progress, but there was no firing from the ground. Another 3,300 sorties would be undertaken over the next nine days – 3,156 of them by Avro Lancasters. Bomber Command dropped 6,680 tons of food during the operation.

Alan Fearnley

Portrait of Winston Churchill
Cuthbert Orde

Winston Churchill was invited to become Honorary Air Commodore of No 615 (County of Surrey) Squadron AuxAF upon its transfer to Fighter Command in 1939. He immediately accepted and gave a great deal of his time and correspondence to what became known as 'Churchill's Own'. However, by the middle of the war he had often made the observation that virtually all the senior officers of the RAF with whom he dealt had, in addition to their medals and awards, pilot's wings on their chest. Eventually, and with the King's approval, in March 1943, to coincide with the 25th anniversary of the formation of the RAF, he was awarded 'honorary wings' by the Air Council. In his letter of thanks he said:

"I am honoured to be accorded a place, albeit out of kindness, in that comradeship of the air which guards the life of our island and carries doom to tyrants, whether they flaunt themselves or burrow deep."

A keen advocate of aerial power projection and air defence, fostered during his tenure as Secretary of State for Air between 1919 and 1921, Churchill's appointment as Prime Minister in May 1940 guaranteed that the Royal Air Force would get the resources it needed, not only in the early years to defend the United Kingdom, but as a means of taking the war to the enemy and then as a vital element of the forces that went on to liberate Europe, Africa and Asia.

Churchill wore the uniform of the RAF on his visits to the front in North Africa and to meet, for the first time, Josef Stalin at the Tehran Conference in late 1943.

CHAPTER VII

OLD ALLIES, NEW ADVERSARIES ~ 1946 TO 1957

"A shadow has fallen upon the scenes so lately lighted by the Allied victory ... . From Stettin in the Baltic to Trieste in the Adriatic an iron curtain has descended across the Continent."

WINSTON CHURCHILL, MARCH 1946

THE situation at the end of World War II was similar to that at the end of World War I. The RAF began to reduce its aircraft stocks and its wartime personnel, with one million people being demobilised. Even so, Operation *Exodus* was the first priority in Europe, bringing home PoWs and delivering food and medical supplies to those still in need. The ubiquitous 'demob' suit, tie, felt trilby hat, raincoat and cardboard suitcase became a familiar sight all over the country. By April 1947 the regular RAF was reduced to less than 300,000 people.

The first year or so after peace in Europe and the Far East may have been difficult for those serving in the RAF, but they were also exciting times as the Service moved into the jet age. On 7 November 1945, Gp Capt Hugh 'Willie' Wilson, flying a Gloster Meteor F4, had set a new world speed record of 606.25mph. This record was raised a few months later to 616mph by Gp Capt 'Teddy' Donaldson. The RAF Regiment, which had been created during the war and had proud battle honours from every operational campaign after 1942, was officially announced as a permanent integral part of the RAF on 10 July 1946. In the same year the first jet fighter squadrons of the post-war RAF were formed into all-jet Wings. After the Gloster Meteor the RAF was soon to be equipped with its second jet fighter, the twin-tail boom De Havilland Vampire. However, within a relatively short time both these innovative machines were looking increasingly obsolete when compared with the swept wing designs then coming into service with the USAF and Soviet air forces. The American and Russian acquisition of German World War II jet technology and aerodynamic research was beginning to produce results, with the F-86 Sabre and Mig15 respectively. In an attempt to regain Britain's place at the forefront of fighter technology, two promising designs, the Hawker Hunter and Supermarine Swift, were ordered 'off the drawing board' in 1950.

Both were ordered as a contingency in case one proved unsatisfactory. The first production standard Hunter flew in 1951 and, in 1953, a specially modified version piloted by Neville Duke broke the world air speed record for jet-powered aircraft. This record stood for less than three weeks, before being broken in turn by its competitor, the Swift, flown by Mike Lithgow. Indeed, following the coronation in 1953, HM The Queen reviewed the Royal Air Force at RAF Odiham in 1954. A flypast of 640 aircraft was staged, led by a Bristol Sycamore helicopter flying at a stately speed of 90mph (with a large RAF ensign hanging from its winch cable) and, to great cheers from the crowd, a Swift flying at over 650mph to finish the show.

With such advanced technology it was inevitable that there would be teething troubles and both types had their fair share of these, but both entered service with operational RAF squadrons. However, it was the Hunter that was the most successful of the two types, entering RAF service in 1954 and serving in a range of roles from fighter, to ground attack and trainer. The Hunter was also exported widely. Whilst it was retired from the RAF in the early 1990s, it continued in service with other air forces well in to the 21st century.

Throughout the 1950s, the Hunter and Gloster Javelin of Fighter Command provided the all-weather air defence of Britain.

Bomber Command started the replacement of its Lancasters and Lincolns with the revolutionary new twin-jet English Electric Canberra, which entered service in 1951. In the early years of its service, the Canberra set a number of records, including winning the London to New Zealand air race in 1953, covering over 12,000 miles in less than 24 hours.

The RAF also became the first air force to fly a jet airliner with the introduction into Transport Command service of the De Havilland Comet. However, before these innovations could be introduced a recent ally became a new threat.

In 1948 the RAF was again placed on an operational war footing in two distinctly different spheres. The Russian occupation of East Germany meant that Berlin was isolated within the Soviet Zone. The four occupying powers,

Britain, the USA, France and the Soviet Union, had signed a formal agreement concerning arrangements for flights into the city, principally for safety reasons. However, no such agreements existed for road or rail access to Berlin. The Berlin Airlift was set up after Russia closed off all the land access to the city. In the absence of any agreement on road or rail access, short of starting a Third World War, there was little the western Allies could do on land. In the air, however, the existing agreement meant that the onus would have been on the Soviets to break the agreement if they wished to stop aircraft flying down the established corridors. The RAF, civil airliners and the United States Air Force (which had been formed the year before) jointly flew in nearly half a million tons of supplies to the beleaguered people of West Berlin between 22 June and 31 October 1948. In addition to its Dakotas, the RAF had the Avro York (which was a transport development of the Lancaster eventually transporting over half of the cargo carried by the RAF), and the new Handley Page Hastings. Even the venerable Short Sunderland was used, not only because it could land on rivers and lakes (until they froze during the winter months), but more importantly, because of its maritime role, it was protected against salt corrosion. Thus the Sunderland did sterling service carrying salt and other corrosive cargoes into the city. The original aim had been to supply about 200 tons a day but, at the height of the airlift, approximately 8,000 tons a day was being achieved and, on Good Friday 1949, an incredible 12,940 tons was flown in. As can be imagined, this level of airlift required very precise air traffic control arrangements and very close co-operation between the RAF, civil operators and the USAF. The procedures used for landing constant streams of aircraft at busy international airports, which allow such high density traffic at airports today, were pioneered during this period in Berlin.

The airlift sustained Berlin until May 1949 when the Soviets finally lifted their blockade, but operations continued for a further five months in order to build up Berlin's stocks. However, relations with East Germany and Russia remained very tense. In the light of this, the Western European nations, along with the USA and Canada, determined that an alliance based on collective security would be more effective and, in 1949, the North Atlantic Treaty Organisation (NATO) was formed. When West Germany was integrated into NATO in 1955 the Soviet Union responded and, with its allies, formed the Warsaw Pact.

NATO commitments meant a number of changes in the deployment and role of the UK armed forces. An example of this was the revival of the close wartime co-operation between the Royal Navy and Coastal Command within the NATO command structure. Initially, equipment was confined to Maritime Reconnaissance Lancasters, until 1956, when these were eventually replaced by the Avro Shackleton.

The Berlin Airlift had also demonstrated that many of the former Luftwaffe airfields being used by the RAF in Germany were not well located to face the potential Soviet threat. New airfields were built west of the Rhine and the British Air Forces of Occupation returned to its original designation as the Second Tactical Air Force (2TAF). It would evolve into Royal Air Force Germany in 1959.

Even though the demobilisation had started, not all servicemen were released and, as the first years after World War II showed that peace was not guaranteed, a new form of conscription was created by the National Service Act 1948. From 1 January 1949, healthy males 17 to 21 years old were expected to serve in the armed forces for 18 months, and remain on the reserve list for four years. They could be recalled to their units for up to 20 days, for no more than three occasions during these four years.

In October 1950, in response to the British involvement in the Korean War, the service period was extended to two years; in compensation, the reserve period was reduced by six months. National Servicemen who showed promise could be commissioned as officers. National Service personnel were used in combat operations, including the Malayan Emergency, the Cyprus Emergency, in Kenya against the Mau Mau Uprising, and the Korean War. In addition, National Servicemen served in the Suez Crisis of 1956. It was an experience that few would ever forget, for most it was "... *how are we going to get the toe caps on our boots to shine like a mirror ... how are were to learn to fold blankets and sheets was another mystery – which was quickly unfolded?"* (Peter Alliss, golfing commentator); some believed it to be *"... the time of my life"* (William Woollard, broadcaster), and others *"...the RAF took a boy of seventeen and half and turned out a man. Not always a very sensible or mature one; but somewhere, sometime, at the controls of a Vampire, I think we all crossed the threshold."* (Frederick Forsyth, writer).

National Service ended gradually from 1957 and the last National Servicemen left the armed forces in May 1963.

The next major commitment after the Berlin Airlift was in Malaya and started in 1948. A long campaign was fought against Communist terrorists whose insurgents' attacks were primarily targeted at rubber plantations, tin mines and government buildings. They also assassinated both British and Malay civilians and officials including the British High Commissioner, Sir Henry Gurney. The objective was to damage not only the economy, but also the morale of the population. The subsequent state of emergency took Britain into a joint civil and military conflict that would last until 1960. The aim of the Operation, known as *Firedog*, was to isolate the insurgents from the local population and thus, by denying them any support, eventually force them from their jungle strongholds. The tactics were successful and the Communists never gained the support from the local population they had hoped for.

Headquartered in Singapore, the Far East Air Force provided the RAF's support to the civil authorities and required the whole panoply of RAF air power, from reconnaissance, to transport, to ground attack and bombers. The campaign in Malaya also meant that Britain was only able to make a limited contribution to the UN support to South Korea when it was invaded by the North in 1950. The RAF commitment in Korea included a number of pilots on secondment to the USAF and RAAF, but only comprised three squadrons of Short Sunderlands, and the Transport force undertaking trooping flights between the UK, Japan and Korea, as well as bringing home wounded Allied servicemen.

Many of the airfields in Malaya were little more than strips cleared in the jungle, but they proved ideal for the RAF's short take-off and landing aircraft such as the Scottish Aviation Pioneer, which could land on a 150 yard strip, and its larger derivative the Twin Pioneer.

Malaya was the first theatre in which an air force used helicopters comprehensively. Machines such as the Bristol Sycamore and Westland Whirlwind were used for casualty evacuation and to deploy Army foot patrols into the jungle. Significant operational lessons were learned about helicopter versatility in this period. Foot patrols were landed deep in the interior by helicopter where they were sustained by larger aircraft, such as the Vickers Valetta and the Douglas Dakota, making regular supply drops.

Air strikes were sometimes required on suspected insurgent hideouts or food dumps, but never inhabited villages. Initially, these used the twin piston engined Bristol Brigand and De Havilland Hornet, which were later replaced by jets such as the De Havilland Vampire and Venom. Also used on bombing raids was the Avro Lincoln, a development of the venerable Lancaster. As the insurgents in Malaya were progressively defeated, the country declared its independence from Britain in 1957, although the 'Emergency' did not officially end until 1960.

Whilst its commitments in Malaya continued, the RAF was called upon for yet another operational deployment in 1954: subduing the Mau Mau rebels in Kenya. Several Avro Lincoln bomber units were used to back up the Kenyan forces.

In the Middle East, in late 1954, tensions began to increase with Egypt over the Suez Canal, Russian military aid, and the threat of a further war between Israel and its Arab neighbours. By 1956, Britain and France developed both strategic and regime change aspirations in the region. They also had commercial reasons for wanting freedom of movement through the canal, and as diplomatic efforts to resolve the crisis stalled, both countries built up forces in Malta and Cyprus. When the diplomatic efforts failed, the air and sea-borne invasion (Operation *Musketeer*) to re-occupy the canal-zone was launched at the end of October.

In what became known as 'The Suez Crisis' the RAF's first task (supported by the FAA) was to attack airfields and deny the Egyptian Air Force (EAF) the ability to interfere with the invasion. Within two days, attacks by Canberras, Valiants and Venoms destroyed the majority of the EAF on the ground. The Hastings and Vallettas dropped paratroopers for their successful ground offensive. One of the many lessons learned after Suez was that Britain needed a strong, highly mobile tactical air transport force, able to fly troops to any area at the shortest possible notice. This policy was adopted by the RAF in the following years when Transport Command was expanded and No 38 Group formed, combining transport units with their own fighter tactical support squadrons.

Suez was militarily successful, but the USA's decision not to support Britain and France, coupled with a United Nations Resolution calling for a withdrawal of forces, made *Musketeer* a strategic and diplomatic defeat. 'The Suez Crisis' was a humiliation for Britain and led to the resignation of Prime Minister Anthony Eden. More significantly, it led to a realisation that the UK was no longer the world power it had been for the previous few centuries. This would require an examination of its overall role in the world and decisions for the future on where its efforts should be focussed.

Meanwhile, in January 1955, the RAF had entered a fresh era. The first V-Bomber, the Vickers Valiant, came into service with Bomber Command. It was the first of three major designs, the second being the Avro Vulcan and the third, the Handley Page Victor. These aircraft were intended to convert Bomber Command into an awesome deterrent force.

Designed to lift a nuclear or conventional war load, the Valiant was in service for two years before being joined by the other two V-Bombers. On 11 October 1956 a Valiant dropped the first British atom bomb during trials at Maralinga, South Australia. In May 1957 a Valiant, based on Christmas Island, released the first British hydrogen bomb over Malden Island, Kiribati. These tests meant that the UK became the third recognised possessor of thermonuclear weapons.

Although the Valiant also achieved some notable records such as the first non-stop flight (in 1959) from Britain to South Africa and also pioneered the jet tanker air-to-air refuelling role, it was a fairly conventional design. The same could not be said for the other two V-Bombers, the delta winged Avro Vulcan that entered service in 1957 and crescent winged Handley Page Victor, which was the last of the three types to enter service in 1958.

The re-focussing of the UK's military position after T'he Suez Crisis' was evident in the 4 April 1957 Defence White Paper when the Minister for Defence, Duncan Sandys, proposed a radical new policy, of what was called 'collective defence' with a wider reliance on guided missiles. The 20 fighter squadrons of the Royal Auxiliary Air Force were immediately disbanded and their Gloster Meteors retired. Many promising aircraft projects were cancelled and the British aircraft industry encouraged to retrench for the few projects that would be available in the future. The only new type in development that was spared was the English Electric P1, as it was too far advanced to cancel. The P1 would be developed into the Lightning and become the only all-British Mach 2 aircraft.

A new era for the RAF was dawning and the Defence White Paper looked set to revise the whole future of air policy in Britain. The V-Force was switched to low-level missions to maintain its capacity to penetrate the new Soviet surface-to-air missile defences, while National Service was ended, and the future of manned military air defence was even placed in some doubt.

Avro Yorks at Gatow, Berlin 1948

Michael Turner

Michael Turner's evocative image of the Berlin Airlift shows the intensity of movements at one of the three airfields open to the Western Powers. A mixture of civilian evacuees and freight is being marshalled towards a departing Avro York whilst arriving Yorks pass in the background. During the Airlift of 1948–49, RAF Yorks from seven different squadrons flew over 58,000 sorties to provide the city with over one million tons of vital supplies – nearly half the British contribution. Each aircraft was unloaded by German workers in less than 30 minutes. It is not generally known that 83,405 tons of cargo and 68,000 people were also flown out of Berlin.

Royal Air Force Gatow was the RAF's main airfield in Berlin until 1994 when it was handed over to the Luftwaffe following German reunification. It closed as an airfield two years later and is now a housing estate. Parts of the old infrastructure are still in use, particularly by the Luftwaffe Museum.

The Avro York was designed by Roy Chadwick and developed from the Lancaster. The aircraft shared a number of components including wings, tail assembly, undercarriage and Rolls-Royce Merlin engines. It had a completely new fuselage that provided double the internal capacity of the Lancaster.

AK

Javelin Interception

Mark Bromley

Three Javelin FAW9s peel away from a Soviet Myasishchev M-4 Molot (NATO code name, 'Bison') at high altitude over the northern border between NATO and the Warsaw Pact. These aircraft are from No 33 Squadron based at RAF Middleton St George. No 33 Squadron was equipped with the Javelin from July 1958 until its disbandment in November 1962. Upon its disbandment some of its aircraft and crews went to Geilenkirchen, Germany, to join No 5 Squadron. No 5 Squadron amended its markings to incorporate those of No 33 and this combination was flown until the Javelin was replaced by the Lightning on No 5 Squadron in October 1965.

Designed by Richard Walker, the Gloster Javelin was a twin-engine subsonic night and all-weather interceptor featuring a delta wing and a large tailplane design. It was the result of a priority requirement for a high-performance fighter capable of intercepting strategic nuclear bombers. It made its first flight in November 1951 and was the last aircraft design to bear the Gloster name.

After its introduction in to service with No 46 Squadron and it had completed its series of proving flights the Javelin soon showed it was able to intercept jet bombers, such as the Canberra, over a hundred miles out to sea. With its night fighting capability significantly improved, the RAF retired all remaining night fighter Meteor squadrons.

The last Javelins were withdrawn from service in 1968 being replaced by the supersonic Lightning, capable of more than double the Javelin's top speed. A total of 427 Javelins were built in nine different versions.

B
Q
BROMLEY

Canberra Over Suez, 1956

Neil Foggo

This is a Canberra B2 overflying and bombing the facilities adjacent to the Suez Canal during 'The Suez Crisis' of 1956. The special yellow and black striped markings on the wings and fuselage were carried by all the Allied aircraft in the conflict. They were to enable ground and air forces to identify each other effectively and were reminiscent of the black and white stripes used for the same purpose on D-Day in 1944. Canberra B2s operated from Cyprus and Malta during the crisis and attacked by night and day.

Developed by English Electric during the 1940s to replace the De Havilland Mosquito, the Canberra was a first-generation, jet-powered medium bomber. It was named after the capital of Australia, the aircraft's first export customer.

When the Canberra entered RAF service in May 1951 with No 101 Squadron, it could fly higher than any other aircraft in the world. It was the first jet aircraft to make a non-stop transatlantic flight and it established a number of other world records, including an altitude record of 70,310ft.

Built in 27 versions, the Canberra proved to be a highly adaptable platform serving in a variety of roles including tactical bombing, photographic and electronic reconnaissance, unpiloted target aircraft, radar trainer, target tug, radar calibration aircraft, and electronic countermeasures trainer.

In RAF service, Canberras equipped 35 squadrons and served with Bomber Command in a tactical nuclear and conventional strike role until 1972 when the last bomber versions were retired. The aircraft continued to operate in the reconnaissance role until June 2006 when the last aircraft was retired, 57 years after its first flight.

Due to its capabilities and versatility the Canberra became a popular aircraft on the export market and was sold to more than 15 countries. The type was also licence produced in Australia and the United States, the latter building it as the Martin B-57 Canberra. NASA still operates three extensively modified B-57s for a variety of high altitude roles.

NEIL FOGGO

Star of the Sky
Anthony Cowland

This painting looks suspiciously like a training interception by two students in their Vampire T11 jets on the latest jet transport acquisition by the RAF. The DH Comet C1 would have been, in its day, the equivalent of Concorde in terms of speed, by comparison to its predecessors. Being the first air force in the world to fly jet transports it was logical to use them for practice interceptions as well as their primary role of carrying passengers and freight.

The Comet was designed by Ronald Bishop, and was the world's first commercial jetliner. The prototype made its maiden flight on 27 July 1949 with chief test pilot John Cunningham at the controls. It was powered by four De Havilland Ghost turbojet engines which were built into the wings, avoiding the drag incurred by podded engines and allowing extensive soundproofing. The aircraft was aerodynamically clean, had a pressurised fuselage, large square windows and offered a quiet, comfortable cabin. Passengers used to propeller-driven airliners found the Comet smooth, quiet and quick.

The Comet entered service in 1952 and was initially a commercial success until a number of high profile accidents, involving aircraft breaking up in flight, resulted in the aircraft being withdrawn from service. Investigations revealed the cause of the accidents to be overstressing of the airframe and metal fatigue in pressurised structures. As with all such discoveries the outcome was greater knowledge leading to safety enhancements for all this new generation of aircraft. After extensive re-design, structural reinforcement and replacement of the square windows, the improved Comet 2 and prototype Comet 3 culminated in the Comet 4 series, which made its first appearance in 1958 and remained in service for over 30 years.

Between 1956 and 1975 the RAF operated Comets with Nos 51,192 and 216 Squadrons and adapted them for a variety of military roles including surveillance, VIP, medical and passenger transport. In 1960, after the government-backed consolidation of the British aerospace industry, De Havilland was acquired by Hawker Siddeley, who went on to develop the most extensively modified version of the aircraft, the Nimrod. This specialised maritime patrol aircraft enjoyed an enviable reputation for its anti-submarine warfare, surface surveillance and anti-shipping capabilities. The Nimrod remained in RAF service until June 2011, over 60 years after the Comet's first flight.

670

Sixteen Hunters

Harold Garland

In 1961 No 92 Sqn, the Blue Diamonds, became the official aerobatic team of the Royal Air Force. Under the leadership of Sqn Ldr Brian Mercer they flew 16 blue Hawker Hunter aircraft. This painting illustrates the team performing their characteristic 16 Hunter roll and loop, a unique series of manoeuvres which their leader had brought from his service with their predecessor team, The Black Arrows.

The Black Arrows, the most famous forerunner of the Royal Air Force Aerobatic Team, The Red Arrows, was formed in 1956 by Sqn Ldr Roger Topp, then Commanding Officer No 111 Squadron (Treble-One). In 1958 they flew a world record formation loop of 22 Hunters at the Society of British Aircraft Constructors' show at Farnborough. This was the greatest number of aircraft looped in formation, and the record remains unbroken to this day. These feats by these, and other, RAF aerobatic teams are remembered fondly to this day.

The Hunter was the first jet-powered aircraft produced by Hawker Aircraft that was procured by the RAF. Entering service in July 1954 it was the first high-speed jet aircraft equipped with radar and fully powered flight controls to enter widespread service. Single-seat fighter versions were fitted with four 30mm ADEN (Armament Development Establishment Enfield) cannon, and nose-mounted ranging radar. The Hunter served with the RAF for over 30 years.

We've Got Him!

Anthony Cowland

Another panel from the RAF Club's Air Sea Rescue triptych depicts a young Marine Craft Section (MCS) crewman gripping the rail with a line coiled around his shoulder, while the whole panoply of the late 1950s, early 1960s, ASR takes place in front of him. In the background, an Avro Shackleton MR3 keeps oversight and control of the events taking place in a rough sea below. A Westland Whirlwind HAR2, with its winchman giving hand signals to his crew, advances towards RTTL (Rescue & Target Towing Launch) 2758 in order to pick up a casualty from the stern decking.

The Westland Whirlwind was a British licence-built version of the U.S. Sikorsky S-55 helicopter. The Royal Air Force Search and Rescue Force used Whirlwinds, often recognised as such by their vivid yellow paintwork, around the coast of the United Kingdom and took part in many relief operations during periods of extremely poor weather, and in a Mountain Rescue role. The Whirlwind was also famous for forming the first rotary element of the Queen's Flight. More than 400 Whirlwinds were built, of which nearly 100 were exported to foreign customers.

Named after polar explorer Ernest Shackleton, the Avro Shackleton was a development, in the late 1940s, of the Lancaster and Lincoln bombers. This was a part of Britain's military response to the rapid expansion of the Soviet Navy. Entering service in 1951, the aircraft was used primarily in the anti-submarine and maritime patrol roles. It was also frequently used for search and rescue, initially taking the role of observation, but when close co-operation craft were on scene it was able to co-ordinate all elements of the rescue. The Shackleton saw service until 1970.

RAF RTTL 2758 was built by Vosper in 1957. It was a 68ft Air Sea Rescue Launch with double planked mahogany hull and aluminium deckhouse mounting a prominent mast with radio and radar aerials. It was powered by twin screws, each driven by a Rolls Royce Sea Griffon Engine. The last roles for the MCS craft were as guard ships and target tugs for the training of the maritime anti-shipping squadrons of the RAF, and its vessels were designated RTTL to reflect this. In 1986 the MCS was disbanded; the last of the RAF's vessels were retired and handed over to civilian contractors for the target towing role. In the rescue role they were replaced by helicopters, and by the RNLI where necessary.

2758
2758
RESCUE

'Meatboxes' Over Sylt

Anthony Cowland

These Meteor Night Fighters are overflying Westerland on the German island of Sylt, off the west coast border between Germany and Denmark. RAF Sylt was an Armament Practice Camp in the 1950/60s and was visited by different squadrons from within NATO. The purpose of their visits was to practise air-to-air and air-to-sea gunnery. This they did by attacking towed targets provided by resident air and marine craft units. Air and ground crews alike affectionately called all the Meteor family of aircraft, 'The Meatbox'.

This Meteor NF.11 was manufactured by Armstrong Whitworth and flown by No 256 Squadron, based at Ahlhorn and Geilenkirchen in Germany between 1952 and 1959. Sylt was its nearest base for armament practice and an ideal location to train its night-fighter crews in airborne interception.

The Gloster Meteor was the first British jet fighter. The NF.11 was fitted with an extended nose containing the AI Mk 10 Air Intercept radar. Four 20mm cannons were mounted in the wings, and a ventral fuel tank and wing mounted drop tanks could also be fitted.

SQUADRON
256 256
ROYAL AIR FORCE
ADDIMUS VIM VIRIBUS

21 Squadron Scramble
David Shepherd

This oil on canvas is famous as David Shepherd's first wildlife painting. The painting shows a Rhino charging a No 21 Squadron Twin Pioneer during its take-off in Kenya. No 21 Squadron was equipped with four of these aircraft and worked closely with 24 Infantry Brigade Group on internal security duties in Kenya. In October 1961 they flew 146 sorties dropping 254,000lb of food to villages stranded as a result of flooding. The painting also illustrates the masterly command of movement, sky, animal, landscape, and machine that David perfected over a long and distinguished career. The painting was commissioned by the Officers' Mess, RAF Eastleigh, Nairobi, for which the artist was paid £25.

The Scottish Aviation Twin Pioneer, affectionately known as the 'Twin Pin', was a Short Take Off & Landing (STOL) transport aircraft. Designed for both civil and military operators, it was developed as a twin-engined version of the single-engined Pioneer light transport. Powered by two Alvis Leonides 531 radial engines, the prototype first flew from Prestwick on 25 June 1955. Flight trials proved that the aircraft had a very short landing run and required an area of only 99ft by 902ft in which to operate.

The RAF ordered 39 aircraft, which were built between 1958 and 1959. In addition to their service in Kenya, they were also used in Malaya, Oman, Bahrain, and Aden, mainly in moving troops and supplies around wilderness areas.

David Shepherd

Let's Get Him Home, Bristol Sycamore, 1955
Mark Bromley

The painting illustrates the pioneering days of SAR helicopter operations by No 275 Squadron. The Sycamore was, by today's standards, underpowered and the early version like this HR14 could barely lift a survivor and the two crew. As can be seen in this picture the survivor has had to place a strop over his head and under his arms whilst the Sycamore hovers above with the Navigator kneeling by the open hatch behind the pilot on the right side of the aircraft. New techniques were learned in these early days and it was not uncommon for the pilot to start the engine inside the hangar on windy days and taxi outside to avoid being toppled over – a process strictly forbidden for any other aircraft. The crews of these early helicopters proved the versatility of the machine in extremely bad weather conditions and challenging foreign climates. The VIP version, operating from London's RAF Northolt, also pioneered the capital's modern 'heli-routes' and demonstrated that helicopters could be flown safely over big cities.

Developed and built by the Bristol Aeroplane Company, and named after the rotating motion of the seeds as they fall from the sycamore tree, the Sycamore was the first British helicopter to receive a certificate of airworthiness. Powered by a single Alvis Leonides piston engine, later versions were capable of seating four or five occupants. It was manufactured with all of the necessary fittings to enable it to be quickly adapted between configurations to perform roles which included search and rescue, air ambulance, passenger transport, freight transport, aerial crane and dual instruction.

RESCUE
B
XE 319
← DANGER
BROMLEY

Jack of All Trades, The Dakota

Eric Day

It was once said that , *"The only replacement for a C-47 is another C-47"*, such was the utility of the aircraft. This watercolour illustrates the aircraft on the ground and in the air, marked in Transport Command livery. It is being loaded with mail sacks or, possibly, parachute loads as it could deliver its cargo by both means.

Used extensively by the Allies during World War II the Douglas C-47 or 'Dakota', in RAF service, was a military transport developed from the Douglas DC-3 airliner. During World War II, the Dakota served with distinction and was vital to the success of many Allied campaigns in the European theatre and was used in a number of specialised roles including para dropping and glider towing. Dakotas were used extensively during the invasion of Sicily and during the Normandy landings where they dropped over 50,000 paratroops. Dakotas were also used to airlift supplies to American forces in bitter winter conditions during the Battle of the Bulge.

The aircraft were also deployed to Guadalcanal and in the jungles of New Guinea and Burma, where they were used to move troops to counter the mobility of the Japanese army. During the Pacific campaign, Dakotas were used for ferrying soldiers to and from the United States. Possibly its most influential role in military aviation was flying 'The Hump' (through the Himalayas) from India to China; the experience gained from this was later put to good use during the Berlin Airlift. About 2,000 Dakotas served with British and Commonwealth forces.

After World War II, thousands of surplus C-47s and Dakotas were converted for civil airline use. Well over 80 military and civil users have operated the aircraft, and there are still a number of airworthy examples.

Beverley & Camels
David Shepherd

Another superb study of forbidding scenery and local wildlife, this Beverley lands in its own sandstorm as its propellers are put into reverse pitch to enable it to land in a short distance and then back up without turning around, if necessary. The Beverley was totally at home in such conditions serving in Kuwait and Kenya and running a weekly service from the UK to Aden.

Built by Blackburn, the Beverley (named after the cathedral town of North Yorkshire) was a heavy transport aircraft, operated by Transport Command between 1957 and 1967. It made its maiden flight from Brough on 20 June 1950. The first operational aircraft was delivered to No 47 at RAF Abingdon on 12 March 1956, becoming the largest aircraft then in service.

The Beverley was designed to carry large bulk loads and land on rough or dirt airstrips. It had an interior cargo area split into two levels, offering around 6,000 cubic feet of space. The main cargo hold could accommodate 94 troops, with another 36 in the tail boom. In operation, it was regarded as 'ungainly but highly effective'. The take-off run at full load was 790 yards, the landing run at full load, 310 yards.

Paratroopers could also be carried, those in the upper passenger area jumped through a hatch in the base of the boom just in front of the tailplane; those located in the main body exited through side doors. In total, 49 aircraft were produced at Brough, the last being manufactured in 1958. The Beverley was retired in 1967 with the final example in RAF service being the last fixed-wing aircraft to land at RAF Hendon in 1968. That aircraft was abandoned when RAF Hendon closed and, because of its corroded condition, could not be maintained by the RAF Museum and was scrapped in 1990. A single example exists and resides at Fort Paull, close to the BAE Systems site at Brough, Yorkshire.

David Shephard

'The Whispering Giant' at Rest

Penelope Douglas

Sitting peacefully on the ramp at what could be any large RAF Station this painting depicts Britannia C1 XM497 of No 99 Squadron based at RAF Brize Norton in the early 1970s. Transport Command's policy at the time of the introduction of the Britannia was to give individual names of stars, such as 'Arcturus', 'Sirius' and 'Vega' to each aircraft. This aircraft was named 'Schedar' after a second magnitude star in the constellation of Cassiopeia. The Britannia was a landmark in turboprop-powered airliner design when it first flew from Filton Aerodrome on 16 August 1952, with Bristol Chief Test Pilot A J 'Bill' Pegg at the controls.

After an eventful first flight which included wild pitching, a smoke filled cockpit and sticking main undercarriage, the prototype was cleared to fly and performed at the 1952 Farnborough Airshow where spectators commented on the quietness of the aircraft. It became known as 'The Whispering Giant' for its quiet exterior noise and smooth flying, and even though the interior was less tranquil, it was popular with passengers.

Three Model 252 and 20 Model 253 aircraft were purchased by RAF Transport Command in 1959 and assigned the designation Britannia C1 and C2. The Britannia was retired from the RAF in 1976. This painting was presented to the RAF Club by Sqn Ldr J M Costley.

660
AIR FORCE
PENELOPE
DOUGLAS

Valiant
John Young

John Young's skyscapes are a trademark of his skill as an artist and this painting illustrates an early Valiant, in its anti-flash white livery, providing the UK's nuclear deterrent high over the skies of NATO territory. The white livery was a form of protection against the flash from the nuclear weapon it carried. Curtains were also fitted to the cockpit windows to be drawn by the crew for their own protection if ever they had been required to deliver the terrible weapon they carried.

The Vickers-Armstrong Valiant formed part of the Royal Air Force's V-Bomber nuclear deterrent during the 1950s and 1960s. The Valiant was the first of the V-Bombers to become operational. Its first flight was on 18 May 1951, piloted by Joseph 'Mutt' Summers, who had flown the first Spitfire. In February 1955, the Valiant was delivered to No138 squadron and it eventually equipped nine squadrons.

The Valiant could carry a single 10,000lb nuclear weapon or up to 21 x 1,000lb conventional bombs in its bomb bay. It has the distinction of being the only V-Bomber to have dropped live nuclear weapons. On 11 October 1956, Valiant B1 WZ366 of No 49 Squadron was the first aircraft to drop a British operational atomic bomb over Maralinga, South Australia. On 15 May 1957, Valiant B1 XD818 became the first ever aircraft to drop a hydrogen bomb (the first British version of this weapon) over Christmas Island. This aircraft is the only preserved example, joining the other V-Bombers in the National Cold War Exhibition at the RAF Museum, Cosford.

The Valiant was adapted to perform other roles including conventional bombing, aerial reconnaissance, aerial refuelling, and electronic countermeasures. Several aircraft were used for testing and development work, including trials of the Blue Steel nuclear-armed standoff missile.

Valiants were used in 1956 for conventional bombing missions over Egypt during Operation *Musketeer* ('The Suez Crisis'). Valiant production ended in August 1957, with a total of 108 being produced. The Valiant was retired in 1965, its duties being continued by the other V-Bombers.

XD823

Vulcan Scramble
Frank Wootton

Famous for the thunderous and ground shaking howl of its four Rolls Royce Olympus engines, the Vulcan is seen here taking off, in a stream of four aircraft. This was the standard Quick Reaction Alert (QRA) undertaken by crews throughout the Cold War, and is still in place today. The objective for the Vulcan crews was to be airborne within two to four minutes of the alert sounding.

Named Vulcan after the Roman god of fire and destruction, it was the second of the V-Bomber force to enter RAF service behind the Vickers-Armstrong Valiant and before the Handley Page Victor; it was considered the most technically advanced. All the V-Bombers were the result of the British nuclear deterrent program that required a medium range bomber capable of carrying one 10,000lb bomb to a target 1,500 nautical miles from base.

Operated by the RAF between 1956 and 1984, 134 production Vulcans were assembled at Woodford Aerodrome. These were 45 B.1s and 89 B.2s, the latter featuring more powerful engines, a larger wing, and improved avionics. Vulcans were initially finished in anti-flash white, but with the adoption of low-level attack profiles in the mid-1960s, they were re-painted a glossy sea grey medium and dark green disruptive pattern camouflage on the upper surfaces, as featured in this painting. A number of countries expressed interest in purchasing Vulcans, including Australia and Argentina, but there were no foreign sales.

CHAPTER VIII

A LONG COLD WAR ~ 1958 TO 1981

"Berlin is the testicle of the West. When I want the West to scream, I squeeze Berlin."

NIKITA KHRUSHCHEV, AUGUST 1963

IN the Defence White Paper of 1957 Duncan Sandys' vision was for Britain's armed forces to be "... *better equipped, better trained and better designed for the tasks that lie ahead.*" Sandys was Winston Churchill's son-in-law and had been an artillery officer until being seriously wounded and discharged early in World War II. His task (as Minister of Defence under PM Harold Macmillan) was to reduce radically the cost of the armed forces. His solution, for the RAF, was to replace fighter aircraft with rockets and missiles.

This new policy started with the acquisition of the US Douglas Thor intermediate-range ballistic missile, operated by Bomber Command. This system had limited capability so close to the Soviet Bloc, for the missiles were based at above-ground launch sites. Furthermore, they were stored horizontally on transporter-erector trailers and covered by a retractable shelter. To fire the weapon, the crew used an electric motor to roll back the shelter, essentially a long shed mounted on steel rails, then a powerful hydraulic launcher-erector to lift the missile to an upright position for launch. Once it was standing on the launch mount, the missile was fuelled and could be fired. The entire launch sequence, from starting to roll back the shelter through to ignition of the rocket engine and lift-off, took approximately 15 minutes. This period was, of course, famous for the 'four minute warning' – supposedly indicating the amount of time between the launch of a Soviet strike and the arrival of missiles on UK soil. Even so, 20 squadrons were equipped with the Thor system, each with three missiles, at over 60 bases throughout East Anglia and Yorkshire.

For air defence the Bristol-Ferranti (later British Aircraft Corporation) Bloodhound Surface to Air Missile (SAM) was deployed within Fighter Command. Unlike the Thor, which was phased out in 1963, the Bloodhound was updated and kept in service until the end of the Cold War; the last ones were stood down in 1991.

Despite the impact of the 1957 review, the RAF recognised that manned aircraft would remain essential for most tasks, so developments went ahead for two important roles: the replacement of the Canberra and the application of Vertical/Short Take Off & Landing (V/STOL) to both fighter and transport aircraft. The first of these became the British Aircraft Corporation TSR-2, which flew in 1964, only to be cancelled by the Government in 1965 and an order placed for the US General Dynamics F-111. This too was ultimately cancelled and replaced by an order for much modified McDonnell Douglas F-4 Phantoms, for both the RAF and the FAA. After much development by Hawker and Bristol Siddeley, later Rolls Royce, the V/STOL concept evolved into the Harrier, which eventually entered service in 1969.

More immediately, in 1959, a new strategic freighter, the Short Belfast, was ordered and Transport Command received its first Bristol Britannia, a four-engined turboprop airliner/freighter. In October 1959 the first major overseas tri-service command since World War II was established. This was British Forces Arabian Peninsula, with its headquarters at the port of Aden in the Indian Ocean, at the eastern entrance to the Red Sea.

Britain was declared one of NATO's four air defence regions in 1960 and Fighter Command's air defence squadrons were assigned to Supreme Allied Command Europe (SACEUR) in 1961. Within this new organisational structure, No 74 'Tiger' Squadron introduced the English Electric Lightning F1 into service in 1960. With its motto 'Fear No Man', the squadron became the official Fighter Command aerobatic team for 1961, flying at shows throughout the UK and Europe. With this new Mach 2 air defence fighter, coupled with updated command and control systems, Britain was well placed to detect and intercept intruders. Crews and aircraft adopted a 24 hour Quick Reaction Alert, (QRA) providing the UK's first line of air defence against the long range Soviet bombers that continually probed the UK's airspace.

The 1957 White Paper, and the large investment in the V-Force, also led to a reduction of six squadrons from RAF Germany in 1961, with the remaining 12 squadrons spread across the bases at Gütersloh, Laarbruch, Wildenrath and Geilenkirchen. To increase mobility for the troops of the British Army of the Rhine (BAOR), in early 1963 RAF Germany gained its first support helicopters, the Westland Whirlwind, which were replaced by the Westland Wessex after a couple of years. Arriving in 1966 were two squadrons of Lightnings to replace the remaining Javelins.

The V-Force continued to provide Britain's independent strategic nuclear deterrent, although while originally intended as a high level bombing force, the increasing capabilities of Soviet air defence systems forced a move to low level tactics. In addition, the Avro Blue Steel stand-off missile, which had a range of 100 miles to give the bomber some protection from air defences, was introduced on the Vulcan and Victor. Tensions were high throughout the Cold War, but during the Cuban Missile Crisis of October 1962, with the US/UK Ballistic Missile Early Warning System at Fylingdales, Yorkshire, in the process of being built, the RAF raised its readiness level to the highest it would reach during this whole geopolitically tense period. In the same way that Fighter Command had prepared its air defence, Bomber Command adopted constant readiness QRA with the V-Force. The bombers were nuclear armed and capable of being airborne in less than four minutes of the alarm being raised. The policy of Mutually Assured Destruction (MAD) was firmly in place.

The new technologies of nuclear weapons did not completely deny the possibility that older weapons systems might also be used. Poison gas had been used widely in World War I and, whilst its use in World War II was confined to The Holocaust, it was not used in military operations by either side. However, all sides had stockpiles of modern versions of the deadly gases and, during the Cold War, the spectre of their use became real again. The training, practice and general use of Nuclear, Biological and Chemical (NBC) equipment became regular facets of all military life. In the RAF regular practice and exercise for those on the ground and in the air became an almost everyday part of duty.

At the same time Britain still maintained global commitments, such as to the South East Asia Treaty Organisation (SEATO), where Victors and Vulcans, supported by Valiant and Victor tankers, deployed to overseas locations such as Australia, Malaysia and Singapore. Despite the drawdown from the Empire, Britain retained a number of overseas commitments and bases, which led to numerous operations throughout the 1960s.

Following the defeat of the EOKA (an acronym in Greek for 'National Organisation of Cypriot Struggle') guerrillas, Cyprus had become an independent republic within the Commonwealth. Britain retained the Sovereign Base Areas in Cyprus, including the airfield of RAF Akrotiri. The importance of these bases to regional security in the Middle East was emphasised on 1 July 1961 when Iraq threatened to invade Kuwait, leading the RAF to airlift an entire parachute battalion from Cyprus to Bahrain and a similar number of men of 45 Commando Royal Marines from Aden to Kuwait. In addition, fighter and ground attack Hawker Hunters, and Blackburn Beverley transport aircraft were deployed from Aden. The speed of the build-up and the size of forces deployed deterred Iraq and demonstrated again the mobility that air power provided.

The RAF also continued to uphold its traditions of aid and humanitarian flights. In October 1961, Operation *Tana Flood* was quickly mounted, when RAF transport aircraft dropped food and supplies to people in Kenya who were cut-off by floods. In November further help was given to citizens of British Honduras (now known as Belize) who had suffered from the devastation brought by 'Hattie', a category 5 hurricane. At home the start of 'The Troubles' in Norther Ireland brought extra threats to the military, both in that Province and the mainland. Regular bomb threats and the need to provide extra vigilance around bases led to extra guarding duties for all ranks and a higher awareness of security.

Nevertheless, by early 1962, the 1957 defence policy was being reversed. The new emphasis was on the essential need for manned aircraft in the immediate future, and the need for long-range striking power against submarines and surface vessels. In December 1962, the situation in South East Asia brought the RAF into action in its tactical ground support role, when Blackburn Beverleys and Scottish Aviation Twin Pioneers airlifted troops at short notice to quell a revolt in Brunei, operations which continued until the spring of 1963.

Shortly thereafter Indonesia began its Confrontation ('Konfrontasi' in Malay) with Singapore and the newly independent Malaysia. British ground and air forces were again called upon, with the RAF undertaking a variety of roles, including air defence and reconnaissance using its Hunters; transport of troops and supplies by helicopters (Bristol Belvedere, Westland Whirlwind and Westland Wessex) and aircraft (Blackburn Beverley and Scottish Aviation Twin Pioneer), whilst being supported by the fledgling Royal Malaysian Air Force. Additional RAF authority was provided by occasional detachments of Canberras and V-Bombers to Singapore. The Confrontation ended by 1966 and had again demonstrated the effectiveness of air power and inter-service and Allied co-operation in deterring insurgency.

In 1964, the mountainous Radfan area west of the port of Aden (now a part of Yemen), which had been a major British base in the Middle East since 1839, became the next area to suffer conflict. The Federation of Southern Arabia, which had been created during the early 1960s by Britain's endeavours to bring political stability to the Middle East, was now threatened. Once again, the Hawker Hunter was called upon to provide close air support to the Army and RAF Regiment troops on the ground; with the twin rotor Bristol Belvedere helicopters providing the tactical mobility to the ground forces that was necessary in such terrain. Effective co-operation between air and ground forces suppressed the rebellious tribes and brought a short term peace to the area.

The Belvedere proved particularly useful in hot and high areas and its lifting capability was admired not only by the troops it supported, but also the general public when, in April 1962, Wg Cdr John Dowling (known as 'Mr Helicopter') and his crew mounted the unconventional 80ft spire (or flèche) on to the new Coventry Cathedral.

On 1 April 1964 the three armed services were placed under a unified Ministry of Defence (MoD) and soon the effects of this change became apparent in the RAF. Continuing contraction of the RAF meant the transfer of servicing and maintenance to new centralised servicing organisations. The result was to move ground crews from the squadrons and place them in conglomerate station establishments. It meant a change in the long tradition of intimate co-operation, loyalty and strong relationships between the air and ground crews. However, this was soon overcome by the personnel involved and better use of resources was thought to be the result.

In 1967 Britain finally withdrew from its bases in Aden, requiring Air Support Command to undertake the largest operation since the Berlin Airlift in 1948. Between May and November, the new range of strategic and tactical transport aircraft such as the De Havilland Comet C4, Vickers VC10, Bristol Britannia C1&2, Short Belfast C1 and Lockheed Hercules C1 evacuated troops and families from Aden, with many flights going to the RAF base at Muharraq in Bahrain. The final lift in November moved 6,000 troops and 400 tons of equipment and ended Britain's connection with the ancient natural harbour of Aden. Britain completed its withdrawal from the Middle East by the end of 1971 and from Malta in 1979, only retaining bases in Cyprus and Gibraltar.

In 1968 the RAF celebrated its 50th anniversary with a second Royal Review by HM The Queen at RAF Abingdon.

With the number of overseas garrisons and bases reducing, it was decided that troops should be held in reserve in Britain and flown overseas when required, to provide reinforcements. Therefore, the principal role of the strategic and tactical air transport fleet was to provide a flexible and timely airlift capability. To demonstrate the ability to reinforce the Far East, one of the largest peacetime exercises was undertaken in April 1970. RAF Air Support Command's VC10s, Britannias, Hercules and Belfasts flew 4,500 flying hours and delivered 2,800 troops, 1 million lbs of freight, 350 vehicles and 10 Wessex helicopters to Singapore. Further protection for the transport force was provided by Phantoms, supported by Victor tankers, undertaking a non-stop 8,000 mile flight in 14 hours.

In the 1970s, the Far East, Middle East and Near East Air Forces were all disbanded as units were progressively withdrawn, leaving RAF Germany as the only overseas Command, with a small residual Far East presence in Hong Kong. These vast cuts in RAF commitments had a commensurate impact on the RAF's strength in manpower, which reduced from 148,000 in 1962, to 120,000 in 1968 and 90,000 by 1976. Similar impacts were felt on its aircraft fleets and, as an example, the transport fleet was reduced by half with the withdrawal of the Comets in 1975, with the Britannias and Andovers following in 1976 and the Belfasts in 1977.

The provision of Britain's independent strategic nuclear deterrent passed from the V-Force to Royal Navy Polaris submarines in 1969. However, the RAF retained an important role through the provision of Maritime Patrol and Anti-Submarine Warfare protection for the Polaris fleet. Initially this was carried out by the Shackleton and from 1971 the Hawker Siddeley Nimrod (named after the biblical figure known as " *... a mighty hunter before the Lord ...*").

The Nimrod was developed from the Comet airliner and not only took over the role, but also provided a significant leap in both technology and capability to counter the burgeoning sophistication of Soviet submarines and surface vessels. The threat from increasingly capable Soviet surface ships also led to the introduction, in 1969, of the Blackburn Buccaneer in the maritime attack role. In addition, a small number of Victors and Vulcans were also used in the long range maritime reconnaissance role.

With the knowledge that the most likely land threat would come via East Germany, a significant re-equipment programme took place in RAF Germany. From the late 1960s, the arrival of the first squadrons of Hawker Siddeley Harriers gave the RAF the unique ability to readily deploy fast jets to temporary airfields, or even forest-strips, much closer to the border.

In the early 1970s the first of the McDonnell Douglas F-4 Phantoms and Buccaneers arrived to replace Canberras in conventional and nuclear strike roles. The Anglo/French SEPECAT Jaguar strike/attack aircraft then replaced some of the Phantoms. In turn, the Phantoms replaced the Lightnings in the air defence role. Recognising that the RAF Germany airfields would be important targets, Bloodhound SAMs were deployed to protect them and, by the mid-1970s, each of the airfields also had an RAF Regiment squadron armed with short range BAC Rapier air defence missiles.

Equipment upgrades were not just confined to the fast jet fleet, and in 1980 the Aérospatiale Puma helicopter arrived to replace the "Mighty Wessex" (as it is still known by its crews).

Back in Britain, the UK Air Defence Region (UKADR) was established in 1975, recognising the country's strategic position in NATO's defensive posture should a conventional war arise with Warsaw Pact forces. Key threats were posed by Soviet long range reconnaissance missions and the capability of their bombers to launch air-to-ground missiles at targets in Britain from many hundreds of miles away. The main elements of the UKADR were early warning radars, SAMs and a long and short range fighter component. The early warning radars comprised long range systems that stretched from the Shetland Islands to Cornwall and the shorter range systems along the eastern coast. As had been done in Germany, the defence of airfields was provided by the BAC Rapier system, which was also deployed to protect USAF bases in Britain. From the 1970s onwards, the fighter component was provided by the Lightning and Phantom, supported by Victor tankers. From the late 1970s, the fighters could be supplemented by British Aerospace (BAe) Hawk, armed with Sidewinder missiles.

Relying only on Britain's ground based early warning radars, the RAF had no Airborne Early Warning (AEW) aircraft until 1970. However, with the drawdown of the Royal Navy's carrier fleet in the 1960s, the RAF was tasked to develop a long range AEW capability, to protect the fleet and supplement the ground based radars. Taking radars from retiring FAA Fairey Gannets, a small number of Avro Shackletons were refurbished and declared operational in 1972. Intended as a stop gap measure until it could be replaced by the new Nimrod

AEW aircraft, ordered in 1977, the unfortunate failure of the latter meant that the Shackleton soldiered on for many years. During the Cold War they were often scrambled up to five times a week to detect Soviet long range reconnaissance and bomber aircraft entering UK airspace, generally through the Iceland/Faroes gap. Controlling the intercepting fighters, Lightnings and Phantoms, as well as their associated tankers, the Shackletons were also tasked with surface surveillance and trained with the Buccaneers in their low-level anti-shipping role. In addition, the Shackleton was able to undertake the long range Air Sea Rescue duties, carrying the necessary equipment in its bomb bay.

In 1981 the Tri-national Tornado Training Establishment (TTTE) was formed. It was set up to train pilots and Weapon System Operators (WSOs) to fly and operate the new Panavia Tornado Multirole Interdictor Strike aircraft. The Tornado was a European collaboration between Britain, Germany and Italy.

At the start of the 1980s, as the Service reduced in size, Trenchard's 'Air Force Spirit' remained, and the quality and morale of both personnel and equipment rose despite the tampering of successive governments. A much smaller, but well equipped, RAF had adjusted to its exit from Empire and re-established itself as an important part of NATO's air defence and strike capabilities. However, world events were about to lead to a return to the expeditionary warfare it had just exited. Delivery of the new Tornado began in January 1982, barely three months before Argentinian forces invaded and occupied the Falkland Islands.

Venoms Over Aden
Anthony Cowland

Two DH Venoms swoop low over an Arab dhow off the coast of Aden. During the Oman rebellion of 1957 these aircraft, of Nos 8 and 249 Squadrons were based at RAF Khormaksar.

The Venom was produced as a successor to the widely-used Vampire and whilst similar in appearance was a completely new design. It was fitted with the Rolls Royce Ghost engine and showed a great advance in performance. It made its first flight on 2 September 1949 and, in 1956 took part in the Suez operations, attacking Egyptian airfields. The last Venoms were retired from RAF service in July 1962.

Lightning At Binbrook 1987

Mark Bromley

Becoming famous for its exceptional rate of climb, acceleration and speed, the English Electric Lightning was the only all-British fighter aircraft capable of flying at Mach 2, which it first reached in November 1957. Designed as an interceptor to defend UK bomber bases, range was not a particular consideration, with the original requirement being only for a radius of operation of 150 miles from the V-Bomber airfields.

The Lightning F1 entered service with No 74 Squadron at RAF Coltishall in July 1960 and, as the Squadron was the official Fighter Command aerobatic team for 1961, it was flown at airshows throughout Britain and Europe during that year. The Lightning's performances at airshows made it one of the most popular RAF aircraft with the public of the time. Equipped with the F6 version by 1967, No 74 Squadron was based in Singapore at RAF Tengah between 1967 and 1971, when it handed its aircraft over to No 56 Squadron at RAF Akrotiri in Cyprus, and it was then disbanded.

Lightnings were also based in West Germany and, in 1972, one was tasked to shoot down an RAF Harrier which had continued to fly towards East Germany after the pilot had ejected. In 1984, in a testament to the Lightning's capabilities, a Lightning intercepted a Lockheed U-2 at an altitude of 66,000ft, a height at which the U-2 crews had previously considered themselves safe from interception. Similarly, in April 1985 British Airways was undertaking trials over the North Sea with the BAC Concorde and offered it as a target aircraft to NATO fighters. Although various nations and aircraft types tried, only the Lightning managed to overtake the Concorde, flying at Mach 2.2 at 57,000ft. Both of these flights were carried out by the same pilot, FL Lt Mike Hale, in the same Lightning, XR749 which he described as "*the best of the best*". On the other hand, RAF Engineering Officer 'Taffy' Holden had a less satisfying experience when in July 1966 he carried out a ground test on Lightning XM135 and inadvertently became airborne. Some Engineering Officers, in those days, were given flight training and 'Taffy' was a qualified pilot, but not in the Lightning. It says a lot for his ability, and the handling of the aircraft, that he managed to bring the aircraft in to a safe landing at RAF Lyneham.

This scene depicts the Lightning towards the end of its service, when the remaining aircraft were operated by Nos 5 and 11 Squadrons at RAF Binbrook until 1988. Under a characteristically grey sky and wet runway following rain, this aircraft displays the late camouflage scheme carried by the Lightning, with the black and yellow markings of No 11 Squadron on its fin.

Following its withdrawal from RAF service, British Aerospace operated four Lightning F.6s as radar targets between 1988 and 1992 during the development of the Tornado Air Defence Variants AI.24 Foxhunter radar.

BL

Work Horses In Aden

Mal Grossé

As part of the British Forces Middle East Command supporting the Aden protectorate, the RAF operated its tactical and transport units from RAF Khormaksar, in Aden, Yemen, with nine squadrons based there. Khormaksar also acted as a staging post for transit between the UK and Singapore. This scene illustrates a busy ramp at the base, occupied by an Armstrong Whitworth Argosy, Blackburn Beverley and Handley Page Hastings; these are being overflown by a Westland Whirlwind SAR/utility helicopter, and pair of Hawker Hunters.

In support of the transport requirements, units operating from the base included No 84 Squadron, which flew the Blackburn Beverley between 1958 and 1967. Moving from the UK to Khormaksar in June 1962, No 105 Squadron operated the Argosy ('the Whistling Wheelbarrow'), where maximum use was made of its medium lift capability.

For tactical duties, No 8 Squadron operated from the base using Hunter FGA9s from the early 1960s. They were joined by No 43 Squadron in 1963, also flying the same variant from Cyprus. Khormaskar closed in November 1967 with Britain's final withdrawal from Aden.

RAF
RESCUE
ROYAL AIR FORCE
MIDDLE EAST
— Mal Grossé —

The Ramp, RAF Muharraq, 1970

Mal Grossé

This scene depicts a number of RAF Transport Command aircraft, including the Short Belfast, Armstrong Whitworth Argosy, Bristol Britannia, and a Vickers VC10 C1. They all rest on the dispersal pan at RAF Muharraq, in Bahrain. The artist was based there and this is the view from the balcony of No 8 Squadron's crew room, with one of their Hunter F.6s in the foreground. Following Britain's withdrawal from Bahrain, the site became the International Airport.

The Armstrong Whitworth Argosy was used by the RAF and a number of commercial operators. Designated as the Argosy C Mk 1, 56 aircraft were produced for the RAF, serving with six squadrons, three in the UK and one each in Aden, Cyprus, and the Far East. With the continued drawdown of Britain's overseas commitments during the 1970s, the Argosy was withdrawn from service in 1975 as an economy measure.

Unlike other RAF Transport Command platforms, the Bristol Britannia was designed originally as a medium to long range airliner, and not born out of a military specification requirement. The Bristol Britannia was acquired by Transport Command in 1959, and continued in service as the Britannia C2 until final retirement in 1975.

The Short Belfast was designed as a heavy lift turboprop freighter, built by Short Brothers in Belfast, Northern Ireland. Only 10 aircraft were constructed, all of which entered service with the RAF in January 1966. Operating under the designation Belfast C1, it served until 1976.

The first RAF Vickers VC10 C1, was delivered in November 1965 and the aircraft entered service with No 10 squadron in December of the same year. In addition to the strategic transport role, the VC10 routinely served in aeromedical evacuation and VIP roles, and was later converted for AAR tanker support, in which role the type retired from the RAF in 2013.

The Hunter F.6, and subsequent variants, were used extensively by the RAF, and the aircraft was also a major export success. In RAF use, it served on many overseas deployments and operations including 'The Suez Crisis', Borneo, Malaysia and Aden. The Hunter F.6 was retired from its day fighter role in the RAF by 1963, being replaced by the Lightning. However, many Hunters went on to continue in service as the FGA.9, in the close air support role, as well as serving in the aircrew fast jet training role, which saw the last Hunters retire in the early 1990s.

ROYAL AIR FORCE
SUPPORT COMMAND
106
XV106
Mal Grossé

Golden Jubilee 1968, RAF Abingdon
Frank Wootton

The RAF celebrated its 50th anniversary in 1968 and, as shown in this scene in June of that year, the Queen conducted a review at RAF Abingdon, Oxfordshire. On the left hand side of this painting can be seen one of the RAF's first successful fighters, the Sopwith Camel, with the RAF's final biplane fighter, the Gloster Gladiator, behind it. On the right of the picture is the latest air defence fighter of the day, the English Electric Lightning, with the Bristol Bloodhound air defence missile system visible in the background.

The Gladiator entered service with the RAF in February 1937, replacing the Bristol Bulldog. No 72 Squadron, based at RAF Tangmere, became the first squadron to be equipped with the Gladiator. With the swift technological advances of the era, the RAF had begun to receive its first deliveries of the Hurricane and Spitfire by the late 1930s, with emphasis being placed on quickly re-equipping half of the Gladiator squadrons with the new monoplanes. Therefore, although largely obsolete by the start of World War II, the Gladiator saw action with the RAF in France, Norway, Greece, the Middle East, and in the brief Anglo-Iraqi war. A single Flight from No 247 Squadron, with only six pilots, was the only unit to operate the Gladiator in the Battle of Britain. Most famous was the defence of Malta by Gladiators. Following the concerted attacks on the islands, a small force of Sea Gladiators provided the sole form of air defence for a month, in June 1940. Legend has it that there were only three Gladiators named 'Faith', 'Hope' and 'Charity' but, in fact, there were more and they were supplemented by Hurricanes by the end of June. Nevertheless, the siege of Malta, its resilience, by all forms of defence, and the stoicism of the population were recognised by the unique award of the George Cross to the Islands. 'Faith' is displayed at the National War Museum, Fort St Elmo, Valletta.

The English Electric Lightning was the only all-British Mach 2 fighter aircraft and was used by the RAF as its primary fighter interceptor for more than two decades. The first aircraft to enter service with the RAF were three pre-production P.1Bs, which arrived at RAF Coltishall in December 1959. During its RAF career the Lightning served not only in the UK, but Germany, Singapore, and Cyprus. The Lightning had a slow phase-out from front-line service, between 1974 and 1988.

The Bristol bloodhound was the UK's main air defence weapon from the 1950s through to 1991. It was designed to protect the V-Bomber bases from Russian aircraft that made it past the Lightnings defending Britain's airspace. The Bloodhound was an advanced missile for its era, incorporating a continuous wave semi-active radar homing system, which gave good resistance to Electronic Counter Measures (ECM). However, being a relatively large missile, it was restricted to static sites. The Camel, Gladiator and ceremonial Land Rover featured at the 1968 Royal Review are all now in the RAF Museum collection.

B
F6314

Harrier Field Ops

Stuart Brown

On exercise, these No1 Squadron Harriers are dispersed to unprepared fields and hidden in camouflage hides. Pierced Steel Planking (PSP) has been laid on the ground to provide a firm surface for their movement to a take-off position. Whilst ground crews carry out their inspection, the pilot in the foreground fills in the Form 700 (Technical Log). The aircraft in the background is attached to a tug for pulling/pushing in and out of the hide. These dispersed units would have been self-sufficient for short periods of time. The Harrier's ability to operate from unprepared ground with minimal ground facilities made it ideal for front-line deterrent duties in Germany.

The Hawker Siddeley Harrier was developed from the P.1127 technology demonstrator that proved the concept of a Vertical/Short Take Off and Landing (V/STOL) aircraft and the subsequent Kestrel tripartite evaluation programme between the UK, USA and Germany. The Harrier was the first close air support and surveillance combat aircraft with Vertical/Short Take Off and Landing (V/STOL) capabilities to enter service with the RAF.

The initial production variant, Harrier GR.1, made its first flight in December 1967 and officially entered service with the RAF in April 1969 with the Harrier Conversion Unit at RAF Wittering.

During the Cold War, the RAF deployed most of its Harrier fleet to West Germany to defend against a potential invasion of Western Europe by the Warsaw Pact in a close air support role.

The RAF had their GR1 aircraft upgraded to the GR3 standard, which are shown in this painting. The GR3 featured improved sensors, a nose-mounted laser tracker, the integration of electronic countermeasure (ECM) systems and a further upgrade to the Rolls Royce Pegasus engine.

The Harrier GR3, modified for naval operations, operated from the aircraft carrier *HMS Hermes* and, subsequently, from Port San Carlos during the 1982 Falklands War, providing close air support to the ground forces alongside the Royal Navy Sea Harriers in the air defence role.

All In a Day's Work, Sek Kong 1982

Frank Wootton

This image shows No 28 Squadron Wessex HC2s at RAF Sek Kong in the New Territories of Hong Kong. The Squadron's role was 'jack of all trades' around the British territory, ministering to the needs of the colony itself, though primarily tasked with assisting the Army and SAR. In this instance Ghurkha soldiers with their working dogs are awaiting dispatch on a training mission in 1982. No 28 Squadron was the last RAF squadron to leave Hong Kong when it was handed back to the Chinese in 1997. These aircraft were sold to Uruguay.

The Westland Wessex was a UK licensed built version of the Sikorsky H-34 / S-58. In the United Kingdom, this type was initially built for the Royal Navy, and then for the RAF, which took delivery of its first aircraft in 1962. The Wessex served with nine squadrons as well as the Queen's Flight. They replaced the Westland Whirlwind, providing a better payload capacity and distribution, as well as being quieter in operation, having been re-engined with the Napier Gazelle turboshaft engine.

In RAF service, the Wessex undertook land and sea rescue duties in the UK and overseas, and was well suited to flying in mountainous terrain. It was also used as a utility transport helicopter for battlefield operations, delivering supplies, equipment, and troops. The Wessex was used in surveillance duties in Northern Ireland supporting security operations, which led to further modification to include self defence systems.

The Wessex HC 4 version, with upgraded interiors and avionics was used by the Queen's Flight to transport the Royal Family and other VIPs. It served in this role until 1988.

The standard Wessex fleet began to be replaced by the Westland Sea King, from the late 1970s. During its service in the RAF it operated in a wide variety of operational environments, including Hong Kong, Cyprus, Borneo, Malaysia, the Falklands and Northern Ireland.

ROYAL AIR FORCE
H

RAF Germany

Frank Wootton

This Jaguar sits outside its hardened aircraft shelter (HAS) with the usual attentive ground crews preparing it for flight. Its tug has detached; it is connected to its ground supply unit and a fire extinguisher is available if anything unforeseen should happen. It is a typical scene at any Jaguar base in the UK or Germany. As a Tornado is flying low over the scene it is highly likely that this is RAF Bruggen as both types were operational at this German station at the same time.

The RAF accepted delivery of the first of 165 single-seat Jaguar GR-1s with No 54 Squadron in 1974, supplemented by 35 two-seat Jaguar T2s over the following years. After being declared operational the Jaguar squadrons were all capable of delivering the WE177 free fall nuclear weapon.

From December 1983, 75 Jaguar GR.1s and 14 T2s were updated to the GR.1A and T2A standards with new navigation and attack systems. They were also re-engined with Adour 104 engines and were fitted with the ability to carry Sidewinder short range air-to-air missiles and electronic countermeasures pods under the wings.

The RAF's Jaguar fleet began to reduce in 1984 when Nos 17, 20 and 31 Squadrons exchanged their Jaguars for the Tornado GR1, although their operational role remained unchanged. The two other RAF Germany Squadrons, Nos 2 and 14, were also re-equipped with the Tornado in 1985 and 1989, which left the operational Jaguar force concentrated in Nos 6, 41 and 54 Squadrons at RAF Coltishall, Norfolk.

Nimrod, The Mighty Hunter

Mark Bromley

The Hawker Siddeley Nimrod was derived from the De Havilland Comet, the world's first operational jet airliner, and was designed in response to an RAF requirement to replace its fleet of Avro Shackletons. The Nimrod MR1 and the later upgrade to MR2 standard were primarily intended to undertake Anti-Submarine Warfare (ASW) operations in support of the UK's submarine independent nuclear deterrent, as shown in this painting with an MR2 flying over *HMS Repulse*. Nimrod's secondary roles included long range maritime surveillance, anti-ship warfare and search and rescue.

The Nimrod entered service in the early 1970s, and was operated by a number of maritime reconnaissance units over the years, including Nos 38, 42, 120, 201, and 206 Squadrons, based at RAF Kinloss in Moray, and RAF St. Mawgan in Cornwall. A modified Electronic Intelligence (ELINT) version known as the R1, served with No 51 Squadron, operating from RAF Wyton and later RAF Waddington.

The Nimrod MR2 was withdrawn in 2010 and it is now planned to replace it with the Boeing P-8A Poseidon.

BROMLEY

CHAPTER IX

UNEXPECTED CONFLICTS IN FAR OFF LANDS ~ 1982 TO 1991

"We have to recover those islands ... for the people on them are British... . When you stop a dictator there are always risks, but there are great risks in not stopping a dictator. My generation learned that a long time ago."

MARGARET THATCHER, 5 APRIL 1982

THE Falkland Islands are some 8,000 miles away from Britain at 52° south of the Equator, about 300 miles east of Argentina. They are a self governing British Overseas Territory. The islands take their name in honour of the 5th Viscount Falkland who, as Treasurer of the Navy, funded an English expedition there in 1690. The Argentines also claim them as the Islas Malvinas, a Spanish name derived from a French title given to them in 1764. The islands served an important role in British maritime, commercial and foreign affairs for three centuries. However, as their importance waned and budget cuts were considered in Westminster, sovereignty talks with Argentina were started in the late 1970s. These broke down in 1981 and tensions with the Argentine ruling military junta grew. The Generals in the junta were anxious to deflect public opinion away from their miserable human rights record and the economic failure of their dictatorship. In April 1982, Argentina invaded the Falkland Islands and South Georgia, which is a further 800 miles to the south-east. Britain responded to the invasion and occupation by sending a task force. It was ordered to repossess the islands by peaceful means if possible, but in the end force would have to be used.

The operation to liberate the islands was given the operational name *Corporate* and depended significantly on the little used South Atlantic airfield and harbour at Ascension Island which was roughly half way between the UK and the Falklands.

Ascension Island is named after the day of its recorded discovery, Ascension Day 1501. It is situated 8° south, 1,000 miles from Africa and 1,400 miles from Brazil. Ascension Island was garrisoned by the Admiralty from 1815 to 1922, especially during Napoleon Bonaparte's exile on St Helena, 800 miles to its south-east. It played a role as an important safe haven and coaling station to mariners and for commercial airliners during the days of international air travel by flying boats. During World War II it was an important naval and air station, especially providing anti-submarine warfare bases in the Battle of the Atlantic.

In 1982 the main user, under a lease arrangement with the UK, was NASA and Wideawake airbase (named after the local colony of sooty terns, whose constant day-and-night chatter keep humans awake) which was specially extended and carefully maintained as an emergency diversion for the Space Shuttle. Thus the island was propitiously well situated both geographically and logistically to act as a 'bridge' to the South Atlantic. Thus the first task was to establish an operational hub on the island.

The initial elements of the Task Force, which eventually consisted of 127 ships, set sail within three days of the invasion and the RAF base at Ascension Island was fully operational within two weeks. Frantic modifications were made to all the aircraft participating, with industry, civilian contractors, and military technicians working night and day to produce innovative solutions to the problems of, amongst many things, range, reconnaissance and air defence. In an example of close co-operation between the RAF and British industry, during a 14 day period, the RAF Harriers were modified to carry air-to-air missiles and transported by sea to the aircraft carriers, while the RAF pilots were also trained to fly from the carriers. Later in the campaign, supported by tankers, other Harriers flew directly from Britain to Ascension and then made the onward nine hour flight south to the Task Force.

Whilst it was clear that the Royal Navy would bear the brunt of the air war over the Falkland Islands the then CAS was quick to recognise what the RAF could contribute at such a huge distance. MRAF Sir Michael Beetham was a veteran of Bomber Command, who had flown a tour on Lancasters during the Battle of Berlin, at the height of the Combined Bombing offensive. In post-war years he had commanded the squadron which pioneered jet air-to-air refuelling (AAR) and held a number of long distance records. He was probably the most experienced airman in the RAF when it came to considering strategic bombing attacks. Despite some scepticism in Whitehall Beetham championed the idea of mounting long range attacks on the Falklands from Ascension Island using AAR. He did this knowing that the AAR capability of the RAF had diminished in recent years, and that his crews would have to re-learn techniques mastered by their predecessors from the few that still served. However, not only would crews need to be trained, but the Vulcan Force had not practised AAR for twenty years and the aircraft were missing key equipment. In fact their AAR hardware had either been removed or made redundant. An immediate 'scrounging' exercise was mounted and items such as refuelling probes, pipework, valves etc. were sought from a variety of obscure places such as spares stores, maintenance facilities and museums. Avionics and navigation systems needed radical change to operate at such long distances and over featureless water. All this had to be accomplished at great speed.

As a result, the RAF's participation in the Falklands Conflict is perhaps best remembered for the five *Black Buck* raids, in which single Vulcans, each supported by up to 13 'leap-frogging' Victor tankers undertook what was, at that time, the longest range bombing missions in history. Beetham also convinced Prime Minister Thatcher, the War Cabinet, and his fellow Service Chiefs that raids on Port Stanley would not only do tactical damage to the Argentine's main airfield and HQ, but also demonstrate a real and present danger to mainland Argentina. His message was simple: if the RAF could mount a bombing raid on a target 8,000 miles away and safely return to base, a 7,000 mile journey to Buenos Aires was also possible. Knowing the parlous state of the controlling military junta and finding a way to change public opinion against them whilst, at the same time, damaging the morale of the invaders on the ground, was a key strategic goal of the *Black Buck* missions.

The raids were specifically mounted against the runway and airfield radars at Port Stanley airfield to deny its use to Argentine forces, with the Vulcan dropping conventional 1,000lb bombs and anti-radar missiles. As in the case of the Harriers, once again innovative modifications were made to the participating Vulcans to prepare them for the missions. During the original design phase for the aircraft hard points had been incorporated into a number of airframes to carry the Douglas Skybolt air-launched ballistic missile. Skybolt could only be carried externally by the Vulcan and so the mounting points were incorporated under the wings; these hard points were covered up, never to be used because Skybolt was cancelled before it could even be tested on the Vulcan. However, for the *Black Buck* raids, these hard points were used to mount Dash 10 Electronic Countermeasures (ECM) pods and Shrike anti-radar missiles.

The raids demonstrated outstanding planning and airmanship, providing strategic success in forcing Argentina to re-deploy fighters, as well as a morale boost to British forces and the public. They were also the Vulcans' first and last combat missions as, following a short service as an air tanker, they were withdrawn from service in 1984.

The RAF Air Transport fleet was another crucial element to the operation for, in addition to bulk supplies taken by sea, Hercules and VC10s flew a constant stream of personnel and equipment between Britain and Ascension. The Task Force could then be supplied at sea with drops made from AAR equipped Hercules. These airdrops continued when the Task Force arrived off the Falklands, which necessitated 25 hour non-stop flights of 8,000 miles. Wounded personnel were flown back to the UK, either from Ascension or, under International Red Cross rules, from Uruguay in the VC10s.

The Victors also provided long range maritime reconnaissance, until the Nimrods had been modified for in-flight refuelling. These Nimrods then undertook 19 hour flights, supported by Victor Tankers, to provide the maritime surveillance for the Task Force as it reached the Falkland Islands. They provided the task force commander with intelligence of enemy activity, within the radius of their surveillance systems. In addition to their normal anti-submarine weapons fit, the Nimrods were fitted with Sidewinder missiles for self-defence. Whilst, initially, the AAR role was undertaken by the Victors, the extreme workload on the crews was relieved when some Hercules and Vulcans were quickly modified into tanker aircraft.

The Air Defence of the Task Force against the significant threat posed by Argentine air power fell to the British Aerospace Sea Harriers of the FAA, operating from the carriers. To augment the overstretched Sea Harriers RAF Harrier GR3s, operating from *HMS Hermes,* took on the task of flying offensive sorties against the Argentine forces on the Islands. Later in the campaign, after the British landing at San Carlos, the RAF Harriers also operated from a temporary landing strip near the original beachhead.

Despite the efforts of the RAF and FAA Harriers, Argentine aircraft continued to attack the Task Force throughout the campaign, sinking several ships, including, on 25 May, the container ship *Atlantic Conveyor*. Amongst its cargo three of the RAF's new Boeing CH-47 Chinook medium-lift helicopters were destroyed but, fortunately, one of the Chinooks was undergoing an air-test and diverted to the carrier *HMS Hermes*. Using considerable efforts and borrowed tools, this aircraft, 'Bravo November (BN)', was kept flying throughout the remainder of the campaign and undertook ferrying of supplies and also supported assaults – on one occasion with three 105mm light guns (two external and one internal), along with 22 troops. In a number of subsequent conflicts 'BN' continued to perform sterling service and Distinguished Flying Crosses have, so far, been awarded to four of her Captains in three different operations. 'BN' is still serving, 36 years after entering service.

As a consequence of the well-coordinated efforts between the Armed Forces, the Merchant Navy and industry, the Joint Task Force achieved a swift and overwhelming victory. The Argentinian surrender, on 14 June, was first witnessed by the pilot of an RAF Harrier who radioed the Task Force that white flags were being waved in Stanley. Once again, air power had played a decisive role in conflict.

Soon after this campaign, and acting upon experience gained, a significant upgrade was undertaken on the Nimrod that included modifying it to carry the Harpoon anti-ship missile and the Stingray torpedo. However, continued pressure on the defence budget saw the number of aircraft reduced and operations consolidated in a single Nimrod base at RAF Kinloss in Scotland. The necessity of strategic AAR capability had also been demonstrated and nine surplus Lockheed TriStars were acquired from British Airways and PanAm. A number of VC10s were also purchased from airlines and converted to tankers. Changes were also happening in the deployment of personnel in the transport fleet when WRAF Loadmasters joined the crews of the Hercules fleet in 1982.

The need for AEW to protect Royal Navy/NATO ships when out of home waters had also been identified and a programme undertaken to develop an AEW version of the Nimrod. After an estimated £1 billion had been spent on the Nimrod AEW project, and no consensus on a final delivery date or price, the project was cancelled in 1986. An order was then placed for the 'off-the-shelf' Boeing E-3D Sentry, with its distinctive rotating radome on top of the fuselage, and the first aircraft was delivered in early 1991. With the E-3 already operated by the USAF and NATO, Britain was able to benefit from the experience of other nations operating the aircraft.

During 1983 the first Tornado GR1s were delivered to RAF Germany and based at Laarbruch. The build-up continued between June 1984 and November 1985 by which time six squadrons were stood up, with the seventh following at Bruggen in October 1986; two squadrons with the tactical reconnaissance GR1A version were formed at Laarbruch in August 1989.

With the Phantom fleet ageing, Britain looked to develop a long-range interceptor variant of the Tornado to undertake the Air Defence role. The first squadron to re-equip with the Tornado F3 Air Defence Variant (ADV) was declared operational in November 1987. By Early 1991 a further six squadrons had been equipped with this version of the Tornado.

The momentous events in Berlin in November 1989, signalled an end to over 40 years of the Cold War. The NATO posture and the RAF's position on the front line between east and west now took on a very different aspect. There was a genuine feeling that there would be a 'peace dividend', especially when East and West Germany were re-united and many of the old Warsaw Pact countries looked to the West for their new forms of government.

For a short period the concept of Mutually Assured Destruction (MAD) and the threat of a possible Third World War against the Soviet Union and the forces of the Warsaw Pact seemed to have disappeared as the eastern Bloc was demonstrably weakened. Thus the RAF entered the 1990s with considerable strength. The frontline comprised nine Tornado strike/attack squadrons, five offensive support squadrons of Harriers and Jaguars, five reconnaissance squadrons and two Buccaneer maritime attack squadrons.

The 11 Air Defence squadrons consisted of seven, with the Tornado F3, and four still with the Phantom. The Nimrod force provided maritime protection and the E-3 Sentry fleet was being delivered for AEW role. The transport force had four squadrons of Hercules, one of VC10 and one of TriStar, with the AAR force having two dedicated Victor squadrons. The rotary wing fleet comprised two of Chinooks, two with Pumas and one with Wessexes, with a further Wessex and a Westland Sea King squadron for the SAR role. The RAF's presence in Germany would be examined and there were still detachments disbursed in such faraway places as Belize, the Falklands and Hong Kong, but it seemed the prospect of war was receding at an ever-increasing pace.

The optimism lasted a very short time for in August 1990, Iraqi troops and aircraft attacked and invaded Kuwait whilst a shocked world looked on. As had happened so many times in the past, the RAF was required to make a rapid response to an aggressor many thousands of miles from Britain's shores. As part of a multi-national force led by the United States, a 17 nation Coalition deployed to the Kingdom of Saudi Arabia (KSA) to deter further Iraqi aggression. The build-up of forces necessary to drive Iraq out of Kuwait began under Operation *Desert Shield*. Britain's contribution was called Operation *Granby* and with a Joint HQ established at HQ RAF Strike Command, High Wycombe, the first RAF Tornado F3s arrived at King Abdul Azziz Air Base, Dhahran, KSA just over a week after the invasion. Within two hours these aircraft were flying Defensive Counter Air operations over the Saudi border with Iraq. Two days later, RAF Jaguars arrived in Oman, providing an offensive capability.

Also deploying to Oman were Nimrods, which gathered intelligence for Coalition navies on the movement of shipping in the Arabian Gulf and Gulf of Oman, and helped to enforce the UN embargo on Iraq and Kuwait. Victor, VC10 and TriStar tankers both supported RAF aircraft deploying to the Gulf, and then provided AAR to virtually all the other coalition air forces, flying around four times their normal peace-time flying rate. A huge air transport effort was also required to move personnel and supplies, with VC10s, Hercules, TriStars and civilian contracted flights providing the strategic lift, and the tactical contribution provided by Puma and Chinook helicopters. Hercules and helicopters also supported the operations of Special Forces, troop insertions, re-supply and casualty evacuation. During the period of Operation *Desert Shield* the air transport fleet exceeded the efforts of the massive 1948 Berlin Airlift.

The UN continued its efforts to bring about a diplomatic solution to the crisis but, in November, issued Iraq with an ultimatum to leave Kuwait by 15 January 1991, or they would be forced out. With Iraqi forces showing no sign of leaving, the Coalition's campaign to liberate Kuwait, known as Operation *Desert Storm* commenced in the early hours of 17 January 1991. This was a complex operation involving missions to achieve air superiority, destroy Iraqi capabilities (including 'Weapons of Mass Destruction' (WMD) sites), air defences and land forces in Kuwait, and then support Coalition ground forces during the land campaign.

Since its famous low level precision bombing attacks of World War II the RAF had forged a reputation for highly effective audacious attacks on high value targets. During the Cold War it had continued to demonstrate extremely effective tactics against specific enemy assets and was the means by which, in the event there had been a conflict with the Warsaw Pact, the enemy's airfields would be destroyed at the very start of hostilities. As a result, the RAF's specialist role in airfield denial by low level strikes was factored into the initial invasion plans for *Desert Storm*.

Attacks on the huge Iraqi airfields involved the RAF Tornado force flying very low-level missions at night against heavily defended targets. Some attacks were made with 1,000lb bombs, but many were made with their specialised JP233 runway denial weapon. These attacks were very demanding on the RAF crews, who made repeated missions to ensure the runways were not repaired. Six aircraft and five aircrew were lost during the campaign. Disturbing scenes were shown on television around the world as Iraq flouted the Geneva Convention by torturing prisoners of war and exhibiting captured and injured RAF aircrew.

From their base in Bahrain, the Jaguar force carried out daytime raids against supply dumps, SAM sites, artillery positions and anti-ship missile positions. They also undertook anti-shipping strikes against Iraqi naval vessels and provided some tactical reconnaissance. The new Tornado GR1A with its advanced day/night reconnaissance capabilities had been deployed just before the start of hostilities, and provided a major element of the efforts to counter the Iraqi Scud missile attacks on KSA and Israel, as well as being used against enemy defences, supply routes, bridges and for damage assessment.

The overwhelming air offensive was so effective that by 21 January, the Iraqi Air Force and its integrated air defence system had effectively been destroyed, meaning the Coalition could use the middle and upper air space at much reduced risk. This enabled the Tornado force to fly during the day, and at medium level using conventional weapons, until the arrival of the veteran Buccaneer with its laser designator pod (LDP). The LDP could laser mark a target for precision weapons, either for the Buccaneer carrying it or for a Tornado equipped with a laser guided weapon. This enabled the Tornado to undertake precision attacks with laser guided bombs against specific targets such as bridges and hardened aircraft shelters. Because the Buccaneers' pod was only suitable for day-time use a solution needed to be found to enable the Tornado to carry out night-time precision attacks from higher level. As In 1982, the RAF and industry solved the problem very quickly when the new GEC-Marconi Thermal Imaging Laser Designator (TIALD) pod, which had a night capability, was rushed into service on the Tornado.

After 38 days of what is known militarily as 'rapid dominance' or 'shock and awe' inflicted by the Coalition's air forces, the ground offensive was launched. The RAF rotary wing force of Puma and Chinook helicopters supported the army by ferrying troops, supplies and weapons to the front. It soon became clear that the air campaign had destroyed so much of the Iraqi armed forces' capabilities and morale that the Coalition governments halted the land campaign after only 100 hours.

The successful liberation of Kuwait and defeat of Iraq encouraged the Kurds of northern Iraq to attempt to overthrow Iraqi dictator, Saddam Hussein. The Kurds failed and the Iraqi army mounted a counter offensive. This led to a significant refugee crisis with Kurds seeking to escape to Turkey. The UN declared a secure area in northern Iraq for the Kurds where they would be free from attack. Known as Operation *Provide Comfort*, Britain's contribution included helicopters, air transport and the Royal Marines, with the safe haven established by September 1991.

The Iraq conflict marked a watershed in RAF operations which saw a definitive shift from the Cold War focus on Europe to a new era of 'expeditionary warfare' and the increasing use of precision-guided munitions.

Black Buck 1, 1982
Keith Woodcock

During the Falklands War in 1982, the RAF mounted Operations *Black Buck 1* to *Black Buck 7* with the aim of attacking the airfield at Port Stanley and its associated defences to deny its use to the Argentinian forces.

Of the seven raids, five were completed successfully, with one being cancelled before take-off due to weather and the other having to be abandoned five hours into the mission due to a fault with a Victor tanker. Of these five raids, three attacked the runway, stores and aircraft, and two attacked the anti-aircraft radar.

This painting shows *Black Buck 1*, undertaken between 30 April and 1 May 1982, by Vulcan B2 XM607 of No 44 Squadron, preparing to refuel from Victor K2 of No 57 Squadron, on its return from the successful bombing of Port Stanley runway. This painting was presented to the RAF Club by the manufacturer of AAR equipment, Cobham plc.

Keith Woodcock

Oilfield Patrol

Alan Fearnley

The McDonnell Douglas F-4M Phantom FGR2 was procured to replace the Hawker Hunter in the Close Air Support role. British Phantoms were significantly different from those of the USA, being heavily redesigned to accommodate Rolls Royce Spey engines and other British systems. Hawker Siddeley Aviation undertook the role of 'Sister Design Authority' and the British Aircraft Corporation built much of the redesigned fuselage.

The F-4M entered operational service with No 6 Squadron at RAF Coningsby in May 1969, and RAF Phantom squadrons were based in Britain and West Germany to carry out tactical reconnaissance and tactical nuclear strike. In these roles they were painted in the grey-green camouflage scheme suited to the Western European terrain over which they operated. This is depicted in this painting showing a pair of Phantoms undertaking a low level flight across the North Sea, passing an oil rig.

During the early 1970s, the introduction of the Jaguar and Buccaneer into service enabled the RAF to transfer more Phantoms to the air defence role, replacing Lightnings in both Britain and West Germany. While No 43 Squadron had operated the Phantom in the air defence role since 1969, it had used ex-FAA Phantom F-4K FG.1s and, with the retirement of *HMS Ark Royal*, the remainder of the FAA Phantoms transferred to the RAF.

Following the Falklands War, Phantoms were based at RAF Mount Pleasant to provide air defence for the Islands. This led to the purchase of 15 used Phantoms from the US Navy, as manufacturing them to the same standard as the existing aircraft was not possible. These aircraft were operated by No 74 Squadron between 1984 and 1991, being replaced by Phantom FGR.2s as other Squadrons converted to the new Tornado F.3 Air Defence Variant.

The end of the Cold War and the 1990 'Options for Change' Defence Review brought about a faster withdrawal of the Phantom squadrons than had originally been planned. However, the invasion of Kuwait by Iraq in 1990 gave the Phantom a brief reprieve, when six aircraft from Nos 19 and 92 Squadrons were used to provide air defence of RAF Akrotiri in Cyprus, as their resident Tornados had been sent to bases in the Gulf.

Alan Fearnley

"*Blue, Fire!*" 208 Squadron

Michael Rondot

This scene depicts maritime attack Blackburn Buccaneers of No 208 Squadron in action, launching Sea Eagle missiles at low level. The British Aerospace (BAe) Sea Eagle anti-ship missile entered service with the RAF in 1985, with the Buccaneer being the first aircraft to carry it. The Sea Eagle was powered by a jet engine and once fired was completely autonomous.

The Buccaneer was originally designed for the Fleet Air Arm to undertake low level, high speed strikes from aircraft carriers against Soviet warships. Despite the RAF deciding against ordering the Buccaneer, with the planned drawdown of the Royal Navy carrier fleet and the cancellation of the planned purchase of the General Dynamics F-111K, in 1968 it was decided that the RAF would receive the FAA Buccaneers, along with some new-build aircraft. They were to replace the Canberras that were still operating in the low level strike role.

The Buccaneer entered RAF service with No 12 Squadron at RAF Honington in 1969, equipped with ex-FAA S2A variants in the maritime strike role. With more squadrons being formed, Buccaneers also served with RAF Germany, operating in support of land forces and armed with the WE177 freefall tactical nuclear bomb.

In the early 1980s, the Buccaneer's land attack roles began to be taken over by the Tornado, which was entering service, leaving just Nos 12 and 208 Squadrons in the maritime role. During the 1991 Gulf War Buccaneers provided laser designation for Tornados and also dropped their own bombs on a range of targets.

The end of the Cold War saw the Buccaneer retired earlier than expected with the last operator, No 208 Squadron, disbanding in March 1994. The maritime strike role was taken over by the Tornado GR1B, which continued to use the Sea Eagle, until the missile was withdrawn in 2000.

TIALD On Target, Baghdad, 1991
Michael Turner

As the first Gulf War started, the first phase of the quest for air superiority was to deprive Saddam Hussein of his airfields. RAF Tornado GR.1s attacked airfields using unguided bombs and the JP233 runway denial weapons system. The JP233 could only be delivered by flying directly over the target, which exposed the Tornado to a high risk from enemy ground based air defences. In a short time the Tornados switched to medium level operations using laser guided bombs. They flew in pairs with Blackburn Buccaneers, which were equipped with the Pave Spike laser designator pod to provide a daylight only targeting capability. Later, two Thermal Imaging Airborne Laser Designator (TIALD) pods were delivered and used by the Tornados to self-designate, including at night, as shown in this painting.

This painting was presented to the RAF Club by the manufacturer of the TIALD pod, GEC Ferranti.

Liberation, February 1991
Roger Steel

As the Gulf War progressed and air superiority was achieved, the Coalition ground troops invaded Iraq. Preceded by tanks, quickly followed up by infantry in Armoured Personnel carriers, they made good speed across the desert. This painting captures the armoured columns advancing towards the border with Tornado support above.

The Panavia Tornado GR1 was a swing-wing, multi-role Interdictor Strike (IDS) aircraft that entered service with the RAF in 1981. It was designed and manufactured by a European collaboration between Britain, Germany and Italy, for delivery of conventional and nuclear weapons, penetrating enemy airspace at low level. In addition to these roles, since entering service with the partner nations, it has taken on multiple roles such as reconnaissance, maritime shipping and close air support operations. For RAF service, it was also developed into the Tornado F.3 Air Defence Variant.

ROGER STEEL

CHAPTER X

ENDURING OPERATIONS ~ 1992 TO THE FUTURE

"The option of war can appear initially to be the swiftest. But let us not forget that, after winning the war, peace must be built."

DOMINIQUE DE VILLEPIN (MINISTER OF FOREIGN AFFAIRS, FRANCE), 14 FEBRUARY 2003

THE Coalition's objective was to drive Saddam from Kuwait, and also to ensure continued peace by leaving his armed forces partly intact and paid for by the West. Thus a part of his military forces was disarmed and allowed to return to Iraq in the hope that Iraqi Army military control could be exercised with assistance, and guidance, from members of the Coalition. This plan was not pursued after a change of policy on the part of the USA, and Saddam remained in power and continued to take military action against his own people. His vengeance was particularly directed at ethnic groups opposed to his secular Ba'ath Party.

Whilst Saddam used Muslim quotations from the Koran to exhort his troops, and had undoubtedly strong resentments against various sectarian groups, it is probable that his attacks against Iraqi minorities were more about their threat to his power than their religious beliefs. However he mounted humanitarian outrages against the Sunni, Northern Patriotic Union of Kurdistan and the southern Shia, Marsh Arabs ('Arabs of the Marshlands'), when, after he had organised the genocidal drainage and resettlement of their homeland they attempted a rebellion in 1991.

This led the UN to establish no-fly zones over Iraq north of the 36th parallel and south of the 33rd parallel known by the Coalition as Operations *Northern & Southern Watch*. Britain's contribution was made with Jaguars, Tornado GR1s and later Harriers and Tornado GR4s, carrying out reconnaissance missions over these zones from 1991 until Saddam was deposed in 2003.

The early 1990s also saw civil war erupt in the Balkans. Following the death of Yugoslavia's President Tito in 1990, a rising tide of nationalism led to the gradual collapse of the country. Croatia and Slovenia broke away completely in 1991 and, then Bosnia-Herzegovina descended into brutal, ethnically-based, insurgencies between its Croat, Muslim, Serbian and Albanian populations, in which widespread 'ethnic cleansing' was undertaken. The objective of the Serbs was to create a Greater Serbia from parts of Croatia and Bosnia. To alleviate suffering in besieged towns and cities, including the capital of Bosnia Herzegovina, Sarajevo, the UN organised a relief effort of food and medicine. Under Operation *Cheshire,* the UK played a major part in this airlift, which ran from 1992 to 1996 and saw the Hercules fleet deliver over 26,000 tons of supplies in nearly 2,000 sorties.

The Bosnian Serbs (mainly Eastern Orthodox Christians), supported by President Slobodan Milosevic's Socialist Party of Serbia, undertook attacks on the Muslim Slavs to drive them out of areas of the country claimed by the Serbs. To stop this genocide the UN ordered an economic blockade, deployed a protection force, and established a no-fly zone over Bosnia-Herzegovina, a mission known as Operation *Deny Flight*. The RAF deployed a force of six Tornado F3s to Italy, between April 1993 and February 1996, to undertake monitoring and enforce compliance with UN Security Council Resolution 816. The F3s were supported by Boeing E-3D Sentry and VC10 tankers, with Nimrod MR2 and Canberra PR9s undertaking maritime surveillance and reconnaissance respectively. RAF Chinooks and Pumas were also deployed to Croatia.

In May 1993 a peace plan was rejected by the Bosnian Serbs, who then increased their actions against Bosnia-Herzegovina; this led the UN to declare six 'safe havens' for fleeing Muslims. However, the UN peacekeeping forces could provide little protection, so NATO was asked to intervene. As part of this, the RAF deployed nine Jaguar GR1s to Italy to undertake reconnaissance and strike missions against threats to the safe areas. While a number of ceasefires were negotiated over the next two years, hostilities always resumed. In June 1995, the Serbs seized one of the safe areas and took UN peacekeepers hostage. The next month they overran two more safe areas and massacres at Srebrenica and Markale were reported. Following a mortar attack on Sarajevo market that killed 38 civilians, NATO reacted with Operation *Deliberate Force* which included RAF Harrier GR7s and Jaguar GR1s bombing Serb targets, in the first use of offensive air power in Europe since 1945.

Between 30 August and 20 September 1995, the campaign (reminiscent of the 'Aerial Policing' pioneered by the RAF in the 1920s) involved 400 aircraft and 5,000 personnel from 15 nations. Over 1,000 bombs (708 of which were precision guided) were dropped on 338 Bosnian Serb targets, many of which were destroyed. Tornado F3, TriStar and Sentry aircraft were also involved and the campaign forced the warring factions to accept the UN brokered ceasefire, in late 1995, that ultimately led to the Dayton Peace Accord by the end of that year.

To enforce the Dayton Accord a NATO Implementation Force was deployed, the air element of which was to police the no-fly zone under Operation *Decisive Edge*, with the RAF continuing to provide Harrier GR7s. In late 1996, the Implementation Force became a Stabilisation Force and *Decisive Edge* became Operation *Deliberate Guard*, with Jaguars replacing the Harriers in early 1997. By April 1998, the situation was sufficiently stable for the RAF to withdraw the Jaguars and their TriStar tankers, but the E-3D Sentrys remained in theatre until 2000.

Although the Dayton Accord had brought some peace to the Balkans area, it remained a volatile ethnic mix. Ethnic Albanians (a Sunni Muslim majority, but a sizeable minority of Roman Catholics) formed the majority of the population in Kosovo, but President Milosevic attempted to alter this by encouraging more Serbs (Eastern Orthodox Christians) to settle, and the Albanians to leave. To resist this Albanians formed a guerrilla movement, the Kosovo Liberation Army, against which Milosevic deployed the Serbian Army and police units into Kosovo, and stories began to emerge of violence against Albanians. Determined to avoid a repeat of the Bosnian genocide, NATO backed diplomatic efforts with the threat of air strikes, using Exercise *Determined Falcon* to demonstrate its strength by overflying Albania and Macedonia. Macedonia had followed the example of its neighbours with an insurgency aiming to give greater rights to the Albanian minority living there.

A ceasefire was agreed in late 1998 and a monitoring team, including RAF personnel, deployed to the region. Despite this, the violence continued and, by January 1999, the situation was deteriorating rapidly, with strenuous diplomatic efforts resulting in peace talks in Paris in February/March. While the Kosovan Albanians unconditionally accepted the Agreement, Milosevic refused. He also failed to accept a NATO peacekeeping force in Kosovo escalating his attacks against the Albanians. The monitoring team was withdrawn and, in March, NATO launched airstrikes under Operation *Allied Force* to influence an end to Serbian aggression against the Kosovars.

NATO had hoped that, as with *Deliberate Force*, air strikes would quickly force Serbia back to the negotiating table but, unfortunately, it did not and *Allied Force* developed into a campaign, with the UK national effort provided by Operation *Engadine*. This included Harrier GR7s, a Canberra PR9, TriStar tankers, E3-D and a Nimrod R1 Electronic Surveillance aircraft. Milosevic responded by increasing his attacks, leaving NATO no option other than to increase the strength of its forces, with the RAF adding additional Harriers and another TriStar, as well as putting RAF Germany's Tornadoes, supported by VC10s, on standby. With a growing humanitarian crisis, RAF Hercules aircraft began delivering aid to sites in Macedonia and Albania.

When spring arrived, operations intensified, with the Tornadosundertaking their first operations against bridges and tunnels used by the Serbs as supply routes, and the Harriers attacking Serb ground forces. With air superiority, by the beginning of May, NATO had flown over 12,000 missions, with the RAF having provided over nine per cent of these. Inevitably the Serbian military capabilities were significantly degraded. However, Milosevic still refused to capitulate and with Albanian refugees numbering almost 500,000, NATO had again to increase its efforts. The RAF added further Tornadoes, Harriers and tankers, and the FAA was also deployed with its Sea Harriers. The rate of NATO sorties increased and by the end of May, in a 68 day period, over 30,000 sorties, including 9,000 attack missions, had been flown.

In early June, a diplomatic outcome was achieved, with a joint EU/Russian delegation advising that Milosevic had agreed to a ceasefire. Operations were scaled back as negotiations continued, only for them to be stepped up again as it appeared that talks were breaking down, until Milosevic finally accepted NATO's conditions. Plans were then put in place for the withdrawal of Serb forces and the deployment of a NATO peacekeeping force.

The RAF had contributed over 50 aircraft and some of its squadrons were subsequently awarded battle honours for their role. A general lesson learned from the conflict, (particularly following the inaccurate targeting, by the US CIA, of the Chinese Embassy in Belgrade) was the need to improve the precision bombing capabilities. With the experience gained throughout the NATO Coalition, the RAF recognised that it needed both new weapons and an increase in the number of Harriers and Tornadosmodified in order to carry them. In time the weapons were acquired and aircraft upgrades were made.

The 1990s also saw the end of British commitments in both Belize and Hong Kong. The threat to Belize from Guatemala was finally considered to have ended in the early 1990s, and the Harrier contingent was withdrawn in mid-1993, and the Pumas a year later. The Sino-British Joint Declaration restored Hong Kong to China on 1 July 1997. RAF Sek Kong, which was the last RAF station in mainland Asia had closed in 1996, with the Wessex helicopters of No 28 Squadron being moved to Kai Tak International Airport for their final year of operation.

Back in the Middle East, in an attempt to force Saddam to hand over his WMD, the UN had sent in a Special Commission of weapons inspectors to oversee their destruction. However, in late 1998, Saddam decided to end co-operation with the inspectors unless UN sanctions against Iraq were lifted. As the situation deteriorated the build-up of Coalition forces commenced; the RAF sent 12 Tornado GR1s and 400 personnel to Kuwait, supported by VC10 tankers and Hercules air transport. In addition, eight Harrier GR7s were embarked on *HMS Invincible*. By the end of the year, the RAF had 24 Tornado GR1s deployed, six in Turkey, six in the Kingdom of Saudi Arabia (KSA) and 12 in Kuwait. With the GR1 fleet embarking on its mid-life update to GR4 standard with British Aerospace, Tornado F3s replaced the KSA based GR1s and provided Air Defence. Operation *Desert Fox* was undertaken by RAF and USAF aircraft in December 1998, with the Tornado force dropping Laser Guided Bombs (LGBs) onto a number of targets including Hardened Aircraft Shelters (HASs).

The RAF had been deeply involved in Northern Ireland since the late 1960s, with support helicopters and transport aircraft. Through the 1970s, firstly Westland Wessexes and then Pumas were based in the Province; by the late 1980s, Boeing Chinooks were also deployed as required. The helicopters provided a range of support and transport roles to ground forces, including the Army and Royal Ulster Constabulary (renamed Police Service of Northern Ireland in 2001), as well as VIP transport, SAR, casualty evacuation and moving ballot boxes. Operating in dangerous conditions, the helicopters often came under attack from small arms fire, RPGs and on one occasion in 1991 a SAM.

The RAF Regiment was also deployed, protecting RAF bases and, on occasion, undertaking street patrols in the Aldergrove area. In late 1999, the Joint Helicopter Force Northern Ireland (JHFNI) was formed from the assets of the RAF, Army Air Corps (AAC) and FAA.

The 1990s were also a time of significant re-equipping for the RAF, with many of the types that had served it well throughout the Cold War being retired. The McDonnell-Douglas F-4 Phantom retired by the end of 1992, and was replaced by the Tornado F3 in the air defence role, with the Blackburn Buccaneer being withdrawn in early 1993 and its anti-shipping role undertaken by Tornados that had been modified to the GR1B standard, to carry the Sea Eagle missile. Also retiring by the end of 1993 were the last of the Victors that had served with No 55 Squadron for 33 years as both a bomber and tanker; this was a record for a squadron continuously operating a single type. Another notable change was the merger in 1994 of the WRAF with the RAF, when female personnel became fully integrated with the same rates of pay and subject to the same regulations as their male colleagues. This change reflected the fact that the RAF had now opened all its roles to women, including flying every aircraft type.

The mid-life update of the Tornado led to the GR4 version which had significant upgrades to its avionics and first flew in mid-1993. This was followed a few months later by the first flight of the newly upgraded VC10 in its K4 version. However, in terms of importance to the RAF's future, the most significant event was the first flight, in early 1994, of the Eurofighter 2000, designed and built by Britain, Germany, Italy and Spain in another example of pan-European co-operation, already demonstrated by the success of the Tornado. Britain's involvement in the Eurofighter was led by BAe and the aircraft was formally named Typhoon in 1998.

Following the election of a Labour Government in 1997, Secretary of State for Defence (SofS), George Robertson, set out the initial defence policy of the new government. The Strategic Defence Review of 1998, amongst other things, determined that the British Military would not be expected to carry out more than two international deployments for more than six months at any one time. Inevitably, this brought significant equipment and organisational changes for the RAF, including the decision to replace the VC10 and TriStar with a new, undetermined, type to be provided under the Future Strategic Tanker Aircraft (FSTA) Private Finance Initiative (PFI). A new Strategic Air Transport was to be procured, initially through the lease of Boeing C-17 Globemaster III aircraft. In addition, the Joint Harrier Force was created to bring together the RAF Harrier GR7s and the FAA's Sea Harrier FA2s, with the support helicopters of all three Services also brought together as the Joint Helicopter Command (JHC).

In another sign of the changing nature of global threats, RAF Bruggen, the last remaining RAF Germany station, was closed in mid-2001. However, the terrorist attacks on New York and Washington DC on 11 September 2001 resulted in an immediate revision by the SofS (Geoff Hoon) and changes were made, particularly in areas such as Special Forces' Operations and Unmanned Aerial Vehicles. Following President George W Bush's announcement of the 'Global War on Terrorism' there followed US-led attacks on the Taliban and Al-Qaeda forces in Afghanistan; these brought the RAF into a protracted operation that lasted until the end of 2014.

The RAF's initial contribution included the veteran Canberra PR9 which undertook high altitude reconnaissance; Nimrod MR2s carried out surveillance missions overland using on-board sensors, with Boeing E-3D Sentrys providing both surveillance and airborne Command and Control. The newly delivered Globemaster IIIs, along with Hercules, deployed to provide a strategic and tactical airlift while, once again, the VC10s and TriStars provided the vital aerial refuelling capability to RAF and Coalition aircraft. The JHC also deployed Chinooks and Merlins, providing support to both regular and Special Forces, and the RAF Regiment secured airfields and provided ground based air defence. As Afghanistan had no operable air traffic control infrastructure remaining, Air Traffic Control was provided from the Regional Air Movement Centre in Qatar, to which the RAF personnel were posted.

In December 2001, the International Security Assistance Force (ISAF) was formed to assist the Afghan authorities in creating and maintaining a safe and secure environment. The British Operations of *Veritas* and *Fingal* were consolidated into Operation Herrick in 2002, which continued until combat operations ceased at the end of 2014. The RAF provided a number of different aircraft types, from Harrier GR7/9 and Tornado GR4 for tactical reconnaissance and close air support, Hercules for in-theatre airlift, and the BAe 146 for in-theatre communications. From 2007, the RAF began using the General Atomics MQ-9 Reaper Unmanned Aerial Vehicle (UAV), and from early 2009, the Raytheon Sentinel R1 to provide a significant enhancement in Information Surveillance Target Acquisition and Reconnaissance (ISTAR) capabilities.

Meanwhile, in Iraq, the UN had continued to try to reduce the threat that the regime posed to the Gulf, especially in view of the need to remove the regime's WMD. This came to a head in late 2002 when the UN passed a resolution declaring Iraq to be in breach of previous resolutions and set new compliance conditions, threatening serious consequences for failure. With Saddam still being un-cooperative, Britain joined the US-led Coalition that was prepared to use force to achieve compliance. In early 2003 Operation *Telic* was launched. With the RAF having maintained forces in the Gulf since 1991, there were already 25 aircraft and 1,000 personnel in theatre, to which a further 100 aircraft and 7,000 personnel were added. These included both Tornado GR4s and Harrier GR7s for offensive roles, Tornado F3s for Air Defence, VC10s and TriStars for AAR, Nimrod R1 and MR2 and Canberra PR9s for reconnaissance, Sentry E-3Ds for Airborne Early Warning and Control, Globemaster IIIs and Hercules for Air Transport. Chinooks and Pumas provided the Support Helicopter role. In addition, six RAF Regiment Squadrons and various other specialist ground support units were also deployed.

The aim of the air campaign was to remove the threats posed by the Iraqi Air Force and its Integrated Air Defence system, enabling the destruction of regime and military targets. However, these were constrained by the Coalition governments' emphasis on the need to minimise civilian casualties and damage to essential services and economic infrastructure. This led to approximately 85 per cent of the RAF's weapon releases being Precision Guided Munitions (PGM) and also the first use of the MBDA Stormshadow stand-off precision air-to-ground missile launched from Tornadoes. In less than a month the Coalition had removed Saddam from power, although *Telic* continued for a number of years under the auspices of 903 Expeditionary Air Wing (EAW), with the final RAF operations taking place in 2009, after which the EAW disbanded, only to be stood up again shortly after in Afghanistan.

In March 2006, No 3 Squadron became the first front line unit to re-equip with the Eurofighter Typhoon at RAF Coningsby, which then became the main base for the Typhoon force. Three months later the RAF's last three Canberra PR9s were finally retired, a remarkable 55 years after the original B2 version entered service in 1951.

On 1 April 2007 Strike Command and Personnel and Training Command merged into the single Air Command at RAF High Wycombe. At the end of the same month the Jaguar was retired after 33 years in RAF service. In June, the Eurofighter Typhoon assumed responsibility for QRA of the southern part of the UK's air defences. Operating from RAF Coningsby the Typhoons remain ready to scramble at a moment's notice, 24 hours a day, 365 days a year, to meet and identify any threat to UK air space, be it a Russian bomber or a hi-jacked airliner.

The Nimrod MR2 retired in early 2010, anticipating its replacement by the MRA4. However, the Strategic Defence and Security Review (SDSR) that was undertaken later the same year was carried out against a backdrop of a global economic downturn and had a significant impact on the RAF. Two of the most severe decisions for the RAF were the retirement of the much loved Harrier by the end of the year and the total cancellation of the Nimrod MRA4. The country was immediately left without any long-range maritime reconnaissance/ SAR capability. This loss had a huge impact, not only on what the Royal Navy, euphemistically, called a "capability holiday", but also on the UK's ability to retain the infrastructure and crews with the experience and technical ability to pursue the full range of tasks previously undertaken by this versatile aircraft. In addition, the SDSR announced the switch of the Lockheed-Martin F-35 Lightning II variant from the STOVL version to the Carrier Version; the early retirement of the Sentinel, once it was no longer required to support operations in Afghanistan, and the withdrawal of the Lockheed Martin C-130J, 10 years earlier than originally planned. However, plans were also announced to procure 22 of the new Airbus Military A400M transport aircraft, to supplement the existing Globemaster III fleet, and additional Chinook helicopters.

In early 2011, civil unrest, referred to as the 'Arab Spring', began in Libya, which was met with considerable violence by forces loyal to Colonel Muammar Ghadaffi, 'Brotherly Leader' of the Great Socialist People's Libyan Arab Jamahiriya (Republic). While the UN sought a resolution to the conflict, the RAF began Operation *Deference* to evacuate British and other civilians to Malta. The evacuations were undertaken by Hercules, with Sentry E-3Ds providing Command and Control. However, with peace efforts failing, in March the UN Security Council passed Resolution 1973 that authorised "... *all necessary measures, short of the deployment of a foreign occupation force, to protect civilians and civilian populated areas from attack*". The Typhoon and

Tornado forces were given warning of deployment and, a few days after the UN Resolution was passed, both types deployed to Gioia Del Colle (GDC) in Italy, with the Typhoons flying Combat Air Patrols (CAP) in support of the no-fly zone. Providing support to these operations were the Nimrod R1, Sentinel R1 and VC10 aircraft.

The campaign, which was called Operation *Ellamy,* was notable for being the first time since the end of World War II that the RAF had launched attack sorties from the UK. These raids were the furthest ever conducted from Britain with Stormshadow equipped Tornadoes, supported by AAR, flying from RAF Marham on a 3,000 mile round trip to attack key installations. Also, in a move reminiscent of the First Gulf War, when Tornado and Buccaneers flew together, these operations saw mixed formations of Tornados and Typhoons working together, using complimentary capabilities to designate and attack targets. As with all operations, the support of the RAF logistics organisation was essential, with the Air Transport fleet transporting over 2.9 million lbs of freight, and the Mobile Catering Squadron deployed to GDC, serving over 37,000 meals a month from its tented facilities.

Ellamy was the final operation for the RAF's intelligence gathering Nimrod R1s, which were finally retired in mid-2011. They were replaced by Boeing RC-135 Rivet Joints, procured under an innovative arrangement with the USAF, where the RAF aircraft were to be treated as part of a common fleet, with operations commencing in 2013. Changes to the RAF AAR and Air Transport fleets were also underway when, after the Airbus A330 Voyagers commenced operations in mid-2013, the ageing VC10s were finally withdrawn later that year after 47 years of service, with the TriStars following in 2016.

The summer of 2014 saw the rapid advance of Da'ish (the Arabic acronym for the Islamic State of Iraq and Syria), through Syria and northern Iraq, provoking strong condemnation from Western and Middle Eastern states. The RAF's initial involvement was with air drops to Kurdish civilians, besieged in the region of Mount Sinjar and Amerli in northern Iraq. Following a request for support from the Iraqi Government, and a UK Parliamentary vote in September 2014 to permit airstrikes against Da'ish, Tornado GR4 and Voyager aircraft operated directly in support of Iraqi and Kurdish forces. Tornado GR4s and Typhoon FGR4s (deployed in December 2015), and flying from RAF Akrotiri in Cyprus, made a significant contribution to the Global Coalition's ongoing fight against Da'ish.

During 2015 the RAF's long-held, and courageously flown, commitment to Search and Rescue (SAR) was contracted to a civilian organisation and the SAR helicopter fleet was stood down. The familiar canary yellow helicopters of the past would no longer be a recognisable sight for any observant viewer as a chapter in RAF history closed. Indeed, for the UK public the RAF's humanitarian efforts are legendary and will not cease following the cessation of SAR services. As historically the RAF has been ever present whenever disaster strikes, (with flood relief, mountain rescue, isolated area replenishment during severe weather, and even firefighting during industrial instability), so the aid to the civil community that has been their hallmark for decades will undoubtedly continue.

As the RAF looks forward to its next century it remains committed to operations against terrorists, particularly in the Middle East. Its value to NATO and its intelligence sharing with other partners marks it out as one of the most capable air forces in the world. It also continues to maintain a flight of Typhoons in the Falkland Islands to provide Air Defence and enable the air-bridge from Britain. Its constant readiness to deliver a response to terrorist attacks on mainland UK, and assist our continental allies whenever necessary, is as high as ever. However, in potentially the highest profile role in defence of the British population and one reminiscent of its 'Finest Hour' in 1940, the RAF uses its ground based radars and QRA Typhoons to secure and protect Britain's airspace from the increased incursions of long range reconnaissance and bomber aircraft from a renascent, and posturing Russia.

Air Battle Management Unit, Iraq 2003

Martin Balshaw

No 1 Air Control Centre (1ACC) is based at RAF Scampton, but is maintained at very high readiness to deploy worldwide in support of operations. In recent years it has provided support to Operations *Telic* and *Herrick* in Iraq and Afghanistan respectively.

The Unit delivers Tactical Air Command and Control which provides increased situational awareness for air and ground domains in support of National, NATO and Coalition Air Operations. This delivers the UK's Deployable Air Surveillance and Control System (DASACS) capability. 1ACC is also on call every day, all day, to provide resilience to the UK Air Defence System, should there be any failure in the primary systems.

The key radar for this deployable capability is the BAE Systems Type 101 Commander, which provides local integrated command and control of air defence forces while operating from prepared or unprepared locations, in static or mobile configurations.

At the time of painting this scene, showing No 1 ACC at Talill air base in Iraq in 2003, the artist was serving with the RAF in Iraq. This painting was presented to the RAF Club by the Fighter Control Association.

© MARTIN BALSHAW
2006

Kacanik Bridge, Kosovo 12 June 1999

Mandy Shepherd

This watercolour depicts a scene on the 12 June 1999 as 5th Airborne Brigade spearheaded the KFOR advance into Kosovo by securing the Kacanik Defile ahead of the ground forces. The Brigade, with the UK support helicopter force of Puma and Chinook aircraft, achieved a rapid strategic insertion into theatre. Kacanik Bridge provided the only access into Kosovo from Macedonia and on to the capital Pristina with the river on one side of the road and cliff wall on the other. Sappers from 9 Independent Parachute Squadron Royal Engineers supported The Paras, along with the Ghurka Rifles, by checking the bridges and tunnels for explosives and booby traps left by withdrawing Serbian Forces.

This painting, commissioned by No 33 Squadron, depicts an accurate interpretation toward the northern end of the defile early in the morning of 12 June. The Puma helicopters continually landed on the bridge, delivering troops, supported by Chinooks of Nos 18 and 27 Squadrons and Apache helicopters of the US Army providing flank protection. NATO armour would soon move along the Kacanik road after it had been secured.

The Puma was selected for RAF service in 1967, with a total of 48 HC Mk 1s being ordered. The first two were delivered in January 1971 to No 33 Squadron at RAF Odiham, becoming the first operational Puma unit in June of that year.

The Pumas were based at RAF Odiham and RAF Benson, with detachments based at RAF Aldergrove in Northern Ireland. The Puma was used mainly for transport duties and by Special Forces as it was found to be ideally suited to covert operations. It has also seen operational deployments overseas in Belize, Iraq, Venezuela, the Balkans, and Zaire, as well as for humanitarian and peacekeeping missions in Africa and the Gulf region.

As a result of an extensive avionics, airframe and engine upgrade programme on the Puma fleet, the first Puma HC Mk2 entered service in late 2012, with the programme completed by early 2014. This enables the Puma to remain in operational service until 2025.

Jaguar Swan Song

Mark Bromley

Following its successful use in the 1991 Gulf War, the need to upgrade the RAF's Jaguar GR.1A fleet was identified.

This started with a 1994 Urgent Operational Requirement (UOR) to introduce the GEC-Marconi TIALD laser designation pod, enabling the subsequent GR1B version to be deployed as part of the RAF contribution to Operation *Deliberate Force*. A No 41 Squadron Jaguar became the first RAF aircraft since World War II to carry out a bombing raid in Europe. In addition, the TIALD pod enabled the Jaguar to designate targets for RAF Harriers.

A series of further upgrades eventually led to the GR3A standard. This introduced new equipment including: Head Up Display (HUD), integrated GPS, helmet mounted sights, datalinks, improved night vision goggle compatibility, and up-rated engines.

The main base of RAF Jaguar operations for many years was RAF Coltishall, which was the home of Nos 6, 41 and 54 Squadrons. However, No 6 Squadron based at RAF Coningsby was the final operator of the type and this painting shows one of that Squadron's aircraft, serial XX729, carrying out a low level flight through mountainous terrain.

The Jaguar was retired from RAF service in April 2007, but many airframes, including this one, remain in use at RAF Cosford for ground instruction use in technician training.

EL
BROMLEY

Last Day at Brize Norton

Kai Choi

The Vickers VC10 served the RAF as a strategic transport aircraft from December 1966 when the first of 14 C1 aircraft entered service with No 10 Squadron. In configuring these aircraft for military use all passenger seats faced aft. This had been standard practice for some years as data had been gathered which showed that survivability in an accident was higher with rearward facing seats. Airlines, when asked to justify their forward facing seats, claimed it was a passenger preference, until configurations in luxury cabins started to place seats in an aft facing position. However, it is a fact that, until recently, seats facing aft for safety reasons had to be more robust and therefore heavier and this was the disincentive for airlines to fit them. The RAF changed their policy after the VC10 came into service and subsequent transport aircraft have standard forward facing seats.

The initial VC10s were soon in use on two regular routes, the first to New York and the other to Hong Kong, via Singapore; later, a weekly service to Washington DC was added. In addition, they were also used in the aeromedical, evacuation and VIP role, including flying Her Majesty Queen Elizabeth II during her bicentennial tour of the USA. All were named after RAF Victoria Cross recipients, carrying the name above the forward passenger door.

As commercial airlines started to retire their VC10 fleets during the 1970s, the RAF purchased nine aircraft from British Airways and East African Airways and contracted British Aerospace (BAe) to convert them to aerial refuelling tankers of the K2 and K3 variant respectively. The conversion of these aircraft included a strengthened floor to support the weight of the extra internal five fuel tanks. In the early 1990s, five additional former British Airways aircraft were also converted by BAe to K4 variants. All these conversions were fitted with wing mounted refuelling pods, a fuselage centreline pod and their own AAR probe, so they too could be refuelled. The differences in Mark principally relate to whether the aircraft has a fuselage freight door and the amount of fuel that could be carried. In addition, during the 1980s and early 90s, the remaining C1s were fitted with wing mounted refuelling pods.

VC10s supported many operations, including the Falklands War, Gulf Wars, Balkans conflicts, Afghanistan and Libya. With the selection of the Airbus A330 as the Future Strategic Tanker Aircraft, the VC10s' days were numbered and, as depicted in this painting at RAF Brize Norton, the home of the RAF's tanking and transport fleet, the final flight in RAF service took place from Brize in September 2013.

Kai Choi VI 2012

Immediate Response
Roy Layzell

The RAF's Joint Helicopter Command Boeing CH-47 Chinook heavy lift helicopters were relied on heavily to support the British forces in Afghanistan, from the start of operations until the last three returned to the UK aboard RAF Boeing C-17 Globemaster IIIs in March 2015.

Due to the threat posed to ground forces by the Improvised Explosive Devices (IEDs) scattered by insurgents, helicopters became highly valued and demanded units, both in the provision of transport and in Casualty Evacuation (CASEVAC). During their time in Afghanistan, the Chinook fleet flew 41,000 hours and extracted 13,000 casualties. This scene depicts one of the many CASEVAC operations carried out during the operations in Afghanistan; it also shows the harsh operating conditions, including 'brown out' that made flying so demanding and which led to numerous gallantry awards. These included 23 Distinguished Flying Crosses (DFC), one of which was only the second ever awarded to an RAF female pilot. This was to Flt Lt Laura Nicholson, for a CASEVAC operation under heavy fire to retrieve a badly wounded United States Marine, followed by an immediate return to retrieve a critically injured Afghan civilian from the same location. This painting was presented to the RAF Club by Boeing Defence UK.

Roy Layzell '10

Coming Home Bearing Gifts, Lockheed L1011 Tristar

Mandy Shepherd

Following the experience in the Falklands Conflict of 1982 it was clear to the RAF that air-to-air refuelling was an absolutely essential aspect of the ability of the Service to operate effectively. With the Victor tankers coming to the end of their operational life and the VC10 fleet requiring augmentation it was decided to purchase ex-airline Lockheed L1011 TriStars. This aircraft offered the flexibility of conversion to several configurations including tanker/passenger and tanker/freighter. The conversions were undertaken by Marshall's of Cambridge and the first fully modified aircraft left them in July 1985. At the time the TriStar was the heaviest (and only wide-bodied) aircraft in the RAF and was allocated to No 216 Squadron at RAF Brize Norton.

This painting shows a TriStar of No 216 Squadron taking off from Afghanistan on a homebound journey carrying personnel returning from Operation *Herrick*. The painting was commissioned to commemorate the disbandment of the Squadron after 96 years of service, and 30 years of them operating the TriStar.

Harrier and Chinook over Kandahar

Ronald Wong

This scene, which was commissioned for the cover of the 2008 RAF Yearbook, depicts a heavily armed BAE Systems Harrier GR9A, carrying Laser Guided Bombs and the Lockheed Martin Sniper targetting pod. The aircraft is just departing Kandahar Airbase in Afghanistan during Operation *Herrick*, which was the UK's contribution to the NATO led International Security Assistance Force (ISAF). In the background can be seen two Boeing CH-47 Chinooks, and a Lockheed Martin C-130 Hercules is on the taxiway.

Joint Force Harrier sent its first Harrier GR9s on operational deployment with No 1 Squadron at Kandahar in January 2007. The GR9s progressively replaced the earlier Harrier GR7s which had also been rotationally deployed since September 2004. Following five years of continuous operations in Afghanistan, the last of the Harrier GR9s were withdrawn from Afghanistan in June 2009, having flown over 22,000 hours on 8,500 sorties. The Harrier force was replaced by RAF Tornado GR4s, which also operated on a rotational basis until November 2014 when the final detachment from No 31 Squadron left Khandahar.

The Harrier GR9 was expected to stay in service until 2018 but was retired from RAF service in December 2010, as an outcome of the Strategic Defence and Security Review of that year.

RONALD
WONG

Sentinel R1 Over its Ground Station

Chris French

The Raytheon Sentinel R1 is an airborne battlefield and ground surveillance aircraft, with its main radar mounted in the canoe fairing that can be seen under the fuselage. It entered RAF operational service with No 5 Squadron at RAF Waddington, and flew its first operational sortie in Afghanistan in February 2009.

Since then it has provided a key role in gathering battlefield intelligence for Allied forces. This painting was commissioned to commemorate the 1,000th sortie and 10,000 flying hours of the Sentinel and was presented to No 5 Squadron in December 2012.

In addition to its use in Afghanistan, the Sentinel has been used to support counter insurgency operations in Libya, Mali and Nigeria, as well as monitoring serious flooding in the UK in 2014. The Sentinel also provides the UK's contribution to NATO's Alliance Ground Surveillance programme. In March 2015, the RAF deployed two Sentinel aircraft as part of Operation *Shader* to provide ground surveillance intelligence to coalition forces fighting against Da'ish.

The Sentinel was originally identified in the 2010 Strategic Defence and Security Review for withdrawal from service once its support to operations in Afghanistan was complete. However, the continued success of the aircraft has led to this decision being re-visited and it is currently expected to remain in RAF service until at least 2021.

FRENCH

Chinooks Over Al Faw, 2003

Charles McHugh

In Gulf War II (the 2003 invasion of Iraq) the Al Faw Peninusla, with the Port of Umm Qasr and its oil pumping station, was a key strategic target for the Allied forces. The aim of securing the oil installations was to prevent the risk of sabotage by the retreating Iraqi Army, creating an environmental disaster in retaliation for the invasion of the country by Coalition forces.

The safety and security of the facility was assured in the early hours of the conflict by the insertion of British, American and Polish forces, attached to 3 Commando Brigade. The UK component comprised Royal Marines from 40 Commando who were airlifted by RAF Chinook helicopters of No 18 Squadron operating from Forward Operating Base (FOB) Viking. The image depicts Chinooks departing the area to pick up more troops and supplies, dwarfed by the massive communications antenna at the station.

The original order for Boeing CH-47 Chinook heavy lift helicopter, to replace the Bristol Belevedere in RAF service, was placed in 1967 but cancelled in the Defence Review later that year. An order for 30 HC Mk 1 aircraft was placed in 1978 and these entered RAF service in December 1980, with a follow-on order for an additional eight aircraft delivered from 1984. RAF HC1s were returned to Boeing for upgrade to HC2 standard, with the first returning in 1993 with additional aircraft including upgraded Mk 2As ordered. In December 2008, a programme to upgrade 46 HC2/2A and Mk 3s to an HC4/5 standard was started. An additional order of a further fourteen HC6 was completed in December 2015.

The RAF's Chinook fleet comprises Nos 7, 18 and 27 Squadrons and forms part of Joint Helicopter Command, based at RAF Odiham. The Squadrons provide heavy lift logistical support and transport, and have seen extensive service in combat and peace keeping operations, including the Falklands, Northern Ireland, the Balkans, Iraq and Afghanistan.

No Hiding Place, Canberra PR9

Mark Bromley

While the RAF retired the last of its Canberra bombers in 1972, it continued its operational use for a further 34 years. This was mainly in Photo Reconnaissance duties, with Squadrons equipped with the much modified PR7 and PR9 variant. UK based aircraft were operated from bases at RAF Wyton and finally RAF Marham.

Amongst many other new sensors, including infra-red line scan systems for low level night flying, the PR9s were fitted with special Long-Range Optical Photography (LOROP) cameras. These were capable of producing images of amazing quality and detail from altitudes between 49,000ft and 51,000ft. Although precise details of these cameras have not been made public, photographs of the clock face of Big Ben's tower taken from an aircraft flying over the Isle of Wight give an indication of their performance.

In addition to their use during the Cold War, in July 1972 the RAF used PR Canberras to search for hidden arms' dumps during the Army's Operation *Motorman* to retake 'no go' areas in Northern Ireland. Following the end of the Cold War, the Canberras were used during the conflicts in the Bosnia and Kosovo Wars in the Balkans as well as the First Congo War in Africa, during the 1990s.

In its final years the PR9 variant, as shown in this painting of No 39 Squadron's XH131, saw service during the 2003 invasion of Iraq in Operation *Telic* and in support of Operation *Herrick* in Afghanistan until July 2006. This aircraft was one of the last three Canberras flying with No 39 Squadron, which finally retired in July 2006 concluding an eventful 55 year service life with the RAF.

AA
XH131
BROMLEY

Typhoons Over Omar Oil Fields

Michael Rondot

Depicted here are a pair of heavily armed Typhoons, carrying Paveway IVs, Litening III laser targeting and reconnaissance pod, AIM-120 Advanced Medium Range Air to Air Missile (AMRAAM) and AIM 132 Advanced Short Range Air to Air Missiles (ASRAAM). In the background, smoke drifts from a strike on a target within the Omar oilfields complex.

Following a period of initial support at BAE Systems Warton under the *Case White* programme, RAF Eurofighter Typhoons moved to RAF Coningsby and in May 2005 entered RAF service with No 17 Squadron, the Operational Evaluation Unit. The first operational squadron was No 3, and it formed in March 2006. Currently the Typhoon serves with Nos 1, 2 and 6 Squadrons at RAF Lossiemouth, and Nos 3 and 11 Squadrons at RAF Coningsby, alongside the Typhoon Operational Conversion Unit, No 29 Squadron, and No 41 Test and Evaluation Squadron. In addition, Typhoons also serve with No 1435 Flight at RAF Mount Pleasant in the Falkland Islands.

The Typhoon undertook its first combat missions in April 2011 during Operation *Ellamy*, which was the UK's contribution to the NATO led 2011 military intervention in Libya.

The first operational missions flown by the RAF's enhanced Tranche 2 Typhoons were in support of Operation *Shader*, which is the UK's military contribution to the fight against Da'ish in Iraq and Syria. In December 2015, Typhoon aircraft with engineering and ground support deployed to RAF Akrotiri and immediately commenced air interdiction and Close Air Support (CAS) missions, striking the Omar oilfield in Syria on 4 December with Paveway IV 500 lb precision guided bombs. Since that first strike Typhoons have been in action on a regular basis, attacking targets with precision guided munitions by day and night.

The Typhoon has achieved over 10,000 flying hours supporting Operation *Shader*, with 100 per cent mission support rate, and delivered more than 450 Paveway IV LGBs. In the last two years, all five Typhoon front-line squadrons have supported Operation *Shader*.

Sea King off the Bell Rock

Anthony Cowland

This main panel from the RAF Club's Triptych depicts the RAF's Westland Sea King HAR 3 undertaking its Search and Rescue (SAR) role, operating in conjunction with a Nimrod MR2 that can be seen in the background. On the horizon an ever watchful Tornado flashes by, heading home to RAF Leuchars. The scene is set in the Firth of Tay, near the Bell Rock Lighthouse that was such a familiar feature to generations of aircrew based in Scotland. The pilot is in a single person liferaft which would have been part of his personal escape equipment, ejected with him from his aircraft.

The Westland WS-61 Sea King was a UK licence-built version of the Sikorsky S-61, built by Westland Helicopters in Yeovil. The aircraft differs considerably from the American version, with Rolls-Royce Gnome engines, British anti-submarine warfare systems and a fully computerised flight control system. The HAR 3 version was introduced into service by No 202 Squadron in 1978 and represented a major change in RAF SAR capabilities over the earlier Wessex's, being a truly long range, all weather aircraft that had an unrefuelled operating radius of 300 miles. The electronics systems fit provided both navigational accuracy and the ability to hover over the sea at night. With the move to a civilian contractor service, the RAF Sea King fleet was retired in March 2016.

The Nimrod MR2 was an upgrade of the earlier MR1 variant and entered service in 1979. From the very start of its service it was a crucial link in SAR operations, capable of searching an area of up to 20,000 square miles. Having located survivors it then acted as the 'at scene' rescue co-ordinator, in conjunction with the Aeronautical Rescue Co-ordination Centre (ARCC) which was based at RAF Kinloss until 2016. The Nimrod could also carry two sets of the 'Lindholme Gear' in its bomb bay, to be dropped near people in the sea. This was an air dropped inflatable dinghy that also contained survival equipment.

ROYAL AIR FORCE
RESCUE
XZ589
E
RAF
RESCUE

CHAPTER XI

CONSISTENT VALUES

"Don't listen to anyone who tells you that you can't do this or that. That's nonsense. ... have a go at everything. Go to school, join in all the games you can. Go anywhere you want. But never, never let them persuade you that things are too difficult or impossible."

DOUGLAS BADER

SINCE its inception, the RAF has embraced excellence, ability, innovation, technology and the importance of its people. It has fulfilled, in every respect, the aspirations and foresight of its founding fathers. Its record of service is exemplary and its family of charities and support organisations reflect the high regard it is held in the hearts of the public.

The first contact most people have with the RAF is probably either through a visit to one of the two RAF Museum sites or at an air show, The RAF maintains a number of display teams that inspire spectators in Britain and, in some cases, around the world. The teams currently displaying comprise the Chinook helicopter, parachute instructors forming the Falcons Team, Tutor representing elementary flying training, the Typhoon representing the ultimate fast-jet and, the two most famous of all, the Battle of Britain Memorial Flight (BBMF) and the Red Arrows. All these interfaces with the public instil a sense of 'air mindedness' which cannot be gleaned from books, or other media.

For any organisation to flourish and secure its future it must have a solid connection with the young. The RAF has achieved this, against mounting pressures, since the founding of the Air Cadets and the University Air Squadrons.

The cadets owe their origin to Air Cdre J A Chamier who had served in the Army, RFC and RAF. He was fascinated by aviation and was determined to help the public become more aware of the RAF and its essential contribution to any future conflict. His aim was to encourage young people to consider a career in aviation by establishing an air cadet corps. With training during World War I having been so limited, he was convinced that, the sooner training began, the better prepared and experienced a person would be in combat. Therefore, in 1938, with World War II looming, the Air Defence Cadet Corps (ADCC) was formed. With high demand for places, Squadrons were established in many towns across Britain and each prepared cadets for joining the RAF or FAA. By the end of 1940, the government had recognised the value of the ADCC and took control of and reorganised it. The re-named Air Training Corps (ATC), with King George VI as its Air Commodore-in-Chief, was established in February 1941. During the war, cadets worked on RAF stations and undertook many vital tasks, such as carrying messages, moving aircraft and filling sandbags. Some older cadets even accompanied Air Transport Auxiliary ferry pilots on delivery flights to help in aircraft that demanded more than one pair of hands. By the end of the war almost 100,000 cadets had joined the RAF.

Officer Training Corps (OTC) units had been established in a number of schools by the Army (since 1859) and, during the 1930s, a number of schools formed Air Sections within their OTCs. During World War II, these OTC Air Sections were absorbed into the ATC. The OTC was renamed as the Combined Cadet Force (CCF) in 1948 and most of the Air Sections became CCF (RAF) units. This structure still exists, with some units having a history significantly longer than the RAF itself.

Girls were able to join the Cadets from the early 1980s and the organisations provide invaluable experiences to young people across the country. Their continuing existence is only possible because of the dedication of their volunteer adult RAFVR(T) members and civilian instructors. One of the key elements of the Cadets is the Air Experience Flights (AEF), which were formed in 1958. With 12 AEF based around the country, mainly at RAF stations, instructors ensure that every cadet gets their annual flying opportunity, including the chance to take control and experience aerobatics. For many years the AEF flew the De Havilland Canada Chipmunk, which was eventually replaced by the Scottish Aviation Bulldog. In turn, the Bulldog has now been succeeded by the Grob Tutor.

Originally formed as a part of the ATC, the University Air Squadrons (UAS) also prepare students at university for a career in the RAF, or in many cases, an entirely different career with a background formed by the ethos and values of the RAF and a lifelong loyalty to the Service. This inspired method of training the future leaders, opinion formers and recipients of a higher education, is much envied around the world and was yet another preparation for World War II. By 1941 there were 23 UAS and today there are 15 providing flying experience, training, sport, leisure and leadership activities for undergraduate students. The majority of recruits to all branches of the RAF have been members of either a UAS or an ATC/CCF Unit.

Flying a military aircraft requires all the same skill sets as a commercial machine, but significant additional expertise is also needed because of the need to operate in considerably more demanding environments. Thus low level flying, aerobatics, weapons delivery and many more facets are added to the military aircrew syllabus. Formation flying and aerobatics are fundamental to every pilot trained in the RAF, and there has been a long tradition of aerobatic displays, starting with the Hendon Pageants between the wars. These were yet another method of instilling 'air mindedness' in the public and they carried on for 17 years during which they were attended by four million people. After the War regular shows were held at Station Open Days and to commemorate the Battle of Britain. During the 1950s and early 60s, a number of teams displayed, such as the Black Arrows with the Hawker Hunter, Red Pelicans with the Percival Jet Provost and the Yellowjacks with the Folland Gnat. On 1 March 1965 the RAF formally established for the first time a Royal Air Force Aerobatic Team (previous teams being associated with specific Commands) which soon became famous around the world as the Red Arrows. Initially based at RAF Fairford, the Red Arrows gave their first public performance at the Biggin Hill Air Fair in 1965. The Gnats flew nearly 1,300 displays before being replaced by the Hawk Advanced Jet Trainer for the 1980 season. In the same year the team adopted the motto 'Éclat', a French word meaning 'excellence'. In 1983, the team moved from its base at RAF Kemble to RAF Scampton, where it operates today.

The Red Arrows have undertaken a number of world tours, where they act as ambassadors for Britain, the RAF and the aircraft industry by supporting exports of the BAE Systems Hawk. They also undertake displays for high profile events in Britain, such as the 2002 flight over London with Concorde to mark Her Majesty The Queen's Golden Jubilee, and the 2012 display for the opening of the Olympic Games, seen by over one billion people around the world.

The 50th season of the Red Arrows was celebrated in 2014, with a special paint scheme on the fin that incorporated both the Gnat and Hawk. Emphasising the team's role as ambassadors, the scheme was revised again for the 2015 season to incorporate a Union Flag inspired design. In 2016, the team undertook a nine-week tour across 17 countries in the Middle East and Asia-Pacific, including a first visit to China.

Similar skills are required to operate precision parachute drops such as those used by Special Forces. No 1 Parachute Training School at Brize Norton is home to a group of senior parachute training instructors who form The RAF Falcons. The Falcons have enjoyed a long and distinguished history as one of the premier display teams in the world. The team was originally formed in 1961 by six instructors from the Parachute Training School when it was based at RAF Abingdon. The team was nicknamed 'The Big 6' as most of the members were shorter than 5ft 6in tall. The team trialled different ways of exiting aircraft, initially jumping from the Blackburn Beverley and Handley Page Hastings. They made their debut display at the Farnborough Air Show in 1961.

The displays performed by 'The Big 6' made them an immediate hit with the public. The demands became so overwhelming that, in 1965, it was decided to increase the size of the team to twelve men. At this point the team was renamed the RAF Falcons, taking the name from a bird of prey which characterised their displays; swift, swooping, elegant and aerobatic in flight.

Within two years of the birth of the Falcons they were setting new records and introducing many exciting innovations into the sport. At the end of the 1966 season the Team started to experiment with formation skydiving. The same year saw the introduction of the helmet mounted camera to film this in-air work.

Display techniques have changed dramatically since the early years. Developments saw the introduction of a close non-contact stack with each parachutist trailing coloured smoke and the coach carrying a flag into very challenging arenas.

The aims of the Falcons have also changed enormously over the decades. In addition to completing displays, there is a requirement for team members to qualify as Military Free Fall Instructors and High Altitude Instructors by the end of their three year tour. During their time on the Falcons, each team member will accumulate 1000 jumps, many of which are on training detachments worldwide. By providing their own unique freefall display, the Falcons remain one of the world's leading free fall display teams and continue to be a major attraction wherever they perform. No 1 Parachute Training School at Brize Norton continues to train all personnel in the UK armed forces who have a requirement to use a parachute.

The Battle of Britain Memorial Flight (BBMF) is based at RAF Coningsby alongside the Eurofighter Typhoons that provide the nation's defence today. The BBMF's Avro Lancaster, Supermarine Spitfires, Hawker Hurricanes and Douglas Dakota provide pleasure to many at displays across the country and are a living memorial to the sacrifices made during World War II.

The BBMF owes its origin to Wg Cdr Peter Thompson DFC, who had flown Hurricanes during the Battle of Britain. By the mid-1950s he was the Station Commander at Biggin Hill where the RAF's last airworthy Hurricane was based; this gave him the idea for an historic flight to keep the Service's greatest Battle Honour commemorated in a suitable way. While authority was given to form the Historic Aircraft Flight (HAF) in 1957, no public funding was available, so all manpower was voluntary. In the same year, the Temperature and Humidity Monitoring (THUM) Flight at RAF Woodvale ceased using the RAF's last three airworthy Supermarine Spitfires and they were allocated to the HAF.

These Spitfires were Photo Reconnaissance (PR) versions, which were not armed, and work to restore three fighter versions was started, with one being completed in time for the HAF to carry out its first commemorative flight for the 1957 Battle of Britain Day when this Spitfire flew with the Hurricane over Westminster Abbey.

The following year the HAF was renamed as the 'Battle of Britain Flight' but, in 1959, both the remaining Spitfire fighter versions were grounded after the annual flypast over London, when one of them suffered a complete engine failure and had to force land in a cricket field.

This left the flight, by now based at Horsham St Faith, with just the original Hurricane and the final PR Spitfire. The flight moved to RAF Coltishall in 1963 and its fortunes began to improve at last when, in 1964, one of the PR Spitfires was returned to the Flight in airworthy condition. The next year Vickers-Armstrong donated another airworthy Spitfire fighter, which was flown to Coltishall by Jeffrey Quill, the test pilot who had been the second person to fly the original Spitfire prototype. Following the filming in 1969 of *The Battle of Britain* movie, the flight was presented with the oldest airworthy type of the Spitfire, which was also a genuine veteran of the conflict. The flight also officially took the name Battle of Britain Memorial Flight (BBMF) in this year. A second Hawker Hurricane joined the BBMF in early 1972 when Hawker Siddeley restored the last one built and presented it to the Flight. The Avro Lancaster joined the BBMF in 1973 when it transferred from RAF Waddington, where it had been maintained by station personnel. Then in 1976, the BBMF moved from Coltishall to its current base at RAF Coningsby.

Following its restoration by apprentices at British Aerospace, one of the PR Spitfires was returned to the flight in 1987. The other PR example was sold to cover the cost of restoring one of the Hurricanes after it was virtually destroyed in a fire following a crash landing in 1991. The Dakota joined the BBMF in 1993 to provide multi piston engine tailwheel handling experience for pilots after the Shackleton retired from service, with further different Spitfire fighter variants joining in 1997 and 2013.

The BBMF commemorated its 60th anniversary in 2017 and demand for appearances by the Flight's aircraft continues to increase. BAE Systems provides support to the BBMF in tribute to both the personnel who flew and maintained these aircraft during World War II, but also to the designers, engineers and workers who built them.

The RAF has its spiritual home in the Church of St Clement Danes in London, where there has been a church on the site for over 1,000 years. The church is mentioned in the Domesday Book (1066) and it was in the care of the Knights Templar for nearly 150 years (1170–1312). Although it avoided damage in the Great Fire of London (1666), it was rebuilt by Christopher Wren in 1681, with the steeple added by James Gibbs in 1719.

The church was gutted by fire from incendiary bombs following an air raid in May 1941, with only the walls and tower left standing. In 1953, the remains were handed over to the Air Council, who launched a worldwide appeal to rebuild the church. Funding swiftly started to come in from both organisations and individuals, with the organ being funded by the recently formed United States Air Force, and within two years restoration began, and the church was re-consecrated in 1958. Whilst St Clement Danes is a church that is in daily use for worship and visitors, its main role is to provide a perpetual reminder of those in Allied Air Forces who gave their lives in War.

With this in mind, there are Books of Remembrance along both sides of the church which contain the names of the men and women who have made this sacrifice: from the days of the Royal Engineers balloonists, through the RFC and RNAS and the entire history of the RAF. Amongst the displays within the church are a number of Queen's Colours and Standards, the names of recipients of the Victoria Cross and the Victoria Tapestry, which remembers London in her finest hour.

In 1972, on the historic site at Hendon, HM The Queen opened the RAF Museum which was, at the time, the most innovative aviation museum in the world. In the intervening years it has grown and now occupies three sites, with another major public museum at RAF Cosford and a storage facility near Stafford. The Museum is one of only a few places where the general public can discover the history, traditions and future plans of the Service.

Also in London is the RAF Club, which was acquired by the RAF in 1919 following a gift made by the first Lord Cowdray who was also responsible for much of the financing of the rebuilding work that was necessary, and which took place between 1919 and 1921. The Club was formally opened by HRH The Duke of York in early 1922, and was also visited by Their Majesties King George V and Queen Mary. This association continues today, with Her Majesty Queen Elizabeth II being the Club's Patron. The Club operated very successfully from the 1920s through to the late 1950s. However, a fall in membership in the early 1960s caused severe financial problems and a working party of serving Officers devised a plan which substantially increased membership during the 1960s.

In the 1980s, the Club managed to acquire the freehold of the building at 128 Piccadilly, and undertook further improvements including the conversion of the basement area into the Running Horse Tavern, named after the public house that stood on the site in the 18th Century. During the 1990s, an extension that provided more bedrooms was opened and a five-year programme to revamp the original bedrooms commenced; the Ballroom and Cowdray Lounge were also refurbished. On 28 June 2012 HM The Queen, The Duke of Edinburgh, and other members of the Royal Family attended the opening of the Bomber Command Memorial in Green Park opposite the Club. Her Majesty, His Royal Highness, and the Royal Family, then attended The Club for a reception and lunch. The Club keeps a permanent watch on the Bomber Command Memorial on behalf of the members of the RAF who are commemorated there. On-going development of the Club continues with a rolling programme of improvements and, in 2017, work started on creating additional bedrooms, a gym and a business centre to open for the centenary of the Club in 2018.

The Club is also home to an outstanding collection of art including paintings, sculptures and squadron heraldic crests that help tell the history of the RAF. The art has been obtained from a number of different sources, with some commissioned by the Club and some purchased. Other works have been donated, or presented. Further examples are on loan from the art collections of individuals and companies.

This book contains one hundred items of this art to tell the story of the RAF and its Club's first one hundred years. Nobody can predict, with any accuracy what the future may hold, but when judged by its past, the RAF can only look forward with optimism and confidence, for its illustrious history as the world's first independent air force has proved its founding principles time and again.

In a speech to the Aero Club of France on 5 November 1908 Wilbur Wright said:

"I confess that in 1901, I said to my brother Orville that man would not fly in fifty years .... Ever since, I have distrusted myself and avoided all predictions."

Colour Presentation, July 2010
Stuart Brown

This painting shows RAF Marham on 18 July 2010 when Her Majesty Queen Elizabeth II presented new colours to the Royal Auxiliary Air Force, and two inaugural standards to No 2623 (East Anglian) Squadron RAuxAF Regiment and No 2620 (County of Norfolk) Squadron RAuxAF Regiment. The significance of the drums is the historical impracticality for armies in the field to erect an altar for their religious services. Drums were laid on the ground as a temporary altar and colours were draped over them; this was called a drum head service. Prior to the presentation of colours they are consecrated and this process requires a similar use of drums to that of a drum head service.

AVM Lord Beaverbrook, Honorary Inspector General, RAuxAF received the Sovereign's Colour for the RAuxAF. The Parade Commander was Gp Capt Gary Bunkell, Inspector RAuxAF. The Sovereign's Colour Bearer was Fg Off Martin Fell RAuxAF; No 2623 Squadron's Standard Bearer was Flt Lt Paul Graham RAuxAF, No 2620 Squadron's Standard Bearer was Flt Lt James Pettit RAuxAF.

Air Experience Chipmunks
Wilf Hardy

This scene shows De Havilland Canada (DHC-1) Chipmunk T10 during its time with No 2 Air Experience Flight (AEF) at Hamble with a trainee getting into the cockpit. No 2 AEF was formed on 8 September 1958 at Hamble and moved to Hurn on 11 December 1978. The Chipmunk was the first aircraft many young people flew in its 40 years of service with the RAF.

The Chipmunk first flew in May 1946 and was intended by the company to be the successor to the De Havilland Tiger Moth, which had been used in great numbers in Canada during World War II as part of the Commonwealth Air Training Plan. Chipmunks were built under licence by the parent company in the UK at their Hatfield and Hawarden sites.

In 1997 two RAF Chipmunks (WP962 and WP833) completed Exercise *Northern Venture* – a circumnavigation of the northern hemisphere through London from London City Airport, the official start point, flying east across the Baltic States and Russia to the Bering Strait, hence across Alaska and Canada to cross the North Atlantic via Greenland, Iceland and the Faroe Islands; the flight lasted 64 days and covered 16,259 miles, visiting 62 airfields en route. This was the first non-Russian air force to fly across Russia from coast to coast, successfully charting an air route for general navigation from Europe to North America across Russia. This also allowed a comparison with the existing route across the North Atlantic, Greenland and Canada. They were also the first Western light aircraft to fly in Russia east of the Ural mountains.

WP962
HARDY

Chipmunk and Bulldog Over Cranwell

Mark Bromley

This painting depicts a De Havilland Canada Chipmunk and a Scottish Aviation Bulldog flying over RAF Cranwell, with College Hall visible in the top centre.

RAF Cranwell was the first Military Air Academy in the world and opened in February 1920. Two years later it was decided that permanent buildings should replace the temporary war-time ones. Although this idea had the backing of the Secretary of State for Air, Sir Samuel Hoare, it took much longer to get Government agreement and funding. In 1929, Hoare gained approval to obtain architects' plans from the Ministry of Works. Along with Hoare, the architect James West visited the Royal Hospital in Chelsea which had been designed by Sir Christopher Wren; the final design for College Hall was influenced by this visit. Construction was completed by September 1933 and it was officially opened in October 1934 by His Royal Highness The Prince of Wales (later King Edward VIII).

Cranwell has a long association with record-breaking and 'firsts', with the pilot of the winning Schneider Trophy flight in 1929 being trained there. Also in 1929, the Fairey Long-range Monoplane made the first non-stop flight to India, with a further non-stop flight to south-west Africa being made in 1933. However, the most famous of all is probably that of the flight of Britain's first jet aircraft, the Gloster Whittle E28/39, in May 1941. Whittle later became the first flight cadet to receive a knighthood.

The College had the distinction of being presented with a Royal Colour by King George VI, becoming the first component of the RAF to receive this honour. Continuing the Royal connection, HRH The Prince of Wales completed his pilot training and graduated in 1971.

Consolidation of training establishments from the 1960s onwards has led to the College broadening the range of Officer candidates and specialisations trained. This has included the Headquarters functions for the University Air Squadrons and the Air Cadets, which both have strong associations with the Chipmunk and Bulldog shown in this painting. In addition, the Central Flying School, which is the parent unit for the Red Arrows, is also now headquartered at Cranwell.

The Bulldogs were built at Scottish Aviation's Prestwick factory and provided valuable service with both UAS and AEFs until 2001.

VII
BROMLEY

The Reds at 50, 2014
Michael Rondot

This painting depicts the Red Arrows during their 50th display season, which was celebrated in 2014. One of the most significant ways in which this anniversary was marked was with a new design on the fin of the team's Hawk aircraft and unveilled at RAF Scampton in February 2014. The new design featured outlines of both the aircraft types the Red Arrows had flown: the Folland Gnat and the Hawk. During that year the Red Arrows flew a number of mixed formations, including with Gnats, and by the end of the season had flown 80 displays in nine countries.

The Hawk was originally designed by Hawker Siddeley to meet a 1964 RAF requirement for an Advanced Jet Trainer to replace the Gnat. Original development was carried out as a private venture and the MoD signed a contract for 175 aircraft in March 1972. The prototype flew in August 1974 and still flies today, with production Hawk T1 aircraft entering RAF service in 1976. The Red Arrows adopted the type in 1979 and the much developed BAE Systems Hawk T Mk 2 is in service at RAF Valley, providing the Advanced Jet Training for the RAF Tornado, Typhoon and F-35 aircraft. A small number of T1 variants remain in service with the RAF including, in addition to the Red Arrows, No 100 Squadron at RAF Leeming.

St Clement Danes

Ken Howard

The Church was designed by Sir Christopher Wren in an elegant neo-classical style; with a tall west tower that rises in stages like a wedding cake. Construction of the church began in 1680 and the steeple on top of the tower was added later by James Gibbs. Gutted during the Blitz, the church was rebuilt and has served as the Central Church of the RAF since its re-opening in 1958.

The floor of the church, of Welsh slate, is inscribed with the badges of over 800 RAF commands, groups, stations, squadrons and other formations. Near the entrance door is a ring of the badges of Commonwealth air forces, surrounding the badge of the RAF.

A memorial to the Polish airmen and squadrons, who fought in the defence of the United Kingdom and the liberation of Europe in the Second World War, is positioned on the floor of the north aisle. Books of Remembrance list the names of all the RAF personnel who have died in service, as well as those American airmen based in the United Kingdom who died during the Second World War. Near the altar are plaques listing the names of RAF, Royal Flying Corps and Royal Naval Air Service personnel awarded the Victoria Cross and the George Cross. In the gallery hang Queen's Colours and Standards which have been replaced, along with standards of several disbanded squadrons (most standards of disbanded squadrons hang in the rotunda of the RAF College Cranwell). Pulpits, pews and chairs in the body of the church have been presented by various people, including past chiefs of the Air Staff, Sir Douglas Bader and the Guinea Pig Club. The armorial achievement of Lord Trenchard is displayed above the main entrance at the west end of the church. The lectern was a gift from the Royal Australian Air Force, the Cross from the Air Training Corps, the altar from the Dutch embassy. The font in the crypt was donated by the Royal Netherlands Air Force. The Paschal Candle was given by the Royal Belgian Air Force.

The earliest records of an organ in St Clement Danes are from 1690, when an organ was installed by Bernard Smith. This went through several rebuildings over the next 250 years, but was finally destroyed in the Second World War. A new organ, situated facing the altar in the gallery, was installed by the builder Harrison and Harrison in 1958. This was a gift from the United States Air Force. The case was made as a replica of the Bernard Smith organ previously destroyed.

Outside the church are a number of statues, including those of Sir Hugh Dowding the Commander in Chief of Fighter Command during the Battle of Britain, and Sir Arthur Harris who led the strategic campaign fought by Bomber Command. There is also a statue of Samuel Johnson, the well-known biographer and political writer of the 1700s, who attended the church.

Ken Howard

CHAPTER XII

INTO THE NEXT CENTURY

"It is not in the stars ... to hold our destiny, but in ourselves."

WILLIAM SHAKESPEARE

IN the hundred years since its foundation the RAF has been both the saviour of the nation and a beacon of innovation. It has been years ahead of almost every other organisation in its use of technology, its treatment of people based on merit, and its lack of any form of ethnic/racial selection was unique in its earliest years. As Trenchard remarked "*We open our ranks widely to all*". When most employers were seeking debentures and fees from trainees the Halton Apprentice Scheme was turning out highly trained young people who were the envy of most industries in the country. To build a military tradition so fast and so solidly took imagination and leadership – traits which are embodied in every member of the Service to this day. For such a young Service, the RAF established its own identity, values, esprit de corps and reputation within the first few years of its creation. During the Battle of Britain it cemented its place in the hearts of the British people forever. Its stoicism and perseverance throughout World War II, right across the world, set a standard of expectation which those who came after found easy to understand and necessary to follow. Their role models had done more than anyone could have expected of them and come through victorious.

The following 40 years of Cold War saw their challenge change as they dealt with the very real possibility that their duties might, ultimately, bring about an apocalypse of nuclear destruction. Still they held their professionalism and purpose and were also deployed to many far-off lands to provide protection or assistance – all the while living up to the reputation set by their predecessors. Even when a task so far away as the Falkland Islands was required of them they not only supported their colleagues in the other Services, but audaciously proved that Britain's projection of air power is very far reaching. As the last quarter of the century commenced, the activities changed again and an agile and flexible approach became so essential with the new conflicts raging in the Middle East and the Balkans. In all instances, and sometimes against huge pressure on equipment and numbers of personnel, the RAF proved up to and usually above the task. Consistently punching above its weight, there is not an air arm in the world that underestimates the Royal Air Force.

So, what of the future after such an auspicious first 100 years? It is not possible to predict such things accurately, but what is certain is that the 'Air Force Spirit' which Trenchard articulated all those years ago, is so strongly embedded in the psyche of each and every person serving, or retired, that future excellence is assured. Things will be very different, of course, but the basic building blocks of the RAF were laid long ago, by master builders of great skill and determination.

As the RAF moves into its second century, it may be, as it has so often been in the past, in the midst of significant changes across all facets of its work. The Typhoon has become a truly multi-role aircraft and is undergoing a programme of continuing upgrades to introduce new capabilities and weapons. A number of these enable it to undertake roles currently performed by the Tornado, which is to be retired from RAF service in 2019.

Complementing the Typhoon Force is the Lockheed Martin Lightning II F-35B, which will be operated by both the RAF and the FAA, in the same way as the Harrier before it. The first Squadron to operate the F-35 has already been stood up and continues the lineage of one of the RAF's most famous numbers, No 617 'The Dambusters'.

In addition, the first Boeing P-8A Poseidons (named after the Greek god of the sea and protector of seafarers) are on order; this will re-create the maritime patrol and anti-submarine warfare capability lost when the Nimrod MRA4 programme was terminated.

In line with its lifelong commitment to new technologies, the RAF is fully engaged with UAVs and, to take this concept even further, it has programmes, such as the BAE Systems *Taranis*, which is exploring the potential for complete Unmanned Combat Air Systems (UCAS). As in the past it also recognises the advantages of sharing the hugely expensive costs of developing such projects by working with allies from across Europe and NATO. Joint projects not only share the costs, but also the intelligence and expertise of the partners involved.

For every person in the RAF who occupies a seat in an aircraft there are 15 who support him or her on the ground. The RAF has never been, and will never be, only about the aircraft it flies and the equipment it uses. It is about the quality of people it attracts, trains, nurtures and supports. From its foundation it brought together a mixture of full-time and reservists and this is still the case today. The sheer variety of tasks undertaken by the RAF mean its workforce must be flexible and possess skills which are equal to or better than those elsewhere. In recent years this need to recruit train and retain the very best people has become, as it was in years past, even more flexible by the re-structuring of Reserve Forces. Alongside their full-time colleagues these people bring their expertise, enthusiasm and training to the exact point where it is most needed.

New plans were announced for Reserve Forces in 2013 which would:

- Increase the Royal Auxiliary Air Force to a target of 1,800 personnel.
- Broaden their geographical footprint with 3 new multi trade Squadrons in Liverpool, Northern Ireland and Wales.
- Restructure and expand roles, with an increase in logistics, RAF Police, intelligence, medical and media capabilities.

The RAF itself has six main areas of focus in the coming years:

- Respond to threats
- Prevent conflict
- Watch the skies
- Deliver aid
- Combat cyber threats
- Work in partnership

This book has attempted to show, through its text and the wonderful selection of works of Art from the RAF Club and BAE Systems collections, how the Service has evolved and performed over its first century. Trenchard said:

"I have laid the foundations for a castle; if nobody builds anything bigger than a cottage on them, it will at least be a very good cottage."

The future of the RAF, after such an eventful and courageous century are proof, if proof were needed, that those foundations are well and truly cemented into the fabric of our national security and the hearts of the people for whom it provides defence in the air.

The Titan Comes Home, Airbus A400M Atlas
Mandy Shepherd

With its distinctive scimitar-shaped, eight-bladed propellers Atlas is intended to replace the RAF's C-130J Hercules in the tactical air transport and special forces' support roles and to complement Voyager and the C-17 Globemaster III in providing air mobility. Predictions are that, in the future, the UK's capability is likely to be more reliant on bulky, heavy, cargoes and humanitarian operations looking to deliver relief rapidly to more remote or desolate regions. With this in mind the Atlas has been built as the ideal means of carrying more than the C130J into landing area which would not suit a C-17.

The Atlas is capable of carrying up to 81,500 lbs of payload. Its cargo hold is optimised for carriage of heavy vehicles, helicopters or cargo pallets along the central cargo area, and troops seated at either side. For combat operations, the aircraft can carry protected vehicles with side armour and top-mounted guns fitted allowing a deploying force to arrive ready to fight. In the humanitarian role, it can deploy a mobile crane or an excavator and large dump truck for clearing earthquake sites. Atlas will often find itself operating from austere or unprepared surfaces and with rudimentary loading vehicles. In these circumstances the air loadmaster can manipulate the landing gear to make the aircraft 'kneel' and 'roll' in order to make load transfers easier and faster, particularly when the aircraft is parked on uneven ground.

One of the most notable differences between Atlas and other turboprop aircraft is that the two propellers on each wing turn in opposite directions (towards each other). This counter-rotation produces a more symmetrical airflow over the wing, which improves lift, aircraft handling, and stability. As well as allowing a reduction in the structural weight of the wing, the arrangement also reduces the adverse yaw in case of an engine failure and gives better control at low speed.

This painting illustrates one of the first Atlas aircraft taking off from RAF Brize Norton following its introduction in to service with No LXX Squadron in 2014.

Heavyweight Arrival, Boeing C-17A Globemaster III
Mandy Shepherd

Because of its short field capability the Globemaster III (C-17) is capable of rapid, strategic delivery of troops and all types of cargo to main operating bases anywhere in the world, and directly to more temporary forward operating bases. The design of the aircraft allows it to carry out high-angle, steep tactical approaches at relatively slow speeds, thus allowing it to operate into small, austere, airfields and onto runways as short as 3,500 ft long and only 90 ft wide. The aircraft can operate into and out of problematic sites such as those surrounded by inhospitable terrain or made difficult by adverse weather conditions. The fully-integrated, electronic flight-deck and the advanced cargo-handling systems allow a basic crew of only two pilots and one Air Loadmaster to operate the aircraft. On the ground, the aircraft can be turned in a very small radius and its four engines are fully reversible, giving it the ability to manoeuvre into and out of restricted parking, or freight-offload areas at undeveloped strips.

Cargo is loaded on to the C-17 through a large rear door that can accommodate military vehicles and palletised cargo. It can carry almost all of the Army's air-transportable, outsize combat equipment, from three Warrior armoured vehicles or 13 Land Rovers, to a Chinook helicopter or three Apache-sized helicopters. It carries all its own role-equipment and can fit centre-line seating, which increases the seating capacity from 54 side-wall seats to 102 seats. The aircraft can also be configured in the Aeromedical Evacuation role to carry a full stretcher fit. The C-17 needs little or no ground support equipment and, if none is available, it can perform a combat off-load where pallets are dropped from the aircraft ramp on to the taxiway or hard-standing.

This painting illustrates a Globemaster III on No 99 Squadron which has been operating the aircraft since 2003 from RAF Brize Norton.

Far From Home

Anthony Cowland

The Airbus A330 was selected by the MoD in January 2004, under the Future Strategic Tanker Aircraft (FSTA) programme, to replace the RAF's VC10 and TriStar aircraft. In March 2008, an agreement was signed to lease 14 aircraft from the Air Tanker consortium, led by Airbus, under a Private Finance Initiative agreement.

The decision to name the aircraft Voyager in RAF service was announced in a ceremony at the Royal International Air Tattoo at RAF Fairford in 2011. The first aircraft arrived at RAF Brize Norton at the end of the same year, started training flights in April the following year and, following completion of certification, began operational flights in May 2013. The RAF's fleet of nine aircraft had been delivered by mid-2014 and are flown from Brize Norton by Nos 10 and 101 Squadrons.

This painting, part of a diptych, by Anthony Cowland, was presented to the RAF Club by Air Tanker. The Voyager is seen providing air-to-air (AAR) refuelling for a pair of Eurofighter Typhoons from No 1 Squadron.

Voyager brings new operational flexibility to the RAF, providing increased reliability and range, and it gives the RAF an enhanced capability in support of troop mobility, the movement of military assets, UK air defence and humanitarian operations. This includes a state-of-the-art AAR capability, supporting the movement of other air assets through AAR trail and towline operations. With a payload of 43 tonnes of freight and 291 seat passenger capacity, plus an aeromedical evacuation capability, Voyager also delivers new flexibility in air mobility to the UK armed forces in support of military or humanitarian operations. One Voyager can also be configured as a VIP aircraft for use by the Royal Family and Ministers.

ROYAL AIR FORCE
ZZ333

Storm Brewing, Lockheed F-35B Lightning II

Mark Bromley

The Lightning II is a 5th Generation short take-off, vertical landing (STOVL) Multi-Role supersonic stealth aircraft which will provide the UK with a hugely capable and flexible weapons and sensor platform for decades to come. It is designed to operate from established land bases, austere strips and the new Queen Elizabeth Class aircraft carriers. The Lightning II will join the Typhoon FGR4 in providing the Combat Air Component of UK defence from 2018.

No 617 (The Dambusters) Squadron reformed in 2018, at RAF Marham, as the first RAF Squadron to be equipped with Lightning aircraft. This painting depicts No 617 Squadron aircraft in front of the Maintenance and Finish Facility at RAF Marham, which is one of a number of new specialist support facilities being constructed at the base, under project *Anvil,* to prepare it for the Lightning II's introduction in to RAF service.

The Lightning II Operational Conversion Unit, which has been operating in the USA, will relocate to RAF Marham in 2019.

BROMLEY

APPENDICES

About The Author

Dr Michael Fopp has had a long and distinguished career in major museums. He has been the Keeper of the Battle of Britain Museum, Director of the London Transport Museum and, for 22 years, Director General of the Royal Air Force Museums. He has been an aviation historian all his adult life teaching the subject in the 1970s and continuing his interest at the RAF Museum. For 10 years he was a visiting lecturer at Masters' level for London City University and President of the International Association of Transport & Communications Museums and the Museums' Documentation Association. He is an expert on the Gloster Meteor and Boeing Washington aircraft, having written books and articles about both. For the 75th anniversary of the RAF he brought distinguished people together to write their reminiscences for the book *High Flyers* and he has edited numerous works covering the history of the Service over the years. He has written for a number of periodicals and magazines including *Aeroplane Monthly, Pilot, Flyer, Flypast, Popular Flying, The Air Pilot* and many international museum journals. He is also a widely published scholar in Museum Studies and Non-Profit Management. Following from his PhD research, his seminal work *Managing Museums & Galleries* is widely used as a standard text around the world. Michael is a qualified commercial pilot with an instrument rating and flew his own aircraft all over the world. In 2010 he was elected Master of the Honourable Company of Air Pilots. He is currently completing the biography of his father who was a Battle of Britain pilot and served a full career in the RAF. Michael is also in great demand as a speaker on historical subjects, not only aviation, but also social and geopolitical history.

Acknowledgements

The gathering together of information, sourcing and choosing works of art, and the general organisation of this project has involved a considerable amount of volunteer time and teamwork. The original working group comprised Wg Cdr Michael Gilbert, Chairman of the RAF Club Art Committee, Dr Michael Fopp, Mandy Shepherd, members of the Art Committee and Gp Capt Tony Banks, Sebastian Cox , Head of Air Historical Branch MOD, John Bulmer in his BAE Systems company heritage role and Howard Mason, BAE Systems Heritage Manager. We were ably supported by Matthew Kent from the RAF Club, and we were an energetic and knowledgeable team with each playing a key role in enabling this book to be produced. Mandy Shepherd's reputation as an artist and her contributions by way of vignettes to the book have been overwhelming. Michael Gilbert and Tony Banks have brought historical knowledge and organisational rigour which can only have been a direct result of their long careers in the RAF, teaching, and service as Trustees of the RAF Club.

In the context of actually writing the book I must single out a number of individuals in addition to the whole team who provided constructive and helpful input at every stage. The basic historical and statistical research for the book was compiled by John Bulmer. His initial texts and the help he received from colleagues, Christopher Chamberlain, Keith Dixon and Malcolm Hill were seminal to the final work and gave the project a timescale which was achievable. Howard Mason lent his considerable organisational talents and the ability to produce important material and photographs in very short spaces of time. Sebastian Cox, was, in modern parlance, 'head of quality control'. Seb, an old friend and colleague, did the final checking and made many helpful suggestions and alterations.

It is also important to recognise the financial and material support from our sponsor BAE Systems, without which we would not have passed the first post. Of course, once written, a book needs to look right and final thanks go to our designer, Mike Brain and publisher, Chris Andrews, for their expert transformation of ideas, images and text into this final form.

This book is, after all, not only a celebration of the RAF's centenary, but also the centenary of the Royal Air Force Club. Both are institutions dear to the hearts of all involved.

Appendix 1: Artists

Martin Balshaw

Martin Balshaw is a serving Qualified Flying Instructor in the RAF. He is a self-taught artist, having followed a scientific, rather than artistic education. He has been a serious painter for more than 20 years and has been a member of Armed Forces Art Society (AFAS) since 1994.

Originally a water colourist, he specialised in military subjects in their operational environments. Gaining recognition, he worked on official commissions for military units and private collectors. However, with a passion for the great outdoors and mountaineering, he diversified into painting wilderness landscapes, which brought him wider recognition.

He uses his qualification as a Joint Service Mountain Leader as an excuse to take his sketch book and camera into the wilds in search of subject matter and inspiration.

Having enjoyed commercial success with his winter mountain landscapes, it was suggested that his work would also suit other mediums. Encouraged by AFAS members, he produced a series of oil paintings based upon his watercolours. Since then he has not looked back, and now paints in both watercolour and oils.

Sir Oswald Birley (1880–1952)

Sir Oswald Birley was born in New Zealand while his parents were on a world tour. He was educated at Harrow School, London and Trinity College, Cambridge. He served in France in World War I, first with the Royal Fusiliers, later transferring to the Intelligence Corps, obtaining the rank of captain and being awarded the Military Cross in 1919. During World War II he served with the rank of major in the Home Guard.

A favourite of the Royal Family, he was well known for his portraits of King George V, Queen Mary, King George VI, Queen Elizabeth the Queen Mother, and Queen Elizabeth II.

He painted several highly regarded portraits of his friend Sir Winston Churchill (to whom he also gave lessons), and many war-time leaders such as Generals Eisenhower, Montgomery and Admiral Mountbatten. He was knighted in 1949.

Mark Bromley

Mark Bromley was born in 1960, in west London. After a fairly average school education, during which his secondary school art teacher's report said, "*he can draw but he can't paint*", he started work in a small precision engineering company. During his year there he put himself through a day release course at Richmond-upon-Thames College, studying Illustration. An opportunity arose at the Hawker site in Richmond Road, Kingston, for which he applied as an apprentice technical illustrator. At the end of the apprenticeship in 1982 Mark joined the Illustration Section in the Technical Publication Department at Kingston. A year later he transferred to the Graphics Department and started to put the airbrush retouching skills learnt at college to good use in creating artwork from scratch. In 1992 the airbrush was replaced with oils and canvas, and a selection of the 300 pieces created since then are reproduced in this book. These are works commissioned by, and a part of, the BAE Systems Collection.

Stuart Brown

Stuart Brown studied Illustration at the Southampton Institute. After graduating he joined a busy commercial design studio producing illustrations for a wide variety of brochures, advertisements and exhibitions. Working full-time with other traditionally skilled artists and designers proved valuable experience. This demanding environment developed the skills necessary to tackle any subject matter, though his passion for military subjects eventually led him to leave the commercial world to focus entirely on commissioned oil paintings.

He developed a style ideally suited to military subjects with a balance of atmosphere and technical accuracy. A series of larger clients, including agencies of the UK MoD, provided a continuous flow of involved and challenging projects over a period of some 15 years. This work tied in well with a passion for aviation and a series of commissioned oil paintings of military and aviation subjects inevitably sparked a new direction for his work. Today, limited edition prints of Brown's work are collected worldwide with original paintings in the collections of HM Forces. He is also a member of a British formation skydiving team; he has over 1,000 jumps and regularly competes at national level.

Kai Choi

No details available from public sources.

Anthony Cowland FGAvA

Anthony Cowland graduated from Brighton College of Art and Design and went into Architecture and Design, working in London and New York. After ten years he became a full time illustrator and, during the subsequent 20 years, has travelled the world for painting commissions.

He believes that first-hand experience, if practical, is important for artists and illustrators. He tackles a wide number of subjects but finds aircraft and automobiles a real challenge. Motorcars are a great interest and restoring vintage cars is one of his many hobbies.

He frequently exhibits his work in London galleries, and has won a number of awards. His work is regularly published in books and magazines as well as limited edition prints. For the past 20 years he has been a War Artist for the British Army and has visited a number of their units at home and abroad. Cowland was recently commissioned, by the RAF Club, to paint the triptych commemorating the cessation of RAF Search & Rescue operations.

Geoffrey Crompton

No details available from public sources.

Roy Cross GAvA

Roy Cross was born in 1924 in Southwark, London and is mainly self-taught. His interest in art began when accompanying his father on walks around the London docks, sketching the boats he had seen when returning home. At the age of 15, he began work for a Thameside shipping office. Here he saw Thames barges and the last of the sailing coasters, and thus in the 1930s was born his lasting love of sea and ships.

After training at the St Martins School of Fine Art, his artistic career became established as an illustrator for journals and books. During World War II he was a technical illustrator for training manuals for Fairey Aviation working on maintenance manuals and pilots' notes, as well as for publications such as *Aeroplane* and *Aviation Week*. He progressed from there to producing advertising art for the aircraft industry and other companies. He also illustrated for the *Eagle* comic.

His detailed drawing of the Gloster Meteor, Britain's first service jet fighter, took him eight weeks to create, was a yard in length, and became acknowledged as a masterpiece of this specialised branch of technical illustration. It is probably his work at *Airfix* for which he is best known. He started in 1964 with box art for Airfix's Dornier Do 217 and his last work for them was the box art for the German heavy cruiser *Prinz Eugen* in 1974. Much of the *Airfix* artwork was destroyed but the lids of many millions of boxes remain.

Eric H Day

Very little can be discovered about Eric Day except that he was quite an eccentric man who worked out of a rather chaotic studio in Market Rasen, Lincolnshire; a location surrounded by RAF stations during his lifetime. He was popular with the RAF for his passionate and expressive depictions of aircraft and ground scenes. Many of his paintings were hung in RAF Messes, but it is not clear how many have survived. Eric Day died in 1995.

Patrick Donovan RSMA

Patrick Donovan specialises in marine and military subjects using watercolour, acrylic, pen, ink, and pencil. He started full-time work as an artist in 1990. He lives near Dover and finds inspiration in watching the ever-changing panorama and shipping on both sides of the Channel. He devotes great effort to research for both historical and modern subjects in order to be as technically accurate as possible. Preparatory work finds him searching archives or armed with a sketchbook and camera on board a variety of coastal and deep-sea craft, including lifeboats and pilot cutters.

Penelope Douglas VPGAvA

Penelope Douglas started painting in Norfolk and was well established as an artist of landscapes and animal portraits, when commissioned for her first aircraft painting.

She works in both oils & water colours, specialising in aviation subjects, with many commissions from the Armed Forces, taking her to a variety of countries for her paintings, including Europe, RAF Masirah, RAF Gan, Ascension Island, the Far East, United States of America, Australia, & Kenya with the SAS. She is a Vice President, Full & Founder Member of The Guild of Aviation Artists with whom she exhibits annually.

She published, *So Many Bridges* in 2000, the story of the 'ups & downs' and privilege of working with the Armed Forces when getting the material for painting commissions.

Alan Fearnley GAvA

Alan Fearnley was born in Yorkshire in 1942, and studied at Batley College of Art. After several years as a commercial studio illustrator he became a full-time self employed artist in 1974. His early works established him as an artist of talent and quality. Over the past 30 or so years he has built up a wealth of subject matter, starting with landscapes and moving later into his well known transport and motor racing paintings. His work reflects not only his artistic skill, but also his love and passion for both motoring and motor sport. He is a member of the Guild of Aviation Artists, has been awarded the B.A.C. Trophy and Qantas Trophy for aviation paintings, and a member and chairman of the Guild of Railway Artists. He has also exhibited with the Royal Society of Marine Artists and the Royal Institute of Oil Painters and had a series of one man shows in London and Monaco.

Denis Quentin Fildes (1889–1975)

Fildes joined the Royal Navy in 1906 and was a midshipman. In 1912, as a lieutenant, he joined the cruiser *HMS Natal* and was serving in her when war was declared with Germany in 1914. On 30 December 1915 she was lying in Cromarty Firth and Fildes was officer of the watch during an afternoon party for local children. The ship blew up and sank causing great loss of life. Fildes was badly burned but survived. In March 1916 he was back in service and continued in the Royal Navy rising to the rank of lieutenant commander in the battle cruiser *HMAS Australia* in 1922. He was then retired with a disability pension, but during the Second World War served as port officer at Harwich and Suez. In civilian life he followed his father, Sir Luke Fildes' profession as a portrait painter. One of his commissions was a full-length portrait of Queen Elizabeth II and Prince Philip for the Royal Naval College at Greenwich. He also made a number of portraits of HM The Queen following her coronation in 1953. The original of the portrait in the RAF Club is owned by the Royal College of Defence Studies and the artist's copy was commissioned for the Club in 1961.

Neil Foggo GAvA

Neil Foggo is a member of the Guild of Aviation Artists and has twice won the Westland Trophy for rotary wing aircraft at their annual exhibition. He is self-taught and focuses mainly on aviation. His work hangs in numerous UK and Commonwealth Service Establishments and private collections. A 33 year career in the RAF, retiring as a Squadron Leader Air Electronics Officer, has infused his aviation compositions with authenticity and life.

Chris French GAvA

Chris French lives in Essex and works predominantly in oils. He specialises in aviation subjects but has been commissioned to cover many other topics including military, naval, automotive, animals, portraits and landscapes. Clients for his work include major companies, the RAF, British Army and Royal Navy as well as private collectors.

He has exhibited aviation paintings at the RAF Museums at Hendon and Cosford, the Fleet Air Arm Museum and various other museums and galleries including the US Air Force Museum in Dayton, Ohio. Chris has won awards in the UK and US for his aviation art including the prestigious Guild of Aviation Artists' 'Aviation Painting of the Year' award. He likes to research his subjects thoroughly and create images that are more than just a representation of the subject.

Harold Garland

Harold Garland is a painter of marine and aviation subjects. There are six of his paintings in the National Collection.

Mal Grossé

Mal Grossé was born in Lancaster and was educated at the Royal Grammar School before joining the RAF in 1962. During the next 27 years, as a pilot, he flew Hunters, Buccaneers and the Tornado, served four years in the Middle East, and attended the Royal Australian Air Force Staff College. He was awarded the Queen's Commendation and the Air Force Cross, retiring in 1988 as a Wg Cdr. Grossé then joined BAe with responsibility for Eurofighter Typhoon marketing, spending his last four years in Australia as Vice President of the Typhoon sales campaign in Australia. Giving up full time work in 2000, he has maintained his aviation passion through oil painting, diversifying with other subjects such as flora and human form. His works now hang worldwide.

Alex Hamilton GAvA

Alex Hamilton was born in Croydon in 1956, and even though he was fairly proficient in art as a school boy, he was actively discouraged by his school careers master. However, his art master had encouraged him to go on to Art College. He applied to Hornsey College of Art for a one year foundation course, but that did not work out and he went through a series of jobs until his old art master suggested a job at an advertising studio in London. After seeing the work they did, he joined them as a junior and started what would become a worthwhile and challenging career.

He continued to work in commercial illustration, and painted in his spare time. In 2003 small commissions started to come his way and there came a point when the two disciplines were conflicting so he decided to become a professional aviation artist.

He has worked for private individuals and some large companies, but he finds working for active service squadrons an honour and a pleasure. He particularly enjoys talking to the aircrew about the painting they want, and their reaction to the finished thing.

George Harcourt RA (1868–1947)

George Harcourt was born in Dunbarton, Scotland. He studied at the Herkomer School of Art, Bushey, and subsequently became an assistant teacher there. He exhibited at the Royal Academy from 1893. He was appointed a Royal Academician (RA) in 1926. He was also well-known abroad, winning medals at the Paris Salons and the Amsterdam International Exhibition.

In 1945 he was elected president of the Royal Society of Portrait Painters. Harcourt was described as so 'naturally retiring' that neighbours were unaware of his artistic distinctions, nevertheless to friends 'his wit was proverbial', expressed in 'caustic, yet exceptionally humorous remarks'.

Wilfred Hardy GAvA (1938–2016)

Wilf Hardy was born in Brentford, West London and contributed many painted pages to *Treasure*, *Look and Learn* and *Speed and Power* magazines. He specialised in painting aircraft and is remembered for his many illustrations, for RAF Museum philatelic flown covers, evocative book covers and posters, for many major air shows.

Elizabeth Lucas Harrison (1923–2016)

Elizabeth Harrison was born in Düsseldorf in 1923 and moved to Belgium in 1933 when Hitler rose to power. She evaded arrest in France in the 1940s, moved to Southern Africa in 1947 and settled in London in 1968. During World War II she was actively involved with the Resistance, serving as a courier carrying messages to Lyon and assisting in distributing air-dropped supplies. After liberation, she worked in a hospital caring for injured troops and German and French civilians, later working for the American Red Cross in the Civilian War Relief department. She was Secretary of the RAF Escaping Society (RAFES) for 18 years from 1978 and was responsible for keeping it going until its 50th anniversary in 1995 and as a charity until 2000.

She was awarded an MBE in 1996 for her work with the Escape Lines Memorial Society, as a founding member and long-standing committee member, for her RAF Escaping Society plaque and for three tandem parachute jumps that she braved in her mid-seventies to raise money for RAFES and two other charities. She was also decorated by the Belgian Red Cross.

A formidable poet and a talented sculptor, Harrison designed the Valençay SOE Memorial, a 30ft monument dedicated to those members of 'F' Section of the Special Operations Executive (SOE) who lost their lives in France.

William John 'Bill' Hooper (1916–1996)

Bill Hooper was educated at a boarding school in Kent. After school he was sent to work as a laboratory assistant in a Windsor medical clinic. This introduction to science led him to begin a degree in metallurgy at Imperial College , London. However, he dropped out of university after just two terms. Hooper then went to Ireland to work as an armed bodyguard, before eking out a living as a painter.

At the start of World War II he joined the RAF as an air gunner, but was soon transferred to ground staff. During the war he met Anthony Armstrong, editor of the training manual, *Tee Emm*, and together they created the character of PO Prune as a way of instructing wartime pilots what not to do if they wanted to save their lives and their aircraft.

In the post-war years, Hooper and Armstrong produced a number of successful books. Hooper worked as political cartoonist for the *Sunday Chronicle* , and later for the BBC as presenter of the series *Willy the Pup*. He also formed a studio of artists to create animations for BBC programmes. He produced a strip cartoon for *The Star* newspaper before returning to television as, first, an artist and later a presenter. He was also worked for several years as a columnist for the *Sunday Pictorial.*

Hooper's comprehensive collection of cartoons and incredibly detailed puppets of all his 'Prune' characters was acquired by the RAF Museum shortly before his death in 1996.

Professor Kenneth Howard OBE RA

Ken Howard was born in London in 1932. He studied at the Hornsey College of Art and the Royal College of Art. In 1958 he won a British Council Scholarship to Florence. He spent his National Service in the Royal Marines. In 1973 and 1978 he was the Official War Artist to Northern Ireland, and between 1973 and 1980 worked in various locations, including Hong Kong, Cyprus and Canada with the British Army. In 1998 he became President of the New English Art Club, a post he held until 2003. In 1991 he was elected a Royal Academician.

His work is in a number of public collections including the National Army Museum, Guildhall Art Gallery, Ulster Museum and Imperial War Museum. Howard was appointed OBE in the 2010 Birthday Honours.

Ron Lackenby

No details available from public sources.

Sir John Lavery RA (1856–1941)

Sir John Lavery attended Haldane Academy in Glasgow in the 1870s and the Académie Julian in Paris in the early 1880s. He returned to Glasgow and was associated with the Glasgow School. In 1888 he was commissioned to paint the state visit of Queen Victoria to the Glasgow International Exhibition. This launched his career as a society painter and he moved to London soon after. Lavery was appointed an official artist in World War I. Ill health prevented him from travelling to the Western Front. A serious car crash during a Zeppelin bombing raid also kept him from fulfilling his role as a war artist. He remained in Britain and mostly painted boats, aeroplanes and airships.

Trevor Lay

Trevor Lay was born in Birmingham and still lives in the West Midlands. He has exhibited throughout the Midlands over many years and has a reputation for his atmospheric aviation art. A self taught artist mainly in oils, he was a co-founder of the Saracen Art Group in 1975. In 1978 he founded another art group called 'Artco' touring with another artist, in the Midlands during 1983. Several other exhibitions and one-man shows followed, until in 1992 he turned professional, concentrating on aviation art. In more recent years he has put his talents into landscape and abstract painting.

Roy Layzell

No details available from public sources.

Fred May (1891–1976)

Fred May was a famous caricaturist and painter. Most of his work was done with pencil, brush, ink and white heightening. His earliest drawings were produced for the *North Eastern Daily Gazette* and his first cartoons for the *Tatler* were sent home in 1917 from the trenches where he was serving as an infantry officer. He continued to work for the *Tatler* until his death in 1976. The National Portrait Gallery has 22 of his caricature portraits in its collection, most of famous or distinguished people, including Neville Chamberlain done in 1935.

Charles McHugh

Charles McHugh was born in Whiston, Lancashire in 1959. At 13 years old, he joined the Air Training Corps and was flying gliders solo at age 16. He joined the RAF – initially in Air Traffic Control, and later flying as a Helicopter Crewman reaching CFS (Central Flying School) A2 flying instructor standard on several helicopter types. He retired from the RAF in 2014 after a 37 year career in which he accumulated 6000 flying hours, mainly in the low level environment. Following his retirement his artwork became a financially self-sustaining hobby, that developed and improved over a long apprenticeship. Whilst he received no formal art training he studied many academic aspects of art, developing his own natural aptitude for drawing and painting. He is passionate about ensuring that aircraft, aircrew, and groundcrew, receive the credit they deserve.

Captain Cuthbert Julian Orde (1888–1968)

Cuthbert Orde served throughout World War I and qualified as a pilot for the Royal Flying Corps in a Maurice Farman biplane in May 1916. He was given the rank of temporary major in 1918, but relinquished his commission in 1919 on grounds of ill health, retaining the rank of captain.

Throughout his life Orde strongly identified himself as an artist. In the early 1920s he had a painting studio in Paris. Having been hired to produce illustrations of bomber stations in the summer of 1940, his mastery of portraiture was recognised by the Air Ministry when, at the height of the Battle of Britain with public attention focused on the fighter pilots, he was asked to make a large number of portraits of them. It is unclear how many portraits he drew in the year or so with Fighter Command. Some sources say up to 300, though Orde only lists 160 in his book *Pilots Of Fighter Command.*

The daily peril of these men's lives was apparent. Orde stated that some of his choices for subjects of his work were killed before he had chance to draw them. Many did not live much longer after their portrait was done. However, having flown in combat himself and lost both his brothers in military incidents 20 years earlier, the proximity of death would not have been new to him.

Orde remained a professional artist, and was still taking commissions for military portraits long after the war, such as the one of MRAF Sir John Salmond. He was an inaugural painter-member of the Society of Aviation Artists, formed in 1955.

Major Sir William Newenham Montague Orpen, KBE, RA, RHA (1878–1931)

Sir William Orpen, was an Irish artist who worked mainly in London. He was a fine draughtsman and a popular, commercially successful, painter of portraits for the well-to-do in Edwardian society, though many of his most striking paintings are self-portraits.

During World War I, he was the most prolific of the official artists sent by Britain to the Western Front. There he produced drawings and paintings of ordinary soldiers, dead men, and German prisoners of war, as well as portraits of generals and politicians. Most of these works, 138 in all, he donated to the British government and they are now in the collection of the Imperial War Museum. His connections to the senior ranks of the British Army allowed him to stay in France longer than any of the other official war artists, and although he was made a Knight Commander of the Order of the British Empire in 1918, and also elected a member of the Royal Academy of Arts, his determination to serve as a war artist cost him both his health and his social standing in Britain.

After his early death a number of critics, including other artists, were loudly dismissive of his work and for many years his paintings were rarely exhibited, a situation that only began to change in the 1980s. Today he is a highly regarded war artist and portrait painter whose prolific studies of war have given greater depth to World War I than would have been possible had he not been so determined to record what he saw.

Michael Rondot

Michael Rondot was born in Ontario, Canada but has lived in the UK since the mid-1950s. He developed a lifelong interest in military aircraft that led eventually to his 25 year career as a reconnaissance and ground-attack pilot in the RAF.

He flew the Canberra PR9 and Hunter before joining his first Jaguar squadron in 1980. He flew combat operations in Jaguar fighter-bombers during the first Gulf War in 1991 and retired from the RAF in 1992.

He has been painting professionally for over 40 years, publishing his first limited edition print of a Hawker Hunter FGA9 in 1980.

His work encompasses every type of aircraft from modern combat jets to World War II aircraft, airliners and helicopters. He also includes unlikely subjects such as armoured fighting vehicles and trucks. Above all, he is widely acclaimed for producing powerful and atmospheric images of aircraft in the wet weather conditions that prevail in north-west Europe. The wet runway scenes that feature in many of his early works have given way to a more subtle view of the kind of weather he flew in for much of his flying career but there remains a strong leaning towards impressive storm clouds and threatening weather. He was a member of the RAF Club Arts Committee until 2016.

David Shepherd CBE VPGAvA (1931–2017)

David Shepherd was one of the world's most outspoken conservationists. He was most famous for his paintings of aircraft, steam locomotives, wildlife, portraits (notably HM The Queen Mother) and landscapes. His work has been extremely popular since the 1960s in limited edition print reproduction and poster form, as well as other media. He published five books about his art, including an autobiography.

Shepherd was born in Hendon and won a children's painting competition when he was eight years old. He then attended Stowe School. Upon leaving school he travelled to Kenya with the hope of becoming a game warden, but was rejected as having "*no talent whatsoever*". He returned to the UK but was rejected by the Slade School of Fine Art in London. However, he was taken on by the artist Robin Goodwin (1909–1997) who trained him for three years.

In the years following his training he began painting aviation pictures. The subject was a natural for him, rooted in his boyhood. He was eight years old when World War II began and had lived in London during the Blitz. To paint aviation subjects he obtained a permit which gave him access to Heathrow Airport. He was allowed to wander wherever he chose and was able to capture some wonderful images of the daily life of a busy airport. In 1960 the RAF flew him to Kenya as their guest. He was asked to paint 'local things like elephants' and his first wildlife painting was of an aircraft taking off with a charging Rhino in the foreground. He charged the RAF £25, including the frame, for his very first wildlife painting. That original now hangs in the RAF Club. Shepherd's paintings of elephants and wildlife brought him international fame, but during that same visit to Kenya he found a waterhole poisoned by poachers, around which were lying 255 dead zebra. He realised that, through his paintings, he could repay his debt to the wildlife that had brought him such success. Throughout his subsequent life he raised more than £3 million towards helping to save critically endangered mammals in the wild.

Mandy Shepherd

Mandy Shepherd is a painter of Military and Wildlife. It was the wildlife of the Falklands, in the aftermath of 1982, that took her to the South Atlantic courtesy of the RAF from Brize Norton. Her mission was to research and illustrate a book about the Wildlife and Way of Life in the Islands.

On arrival at Mount Pleasant she was shown around and invited to sketch the various aircraft and personnel serving at the base. This one moment changed the direction of her career and various contacts led to the build-up of an exciting military portfolio and working with all three Services. She has also worked in Iraq, Afghanistan, Oman, Brunei, Bosnia and other locations. She enjoys recording regimental and Squadron history and has captured military hardware at its birth and retirement. Mandy enjoys the challenges of working with people, ships, vehicles and aircraft and most recently has also worked with Special Forces. She is a member of the Arts Committee of the RAF Club.

Solomon Joseph Solomon (1860–1927)

Solomon Solomon was a considerable talent not only in portraiture, but also in the development of camouflage. He had connections with the City of London, painting a large mural for The Royal Exchange. With regard to his work in this book, he may well have been known by the sitter's father, A. Herbert Morgan, who had premises close to the Royal Exchange and was influential in The City. Solomon pioneered camouflage techniques having signed up at the beginning of the War in The Artists Rifles. He so impressed senior officers with his ideas that General Haig instructed that he be given the temporary rank of Lt Colonel in order that he could command what eventually became a full-blown camouflage school based in London's Hyde Park.

Roger Steel

No details available from public sources.

Michael Turner P&FGAvA

Michael Turner was born in Harrow, Middlesex, in 1934. Raised in the suburbs of London during World War II, he was inspired by the exploits of the RAF and developed an early talent for aircraft recognition, drawing aeroplanes in his school exercise books to the chagrin of his teachers. This enthusiasm for aviation found a parallel passion in the thrill of motor racing after a holiday visit to the Isle of Man in 1947, where he chanced to see the first post-war revival of the British Empire Trophy Race. Michael spent a year at Art College followed by two years National Service with the Royal Electrical and Mechanical Engineers. Three years in an advertising studio in London provided valuable experience and in 1957 he went freelance. With a strong belief that there is no substitute for first hand involvement in order to portray such demanding subjects with authority and feeling, he has travelled extensively to the world's major race tracks and has flown in many service aircraft, from Tiger Moth and Lancaster to Harrier and Tornado. He has also flown aerobatic sorties with the Red Arrows to gain first hand impressions for his aviation paintings. Turner also holds a Private Pilot's Licence and flies his own Chipmunk aircraft.

Ronald Wong FGAvA

Ronald Wong's original training was in biochemistry, and it was only after years of working in the NHS that he decided to divert to a career in painting, in particular his childhood passion for aircraft. He developed his own style as a self-taught artist, combining technical accuracy and realism with imagination, colour and atmosphere.

He works independently, unattached to promotional galleries or commercial publishers, preferring instead to preserve his freedom to work from commissions and, usually, directly with the aircrew who are the inspiration behind so many of his works. Aside from the hundreds of paintings he has made over the years, he has also published more than 220 editions of lithographic prints. Apart from aviation, his artistic interests range widely from motoring and marine art, to portraiture, animals and landscapes.

Keith Woodcock GAvA

Keith Woodcock initially trained and qualified as a design engineer. He opted to fulfil his ultimate aspirations of becoming a full time professional artist in 1982, but restricted his choice of subjects to aviation and motoring. This was a deliberate decision rooted in a determination to utilise the knowledge gained during his 26 years of varied employment in the engineering industry and a lifelong enthusiasm for aircraft and cars.

Since that time he has acquired an impressive reputation with solo exhibitions in both the UK and USA plus participation in regular group shows in Germany, France, Italy, Canada and the Channel Islands winning 18 awards including the premier trophies at international exhibitions on both sides of the Atlantic. He has now completed over 2000 paintings, many of which hang in the collections of, companies, organisations and individuals worldwide.

Frank Wootton OBE FPGAvA (1911–1998)

Frank Wootton attended art school in 1928 at the age of 17, winning a travel scholarship and a gold medal from the Eastbourne School of Art and a prize of £25, which he used to fund a three-month trip to Germany, painting murals. In the 1930s, he was commissioned by Edward Saunders to do art and book illustrations. In this time he wrote several books on art instruction, one of which, *How to Draw Aircraft*, became a best-seller. In 1939, he volunteered for the RAF but instead was invited to accept a special duty commission as official war artist to the RAF and RCAF. He painted RAF subjects from England, France and Belgium before travelling to south-east Asia at the end of World War II. Most of his wartime work was done, balanced on his knee, in the field, using minimal materials and, often, aviation fuel to thin his oils. It is for this work advancing the field of aviation art, that Wootton is recognised as one of the finest aviation artist of all time. His other interests were in equestrian and landscape subjects.

John Young GAvA (1930–2015)

John Young was born in Bristol, England in 1930. His love affair with aviation began after a visit to Sir Alan Cobham's National Aviation Day air show in a farmer's pasture near his home in Chesham. Watching US Eighth Air Force B-17s and B-24s operate out of nearby Bovingdon during World War II further fuelled his interest in historic aviation. He painted professionally from 1950 gaining his technical knowledge during service in the RAF. In 1960, after having established a career in illustration for many aviation manufacturers, airlines, air forces, and publishers, he went freelance to further develop his talents and move towards the world of fine art. In the early 1980s he received a commission for 45 paintings by the RAF Museum to illustrate a set of the Museum's first day covers and countless other works by him are in private and corporate collections in the US and UK.

Appendix 2: BAE Systems Timeline

The Air sector of BAE Systems can trace its history back to the advent of flight in the UK, with the pioneer companies being formed at the end of the first decade of the 20th century. Fifty years later, the industry consolidated into two major groupings in order to more effectively support major contracts. A further consolidation took place at the time of nationalisation in 1977 when British Aerospace was formed, and BAE Systems took the industry into the new century after the merger of Marconi Electronic Systems. This timeline illustrates the principal mergers and the many famous names that are today counted as the predecessors of the aviation business of the company.

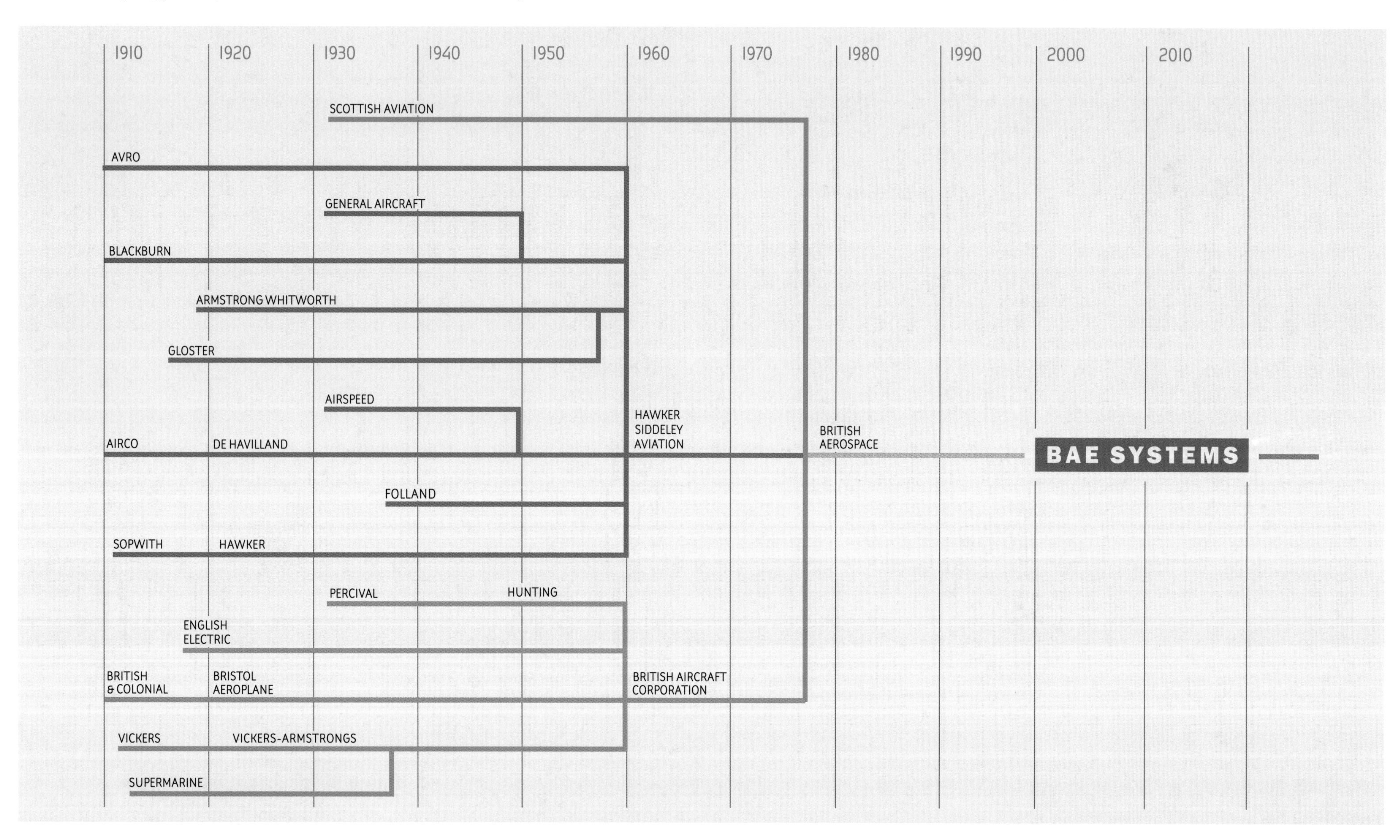

Appendix 3: Glossary

2 TAF	Second Tactical Air Force
2 F1	Sopwith "Ships Camel" designation
3 TAF	Third Tactical Air Force
A400M	Airbus Model 400 Military
AAC	Army Air Corps
AAR	Air to Air Refuelling
AASF	Advanced Air Striking Force
ACC	Air Control Centre
ADCC	Air Defence Cadet Corps
ADEN	Armament Development Establishment Enfield
ADV	Air Defence Variant
AEF	Air Experience Flights
AEW	Airborne Early Warning
AFAS	Armed Forces Art Society
AFC	Air Force Cross
AI Mk 10	Airborne Interception Radar Mk 10
AI 24	Airborne Interception Radar Mk 24 (also known as "Foxhunter")
Air Mshl	Air Marshal
Airco	Aircraft Manufacturing Company Ltd
AMRAAM	Advanced Medium Range Air to Air Missile
AOC	Air Officer Commanding
ARCC	Aeronautical Rescue Co-ordination Centre
ASRAAM	Advanced Short Range Air to Air Missile
ASV	Air to Surface Vessel
ASW	Anti Submarine Warfare
ATC	Air Training Corps
AuxAF	Auxiliary Air Force
AVM	Air Vice Marshal
B1	Bomber Mk 1
B2	Bomber Mk 2
BAC	British Aircraft Corporation
BAe	British Aerospace
BAOR	British Army Of the Rhine
BBMF	Battle of Britain Memorial Flight
BCATP	British Commonwealth Air Training Plan
BEF	British Expeditionary Force
BOAC	British Overseas Airways Corporation
C1	Transport Mk 1
C2	Transport Mk 2
C4	Transport Mk 4
C-130J	Transport (Cargo) – Design Number 130 Series J (US designation)
C-17	Transport (Cargo) – Design Number 17 (US designation)
C-47	Transport (Cargo) – Design Number 47 (US designation)
CAP	Combat Air Patrol
Capt	Captain
CAS	Chief of the Air Staff
CAS	Close Air Support
CASEVAC	CASualty EVACuation
CB	Companion of the Order of the Bath
CBE	Commander of the Order of the British Empire
CCF	Combined Cadet Force
CFS	Central Flying School
CH-47	Transport (Cargo) Helicopter – Design Number 47 (US designation)
CIA	Central Intelligence Agency
CLS	Central Landing School
CMG	Companion of the Order of St Michael and St George
CVO	Companion of the Royal Victorian Order
DASACS	Deployable Air Surveillance and Control System
DFC*	Distinguished Flying Cross (* and Bar)
DFM	Distinguished Flying Medal
DH	De Havilland
DH4	De Havilland 4
DH60	De Havilland 60
DH9	De Havilland 9
DH9A	De Havilland 9A
DHC	De Havilland Canada
DSC*	Distinguished Service Cross (* and Bar)
DSM	Distinguished Service Medal
DSO*	Distinguished Service Order (* and Bar)
E-3D	Special Electronic Installation Mission – Design Number 3 Series D (US designation)
EAF	Egyptian Air Force
EAW	Expeditionary Air Wing
ECM	Electronic Counter Measures
ELINT	Electronic INTelligence
EOKA	National Organisation of Cypriot Struggle (Greek)
F1	Fighter Mk 1
F3	Fighter Mk 3
F6	Fighter Mk 6
F2A	Bristol Fighter early Mark designation
F2B	Bristol Fighter standard Mark designation
F-111	Fighter – Design Number 111 (US designation)
F-35	Fighter – Design Number 35 (US designation)

F-4 Fighter – Design Number 4 (US designation)
FA2 Fighter and Attack Mk 2
FAA Fleet Air Arm
FAW Fighter All Weather
FG1 Fighter / Ground Attack Mk 1
FGA9 Fighter Ground Attack Mk 9
FGR2 Fighter Ground/ Attack / Reconnaissance Mk 2
Flg Off Flying Officer
Flt Lt Flight Lieutenant
FOB Forward Operating Base
FSTA Future Strategic Tanker Aircraft

GAvA Guild of Aviation Artists
GCB Knight Grand Cross of the Order of the Bath
GCVO Knight Grand Cross of the Royal Victorian Order
GDC Gioia Del Colle, an Italian Air Force Base
GEC General Electric Company
GEE GEE (or Gee), navigation aid whose name comes from the letter G in "Grid".
Gp Cpt Group Captain
GPS Global Positioning System
GR1 Ground attack/Reconnaissance
GR1 Ground attack/Reconnaissance Mk 1
GR4 Ground attack/Reconnaissance Mk 4
GR7 Ground attack/Reconnaissance Mk 7

H-34 Helicopter – Design Number 34 (US designation)
HAF Historic Aircraft Flight
HAR2 Helicopter, Air Rescue Mk 2
HAS Hardened Aircraft Shelter
HC1 Helicopter, Cargo Mk 1
HC2 Helicopter, Cargo Mk 2
HC4 Helicopter, Cargo Mk 4
HC6 Helicopter, Cargo Mk 6
HM His Majesty
HM Her Majesty
HMS His/Her Majestys Ship
HP0/400 Handley Page 0/400
HQ Head Quarters
HR14 Helicopter, Rescue Mk 14
HRH His Royal Highness
HSF High Speed Flight
HSL High Speed Launch
HUD Head Up Display

IAF Independent Air Force
IDS Interdictor Strike
ISAF International Security Assistance Force
ISTAR Information Surveillance Target Acquisition And Reconnaissance

JHC Joint Helicopter Command
JHFNI Joint Helicopter Force Northern Ireland
JP233 Hunting Engineering runway denial weapon

K2 Tanker Mk 2
K3 Tanker Mk 3
K4 Tanker Mk 4
KBE Knight Commander of the Order of the British Empire
KCB Knight Commander of the Order of the Bath
KCVO Knight Commander of the Royal Victorian Order
KFOR Kosovo FORce (NATO)
KSA Kingdom of Saudi Arabia

lb Pounds (measure of weight)
LDP Laser Designator Pod
LGB Laser Guided Bomb
LOROP Long Range Photography
LRDU Long Range Development Unit
Lt Lieutenant
Lt Cdr Lieutenant Commander

M-4 Myasishchev - 4 (Russian jet bomber)
MAD Mutually Assured Destruction
MAP Ministry of Air Production
MBDA Matra British Aerospace Dynamics Alenia (Missile Manufacturer)
MC* Military Cross (* and Bar)
MCS Marine Craft Section
MM Military Medal
MoD Ministry of Defence
MR1 Maritime Reconnaissance Mk 1
MR2 Maritime Reconnaissance Mk 2
MR3 Maritime Reconnaissance Mk 3
MRA4 Maritime Reconnaissance and Attack Mk 4

NASA National Aeronautics and Space Agency
NATO North Atlantic Treaty Organisation
NBC Nuclear, Biological, Chemical
NF11 Night Fighter Mk 11

OBE Officer of the Order of the British Empire
OC Officer Commanding
OM Order of Merit
OTC Officer Training Corps

P1 Prototype 1
P-8A Maritime Patrol – Design Number 8 Series A (US designation)
PFF Path Finder Force

PFI	Private Finance Initiative
PGM	Precision Guided Munition
Plt Off	Pilot Officer
PM	Prime Minister
PoW	Prisoner of War
PPRuNe	Professional Pilots Rumour Network
PR9	Photographic Reconnaissance Mk 9
PRU	Photographic Reconnaissance Unit
PSP	Pierced Steel Planking
PTS	Parachute Training School
QFI	Qualified Flying Instructor
QRA	Quick Reaction Alert
R1	Reconnaissance Mk 1
R101	Rigid Airship 101
RA	Royal Academy
RAAF	Royal Australian Air Force
RAeC	Royal Aero Club
RAF	Royal Air Force
RAFES	Royal Air Force Escaping Society
RAFVR(T)	RAF Volunteer Reserve (Training Branch)
RAuxAF	Royal Auxiliary Air Force
RCAF	Royal Canadian Air Force
RDF	Radio Direction Finding
RFC	Royal Flying Corps
RHA	Royal Hibernian Academy
RNAS	Royal Naval Air Service
RNLI	Royal National Lifeboat Institution
RP-3	Rocket Projectile 3 inch
RPG	Rocket Propelled Grenade
RTTL	Rescue & Target Towing Launch
S-58	Sikorsky company designation for H-34 helicopter
SACEUR	Supreme Allied Commander EURope
SAM	Surface to Air Missile
SAR	Search And Rescue
SDSR	Strategic Defence and Security Review
SE5a	Scout Experimental – Model 5 a
SEATO	South East Asia Treaty Organisation
SEPECAT	Societe Europeeenne du Production de l'avion Ecole de Combat et d'Appul Tactique
Sgt	Sargeant
SOE	Special Operations Executive
SofS	Secretary of State
Sqn Ldr	Squadron Leader
STEM	Science, Technology ,Engineering and Mathematics
STOL	Short Take Off & Landing
T11	Trainer Mk 11
THUM	Temperature and Humidity Monitoring Flight
TIALD	Thermal Imaging And Laser Designator
TSR-2	Tactical Strike Reconnaissance
TTTE	Tri-National Tornado Training Establishment
U-2	Utility – Design Number 2 (US designation)
UAS	University Air Squadron
UAV	Unmanned Aerial Vehicle
U-Boat	Unterseeboot (German)
UCAS	Unmanned Combat Air System
UKADR	United Kingdom Air Defence Region
UN	United Nations
UOR	Urgent Operational Requirement
USA	United States of America
USAAF	United States Army Air Force
USAF	United States Air Force
V/STOL	Vertical/Short Take Off and Landing
V-1	Vengeance weapon 1
V-2	Vengeance weapon 2
VC	Victoria Cross
VC10	Vickers Commercial number 10
VIP	Very Important Person
VPGAvA	Vice President Guild of Aviation Artists
WAAF	Women's Auxiliary Air Force
WE 177	Weapon Establishment 177
Wg Cdr	Wing Commander
WMD	Weapons of Mass Destruction
WRAF	Women's Royal Air Force
WSO	Weapon System Operator

Index

AIRCRAFT

PEOPLE

PLACES

RAF STATIONS, UNITS & COMMANDS

SQUADRONS, FLIGHTS ETC.

WORKS OF ART

Title reference followed by Artist reference

BAE SYSTEMS

First published 2018 by Chris Andrews Publications Limited on behalf of
The Royal Air Force Club, Piccadilly and BAE Systems

ISBN 978-1-912584-03-1

Chris Andrews Publications Ltd, Oxford. OX2 0LX. Tel. 01865 723404. www.cap-ox.com

Designed by Mike Brain, Wild Boar Design, Oxford

Paintings photographed by Chris Honeywell

Vignettes (black and white drawings) by Mandy Shepherd

Publishing and project management by Chris Andrews

Printed and bound in the UK by Knockout Print Services

Front cover illustration: Detail from ‘Spitfire Scramble 1940’ by Frank Wootton (p77)